BACKWARDS & IN HEELS

THE PAST, PRESENT AND FUTURE
OF WOMEN WORKING IN FILM

ALICIA MALONE

FILM REPORTER AND CRITIC

Cover Illustration & Design : Hema Patel
Layout Design : Elina Diaz

For permission requests, please contact the publisher at:

Mango Publishing Group
2850 Douglas Road, 3rd Floor
Coral Gables, FL 33134 USA
info@mango.bz

For special orders, quantity sales, course adoptions and corporate sales, please email the publisher at sales@mango.bz. For trade and wholesale sales, please contact Ingram Publisher Services at customer.service@ingramcontent.com or +1.800.509.4887.

BACKWARDS AND IN HEELS : The Past, Present and Future of Women in Hollywood

Library of Congress Cataloging
ISBN: (paperback) 978-1-63353-617-3, (ebook) 978-1-63353-618-0
Library of Congress Control Number: 2017910268
BISAC category code : PER004030 PERFORMING ARTS / Film & Video / History & Criticism

Printed in the United States of America

For my fellow movie geeks.

"Alicia Malone gives me hope for the future of film appreciation. Her knowledge and curiosity are matched only by her enthusiasm for all things cinematic."

— Leonard Maltin

"Alicia is a wonderful human whose voracious appetite for, and knowledge of, cinema and its history is immense and passionate. I can't think of anyone more suited to dig into this very important part of the story of film."

— Elijah Wood

"Alicia Malone has opened my eyes to stories and stats about Women in Film, making me recognize the constant prejudices and imbalances that occur in the film industry even today, but also the ways in which women have been and continue to be celebrated. Proud to be a fellow feminist for film!"

— Maude Garrett, Founder of GeekBomb.com

"Over the years since we both moved here from our respective home countries to report on film, I've watched Alicia Malone grow more and more passionate about the roles women play in the modern movie industry, and what she can do to help better this. Alicia is talented and has a natural love of cinema, to be sure, but she's also dedicated to sharing her insights and knowledge in such a way that you can't help but fall in love with film all over again!"

— Nadia Neophytou, Entertainment Reporter

"A fresh and passionate voice that makes us fully aware of the tremendous contributions of women to movies, while giving urgent notice to the stubborn slights and oversights of the film industry and reminding us of the job that remains to be done. A timely and important work of cultural criticism."

— Molly Haskell, Film Critic and Author of 'From Reverence to Rape'

"Alicia is one of those movie lovers equally adept at discussing Neo from "The Matrix" and Italian Neorealism. Her enthusiasm is infectious; I can't imagine anyone better equipped to welcome a new generation of young women into the world of movies. With *"Backwards and in Heels*," she's done it."

— **Ben Mankiewicz,** Primetime Host, Turner Classic Movies

"Alicia Malone is the champion heroines of cinema deserve. Illuminating, insightful, occasionally maddening, *Backwards and in Heels* is required reading for anyone who wants to call themselves a film fan."

— **Sasha Perl-Raver,** Host, FX Movie Download

"Alicia Malone's expert perspective and inspired, informative take on film history make *Backwards And In Heels* a must read. An outspoken advocate for women in film and an ardent lover of cinema, here she is actively changing the conversation around women's achievements in the business with wonderful insights, wisdom and wit."

— **Miri Jedeikin,** Host, Uproxx

"Women have been creators in the film industry since its inception. In *Backwards and in Heels*, you can feel Alicia Malone's passion for highlighting the trailblazers who have deserved this kind of notoriety for decades. Any lover of film will appreciate this celebration of important figures who have made massive contributions to the art form."

— **Tiffany Vazquez,** Saturday Daytime Host, Turner Classic Movies

"There's a slow but steady shift finally sweeping the industry to invest more in female voices. Having a tool like this fantastic book is invaluable for the continued growth and hope of future generations of creative women. Alicia Malone has been a true champion of female artists, exemplifying the passion, intelligence and class needed to bring people together and create positive change."

— **Amirose Eisenbach,** Radiant J Productions

"Alicia is one of the most knowledgeable film fans I know. Her passion is infectious! Excited that so many people will get to experience that joy in her new book! Go read it in your heels!"

- **Tiffany Smith**, TV Host and Actress

"No one lives and breathes film like Alicia. Her passion and enthusiasm for these notable women is infectious and evident on every page."

- **Josh Horowitz**, MTV

"*Backwards and in Heels* will leave you shocked by the behind scenes stories of misogyny and racism, inspired by the resilience women, and hopeful for next 100 years of female filmmakers."

- **Jacqueline Coley**, Black Girl Nerds

TABLE OF CONTENTS

INTRODUCTION

"After all, Ginger Rogers did everything that Fred Astaire did. She just did it backwards and in high heels..." - Ann Richards

When I think back to my childhood growing up in the suburban capital of Canberra, Australia, my memories are patchy at best. My friends sometimes try to remind me of the time when we did this or that together, but all I can do is stare at them blankly. The one thing that really stands out when I think back are the movies.

I remember our house being filled with movies, hundreds of VHS tapes with films my Dad had recorded from the television, piling up in precarious towers in our spare room; my Mum making trips to the local video store to get a weekly supply of movies; the living room with its multiple copies of Leonard Maltin's Movie Guides; and my bedroom, plastered in film posters. From a young age, I was introduced to the magic that lay within movies, and this ended up transforming my life in so many ways. I would sit transfixed by the screen, watching the glamorous Marilyn Monroe, the icy Hitchcock blondes, and sassy Katharine Hepburn. I loved how these women were powerful, strong, sexy and vulnerable all at once. And sometimes, I related strongly to one of the characters on screen, like the young Liz Taylor in 'National Velvet' at the time I too was obsessed with horses. It's a very powerful thing to see yourself or someone you would like to be reflected as the hero of a movie. She made me feel like I could do anything. And so, if you had asked me what I wanted to be when I grew up (after ditching the idea of a being an Olympic-level horse rider), my answer would have been, "a film director." I wanted to create that same type of special magic, including inspiring heroes and fascinating stories that would appeal to future film buffs; to ignite the same love for movies that I had felt.

This continued throughout high school, when I challenged myself to learn more and more about the art of cinema. I devoured seven movies a week, read all the books I could get my hands on, and sat in the front row of film class, eagerly hanging on to every word the teacher said.

Then, I decided that my school peers needed to love movies as much as I did. I started my own Film Club where I elected myself President, transforming a school badge I found on the ground with white-out and a marker to wear as a symbol of my new self-appointed role. I still giggle to think that I called myself "President," which is not a typically Australian term, especially because all the actual roles at school were "Captain" or "Vice-Captain." Every week, I would book the screening room at school with a movie of my choice. It was always a classic film. And even though I was painfully shy, I forced myself to get up on stage during school assembly to plead my case as to why everyone should see 'Citizen Kane'. Nobody ever came to my club, and eventually the school Principal asked me not to get up in assembly anymore.

Around this time I also began to create my own videos using my step-father's camcorder, interviewing my fellow students with my fist held tight, as if it were holding a microphone, asking hard-hitting questions about their futures. I edited the videos using the method of record/pause/record/pause on my trusty VHS tape player, and showed them eagerly to my classmates.

By the time I graduated high school, I had changed my answer about what I wanted to do with my life. Because after reading all of those film books and watching so many movies, I had come to the conclusion that it was just too hard to be a female director. Or for that matter, a female cinematographer, producer, editor, writer, etc. It seemed like the odds were so stacked against getting work in those jobs, and I wasn't sure I was strong enough to make it. So instead I went to work in television, making my way slowly up the ranks in behind-the-scenes roles.

All of that led to my real dream job. I'm now a film reporter who lives in Hollywood and makes a living talking about films, interviewing movie stars, and traveling the world to attend film festivals. I know, I'd be jealous of me, if I weren't already me. I actually didn't know this could be a real job when I was young; but when I think about it, I am still President of my own Film Club, I just use television, social media, and YouTube to plead my case for people to watch classic and independent movies. And I'm still interviewing people, only now with a real microphone. My original reason for wanting to be a director, to ignite a love of movies in others, is what I continue to strive for every day.

This is exactly what I hope to do with this book. Because amongst all of those film books I read when I was young, I didn't come across many stories of the women who worked in Hollywood. Their absence told me that film was exclusively a man's world, which is simply not true.

This is not meant to be a complete history of women in Hollywood. That would take a good couple of years to research, and multiple volumes of books to tell. There are many women that I have had to leave out, and that was hard, but I wanted to describe the plight of women in film in a different way. I have handpicked a few stories about women from each era of American cinema. These women are inspiring in their accomplishments, and their stories are illuminating as far as what they've had to struggle against. Each story stands for a wider problem or a solution in Hollywood, with statistics and expert opinion weaved in.

15

I'd like this to be a guidebook, an entry into the world of women in film. Some stories you may already know, some you may be surprised by. You can flip directly to the story you want to read, or go from the beginning and work your way to the end. However you do it, I hope you will be as enamored of these ladies as I am, and join me in keeping the pressure on Hollywood to let more women in.

PART ONE : THE PAST

THE FIRST PIONEERS (1890s – 1920s)

What if I told you that in the 1900s through to the early 1920s, there were more female filmmakers actively working at the top of Hollywood than there are today? Admit it, you're surprised. Everyone is when I tell them this, even people who work in the film industry. And here's more: during this time, half of all movies made in the United States were written by women, many famous actresses ran their own production companies, and the first person to be titled 'Film Editor' was a woman.

The beginning of cinema — especially the silent era — offered more opportunities to women than we've seen since. So what happened? Let's start at the birth of cinema and go from there.

The idea of moving pictures was born in the late 1870s, when photographer Eadweard Muybridge set up a series of cameras alongside a racetrack. Eadweard was trying to discover if horses lifted all four feet off the ground at one time while galloping. Spoiler alert: they do. In order to show the photos in quick succession, he made an early projector, to which he gave a catchy name: Zoopraxiscope.

In the 1890s, Thomas Edison invented the first motion picture camera, called the Kinetograph. To play the footage, you needed a Kinetoscope, where one person would squint into a peep-hole to view the images. Shortly after, the Lumiére Brothers in France created the Cinematographe, which projected motion pictures onto a screen, creating a shared viewing experience.

These inventions were sold around the world in touring exhibitions, with companies such as photography studios buying the cameras to start experimenting with them. At first, it was a simple matter of recording what was happening around them. One of Thomas Edison's first films was of a laboratory assistant sneezing.

Then, inspired by the theater, filmmakers started telling stories, approaching them like filmed plays. Makeshift cinemas started to pop up around the country, mostly at vaudeville theater shows, where they were offered as an extension to their live acts. These were called Nickelodeons, because admission cost five cents, and their popularity grew very quickly. By 1910, as bigger theaters were being built, the cheap price of a ticket attracted a large rowdy working-class audience, who often chose the movies over the pub for a good night out.

The growing crowds created a big demand for content. Studios were built, and the process of producing films became more streamlined. Movie-making was both fast and furious, with each studio cranking out at least two short films per week.

During the late teens film production began to center in Los Angeles. This was partly because of its ideal weather for filming and space to build studios, and partly because of Thomas Edison. He had tried to monopolize film production in New York by suing for patent infringement on his inventions, so everyone escaped to Los Angeles where they were free to use his inventions with less likelihood of legal trouble.

Silent films became longer and more intricate, and the films were screened in new movie "palaces," elaborate theaters with lavish aesthetic design features that were designed to attract a more upmarket crowd. To fill the seats, theater owners specifically targeted female audiences.

19

The thought was that if you could entice white middle-class women into theaters, it would push out the raucous working-class crowd. These women would bring their husbands, and the theaters could charge more for tickets, advertising it as an elegant night out. So the palaces were built near shopping centers, coupons were placed in magazines, and free childcare was offered. This completely excluded non-white audiences of a lower class.

Movie studios wanted to cater to this middle-class female audience, so female writers and directors were hired to ensure the content would appeal. Karen Ward Mahar, author of 'Women Filmmakers in

Early Hollywood', says these women were "believed to lend a moral tone to the movies that the middle classes appreciated."

The silent era saw actresses such as Mary Pickford, Lilian Gish, Theda Bara, Greta Garbo, and Clara Bow become hugely popular. The fame of these women was almost a reflection of the changing ideas about ladies during these decades. For example, Mary Pickford was the innocent Victorian-era girl, while Clara Bow was the sexy 1920s "New Woman".

The New Woman was part of the first wave of feminism in the U.S., which saw protests for women's rights grow throughout the teens and into the twenties. The movement was successful in winning the right for white women to vote in August of 1920 with the 9th Amendment.

By the end of the 1920s, silent films featured complex plots, artistic cinematography, and glamorous movie stars, and attracted big audiences. But a new filmmaking technology threatened this silent utopia. The ability to record sound heralded the arrival of "talkies," which forced a complete rethinking of how to make movies — such as where to hide the giant microphones. All of this was wonderfully lampooned in 1952's 'Singin' In The Rain'.

This brings us to why women were pushed out of the industry. Firstly, many filmmakers, writers, and actors struggled to make the transition to this new style of making movies. Secondly, the success of a couple of talkies, such as 'The Jazz Singer', saw a select few movie studios rise to the top, and independent companies (often run by women) just couldn't compete, often as a result of a lack of finances.

The Great Depression caused many of these small studios to go under, and the financial gain of making movies became the biggest focus. Filmmaking started to be looked at as a business instead of a creative enterprise, and corporate structures were implemented, complete with executives in charge.

At this time, women were not perceived as being business-minded or executive material, so positions of power on a movie set, such as directing, now were given to men. From the 1930s onward, Hollywood became a boys' club. And women have been trying to make their way back into the industry for almost 100 years.

Here's just how dramatic and entrenched this boys' club mindset became. Between 1912 and 1919, Universal had 11 female directors who regularly worked for them, and who made a total of 170 films in these seven years. But from the mid-1920s right up to 1982, the studio didn't hire a single female filmmaker.

Reading film history books I learnt all about D.W. Griffith, Cecil B. DeMille, and Georges Méliès, but I didn't know about the ladies who were working with them. When I started to research them, I was amazed by their stories. There were female directors who created techniques that filmmakers still use today. Movie actresses who not only demanded equal pay, but made more than the men. Female action heroes who performed their own stunts. Established women who supported younger women, giving them jobs in the industry. And much of this happened before ladies could even vote.

There are so many wonderful stories about revolutionary women in film who shaped the silent era. My hope is that by sharing a couple of them, you too will be inspired, and help to make sure they are not forgotten.

Alice Guy Blaché:
The First Female Filmmaker

One of the first directors in cinema history was a woman. Her name was Alice Guy Blaché, and her history was lost for many years, because it was erased by the man who hired her.

Alice was born in Paris in 1873; twenty years later, she applied to be a secretary for Léon Gaumont - an inventor and the owner of a photography business. One day, Léon and Alice attended an exhibition put on by the Lumiére Brothers. They were showing off their latest invention, a camera which could record motion pictures. Léon purchased one, and Alice, inspired by the footage she watched, asked if she could borrow it.

With this camera, Alice made a short movie called 'The Cabbage Fairy'. This was 1896. As you may guess from the title, this was a simple scene of a fairy pulling babies out of cabbages. It was created to show Léon's customers what a motion picture camera could do, but now stands as one of the very first movies in history which featured a story. Alice didn't think it was a masterpiece, but said, "the film had enough success that I was allowed to try again."

Around this time the first movie production companies were being set up, and Léon decided to create his own — the Gaumont Film Company. Alice was put in charge of making the films, and she proceeded to direct every single movie out of the company for the next eleven years.

Slowly, Alice's productions became more elaborate, and new technicians were hired to help her out. Alice had gone from being a secretary to a powerful figure at the fledgling studios, and she had to learn how to take charge.

On one of Alice's movies, a camera operator fell ill, and an English man by the name of Herbert Blaché-Bolton was sent in his place. He was new to the equipment, and found his director to be cold and distant. "No doubt he was right," Alice said later, "still young, in a job where I had to give proof of authority, I avoided all familiarity."

Over the course of working together, however, Alice began to trust Herbert, and they fell in love. Unfortunately, their first film wasn't as successful. When the print was developed, it was found to be over-exposed, scratched, and unusable. Alice cited faulty camera equipment — which could be true, cameras were not very reliable in those days — but I prefer the romantic version that she was trying to save any blame from falling on Herbert. Not long after, the two were married, and three days later they set sail for a new life in the United States.

For a few years, Herbert and Alice ran the new Gaumont Film Company in New York. But Alice wanted her own production company, so in 1910, she built Solax Studios in New Jersey. This made Alice the first woman to ever start her own motion picture studio.

At Solax, she oversaw the production of more than 300 films, everything from comedies to dramas and westerns. She directed about 50 of those films and continuously experimented with new filmmaking techniques, such as in her movie 'Beasts of the Jungle', where she used a split screen effect to make it appear as if a lion were on the other side of a family's front door. Really it was two recordings side by side, one of the house and the other of a lion at the zoo.

Alice also coached her performers towards a realistic acting style, with the words "Be Natural" emblazoned on a large banner inside her studio. This was unusual for the time, because in silent film, actors were taught to "pose," using over-the-top gestures to indicate their emotions. But if you look at the acting on one of Alice's films, such as 'Falling Leaves', about a child suffering from tuberculosis, it's toned down and realistic.

In the end, Alice had a sad conclusion to her career. Solax couldn't compete with the major Hollywood studios, so she had to shut it down. Her marriage to Herbert also didn't survive, so Alice moved back to France in 1922.

Five years later, she returned to the U.S. to get copies of her films, hoping she could use them to find work as a director in Paris. But out of her one thousand plus movies, Alice couldn't find a single print.

This was very common during the silent era. Nobody thought movies would become a cultural phenomenon or that the preservation of film history would be important. It's estimated that 90% of all silent films made in America have been lost. Negatives were destroyed after they played in the theater, and if they were nitrate prints, storage was often hazardous. This type of film stock was highly unstable and had a nasty habit of combusting when not maintained in exactly the right conditions. And once nitrate film caught fire, not even water would put out the flames.

So unfortunately for Alice and many other silent filmmakers, most of her work disappeared, and today only around 130 of her movies remain.

Now broke, Alice had to lean on her children for financial help. In 1930, to make matters worse, Léon Gaumont published a history of the Gaumont Film Company which didn't mention anything before 1907. He omitted all of Alice Guy Blaché's work as a director. Consequently, nobody knew for a long time how significant a role she played in setting up his very successful studios and in the birth of film itself.

Ten years before Alice passed away, the French Government discovered her accomplishments, and gave Alice the 'Legion of Honor' in 1953. A year later, Léon Gaumont's son Louis admitted in a public speech, "Madame Alice Guy Blaché, the first woman filmmaker... has been unjustly forgotten," and film historians started to take notice.

In 2011, Martin Scorsese awarded a posthumous Director's Guild of America Award to Alice Guy Blaché. In his speech, Martin called the loss of her history "a tragedy," saying that Alice was "a pioneer in audiovisual story-telling...more than a talented business woman, she was a filmmaker of rare sensitivity, with a remarkable poetic eye and an extraordinary feel for locations."

Lois Weber: Social Issues on Film

In 1916, one of the biggest hits in theaters was a movie about abortion, directed by a woman. That woman was Lois Weber, an actress, producer, writer, and filmmaker who pushed the content of movies from simple entertainment to tackling serious social issues.

Lois began her life in Pennsylvania in 1879, with a father who liked to tell fairy stories. He encouraged Lois to start writing at a young age, and fostered her creative spirit through music lessons. As a teenager, her independence impelled her to move to New York, where she paid her rent by playing piano for the tenants of a boarding house. At seventeen, Lois started touring with a theater company. She got this job through her uncle, who was a theater producer in Chicago and one of the few relatives to support her ambitious drive.

During one of her theater tours, Lois met stage manager Phillips Smalley, and they quickly fell in love, marrying within weeks. When their theater tour ended, Phillips joined another, and Lois tagged along. During these two years spent on the road, Lois kept herself busy by writing scenarios — bare-bones scripts for silent movies. She mailed them to film companies and was surprised when they began to sell.

When Phillips was hired for a new tour, Lois decided not to join him. Instead, she approached the American Gaumont Film Company. This was run by Alice Guy Blaché and her husband Herbert. In Alice, Lois had a role model of a female director, and Herbert was also encouraging of her talent. She joined Gaumont and not only wrote scenarios, but directed and starred in them too.

When her husband returned, this time it was Phillips who followed Lois. He got a job at Gaumont acting in her movies and helping direct. Together they churned out one short film after another. This was around 1910, when a structure for movie production was still evolving. The frantic pace actually gave Lois an advantage. As she said later in her career, "I grew up in the business when everybody was so busy learning their particular branch of the new industry, no one had time to notice whether or not a woman was gaining a foothold."

Lois and Phillips got a chance to work on higher quality filmmaking when they both got jobs at the Rex Motion Picture Company, which eventually became part of Universal Pictures. The head of Rex, Edwin S. Porter, wanted to make tasteful, intimate dramas with small casts, and Lois excelled in that type of movie. She wrote intricate scenarios, pairing them with creative direction and editing. With her own signature style for each of her productions, Lois was an early auteur, or "author" of the cinema.

One of the most impressive films by Lois and Phillips is 1913's 'Suspense'. This ten-minute short is often cited as a film that pushed forward the art of visual storytelling. The movie is about a young mother (played by Lois) who becomes trapped inside her house with a homeless man, and calls her husband, who races home to save her.

In one landmark scene, Lois and Phillips heighten the tension by superimposing three different shots. On the left, the homeless man is seen entering the house. On the right, the wife calls her husband for help. And in the middle, the husband receives the distressing phone call. This was a clever way to show simultaneous action, and it was a technique audiences hadn't seen before.

Though Phillips and Lois were a team for many years, she was often singled out for her talent. Professor Shelley Stamp, author of 'Lois Weber in Early Hollywood', says Lois was truly an innovator of cinematic style. "She had an extraordinary capacity for visual storytelling and was really pioneering in terms of using moving camera and superimposition," Shelley said. "And what strikes me is the way she was able to convey the interior psychology of a character visually, using a whole bunch of techniques to help the audience understand what was going on inside a character's head. That's really hard to do."

It was especially hard given her choice of subject matter. Lois said she wanted to make films which would "have an influence for good in the public's mind." So between 1914 and 1921, she made a series of "social problem" movies, becoming one of the earliest directors in America to tackle morally complex issues. Her 1916 film, 'Where Are My Children?' is the one I previously mentioned, which focused on abortion. This was released around the same time as the arrest of activist Margaret Sanger, jailed for promoting the idea of family planning. Margaret Sanger's story and the debate of legalizing birth control was the subject of Lois' follow-up 1917 movie, 'The Hand That Rocks The Cradle'. Then, in 'The People vs. John Doe', she looked at capital punishment, 'Hop, The Devil's Brew' was about drug abuse, and poverty was her subject in 'Shoes'.

It's amazing to think that these films were made back then, that a movie about birth control written and directed by a woman was not only allowed, but was really successful. You could not picture that happening today.

In 1921, 'Motion Picture' magazine wrote, "When the history of the dramatic early development of motion pictures is written, Lois Weber will occupy a unique position." She started making movies when films were silent, a maximum of 20 minutes long, and not yet a business venture. She finished when they had sound, were feature-length, and were thought of as profitable products. Lois was also the first female director to ever make a feature film in the United States, with 1914's 'The Merchant of Venice'. Her final film was 1934's 'White Heat', about a romance between an interracial couple. She passed away five years later, aged 60.

It's true, Lois Weber's name should be written in the history of film, and she does occupy a unique position in it. She showed how movies can be a powerful medium and how they can candidly explore important issues and engender moral discussion, while also being significant pieces of visual art.

27

Mary Pickford:
The Movie Star Businesswoman

With her blonde ringlets, wide-eyed innocence, and naive childlike roles, Mary Pickford epitomized the pure Victorian girl. But this persona belied who she really was: the most powerful woman to have ever worked in Hollywood.

Mary Pickford's life actually encompassed a lot of opposites. She went from poverty to a President's paycheck. She was the first movie star as well as an independent producer. She was the original "America's Sweetheart" but was actually born in Canada. And she was known as Mary Pickford, when her real name was Gladys Smith.

Her childhood was anything but easy. In fact, it could almost be a plot from one of her later dramas. Gladys' alcoholic father abandoned the family when she was three years old, leaving her mother Charlotte scrambling to care for their children. A year later, Gladys almost died from severe diphtheria. She was so gravely ill that a priest was called for an emergency baptism. When she was six, her father returned, but that jubilation was short-lived, because he died soon after from a blood clot. The night he passed away, Gladys heard her mother's desperate screams, and Charlotte was so overwhelmed by grief that the children were sent away to temporarily live with other families.

Their lives changed when the family took in a boarder to help pay the rent. This stranger was the first person to suggest that Gladys try acting. He was a stage manager looking to hire a child actor for a local production. And because it paid money, Charlotte let her daughter act in the play. From her very first moment on stage, she was a natural, improvising and getting the biggest laugh of the night.

The acting bug had bit, as well as the realization that this might save them from destitution. So the Smith family packed up their bags and went to the stage, touring as their own theater group.

The raw talent that Gladys exhibited had her stealing every show, and critics took notice. One review prophesied that the 11-year-old would "someday make a polished actress... deserving of great credit for her work."

This prophecy began to come true when Gladys won a coveted role in a play on Broadway. The producer suggested that she should change her name from Gladys Louise Millbourne Smith to something a bit catchier. They looked into her family tree and chose Pickford from her grandfather John Pickford Hennessey, and came up with

Mary as a version of Marie, the name the priest had baptized her. And so the legendary Mary Pickford was born.

Once the Broadway play closed, Charlotte encouraged her daughter to look for acting roles in movies. Mary wanted to stay in theater, but movies offered steadier pay, so she approached The American Biograph Company in New York. Director D.W. Griffith was the boss at the studio, and Mary convinced him to give her a screen test. Watching the test footage, D.W. saw Mary's potential to be a star; she just had a presence that was so sweet. He hired her to be a full-time actress.

She was not so sweet when it came to negotiating her salary. Mary pushed for, and won, a pay rate twice as large as the original offer. This was unheard of, but Mary was now the breadwinner in her family, so she was determined to get enough money to support them. She quickly proved her worth by acting, writing scenarios, and learning everything she could about lighting, costumes, make-up, stunts, and the art of movie-making. In her first year, she starred in 50 movies.

Mary was often directed by D.W. Griffith. He was a big proponent of close-up acting, and that tighter shot required smaller expressions and as much real emotion as possible. He was known for his temper and often "inspired" these emotions by being cruel. One famous example of this involves sisters Lillian and Dorothy Gish. As the story goes, they came to his studio for an audition, and D.W. took a gun and fired it several times into the ceiling, just to see their reaction. "You have expressive bodies," he told the terrified sisters, "I can use you."

Mary described her early days at the studio as hostile, putting up with unwanted advances from male colleagues and clashing with D.W. She later wrote that she "wanted more than ever to escape," but knew she had to stay to support her family. So she decided to fight back.

The 1909 movie 'To Save Her Soul' saw Mary cast as a choirgirl opposite Arthur Johnson as her lover. In a pivotal scene, his character is overtaken by jealousy, pulling out a gun in the suspicion that she hadn't been faithful. The problem was that over lunch, Arthur had had a bit to drink, so when he pointed the gun, according to Mary, "he waved it at me as if it were a piece of hose." She found it hard to conjure up genuine fear, and D.W. became frustrated. He ran onto the set and grabbed Mary roughly by the shoulders, shaking her and yelling, "I'll show you how to do this thing! Get some feeling into you, damn it! You're like a piece of wood!"

In response, Mary leaned down, and bit him. "Sir," Mary said defiantly, "if I am not an actress you cannot beat it into me. What gave you the right to lay your hands on me? I'm finished with you and motion pictures and the whole thing!" And she stormed off.

D.W. came to her dressing room later to apologize for his behavior and persuaded Mary to return to the set. Without any rehearsal, he started rolling the cameras, and Mary channeled her anger into improvisation, giving an electrifying performance.

She was strong, but with her five-foot frame and curls, Mary was often cast as a child or a child-like woman. These movies kept her young, de-sexualized, and virtuous, as was the desired female type at the time. But Mary's sassier roles were also popular, where she played feisty ingenues, such as in 1910's 'Wilful Peggy' where she beats up a man with his own hat after he tries to kiss her.

In the early days of silent film, actors weren't listed in the credits. But Mary Pickford became so well-loved, directors and theater owners would make sure her name was prominently displayed. She went from being called the "Biograph Girl" or "the girl with the curls" to Mary Pickford, movie star, and her image graced the covers of magazines and the front pages of newspapers around the country.

The press followed her to California when she left Biograph to work with a variety of different studios. Her mother Charlotte came out to help her get settled, and one day, she overheard an interesting conversation about her daughter on the Paramount lot.

Two executives were talking about block booking, a practice later made illegal. Studios would force theater owners to buy a block of their movies, ensuring release dates for every single film, no matter the quality. If a theater wanted one of their prestige pictures, they had to buy the whole lot. So, the executives were saying, if they had a new Mary Pickford picture, they could rest easy about their other films.

Charlotte realized the unique power that Mary now had. She was so popular with audiences, theaters were desperate to play her movies, and studios were clamoring to make them. In fact, much of the success of selling their other films depended on it. Charlotte encouraged her daughter to be tougher. And in 1916, Mary negotiated a contract which gave her a salary of $10,000 per week plus a $300,000 signing bonus, 50% of the profits from her movies, and the creation of the Pickford Film Corporation. This was more money than Charlie Chaplin was making, and by age 24, Mary Pickford was earning a million dollars per year and was the highest paid star in Hollywood.

It was money well spent, because she continued to have top hits at the box office. Some of her biggest successes came from a collaboration with her friend, writer Frances Marion. Together they made 'Rebecca of Sunnybrook Farm', which gave her the "America's Sweetheart" moniker, and one of her most famous roles, 'The Poor Little Rich Girl' from 1917. Its plot was very melodramatic, with Mary playing a rich girl suffering at the hands of abusive servants. At one point they almost kill her with too much sleeping potion.

At the New York premiere, Mary sat next to Frances, trying to be incognito by wearing dark sunglasses and a hat. She watched in amazement as the audience reacted passionately to her movie, laughing, crying and cheering at all the right moments. When Mary removed her sunglasses to wipe away her own tears, she was instantly recognized by an usher, and a large crowd of crazed fans quickly gathered. They ripped fur from her coat and wanted snippets of her hair, and Mary had to be escorted out of the theater by police.

Though "Little Mary" had reached the pinnacle of Hollywood stardom, she didn't quite have the full creative control she craved. Together with D.W. Griffith, Charlie Chaplin, and Douglas Fairbanks Sr., in 1919 Mary formed the United Artists Corporation (UA). This was the first star-driven production company, and it gave each of those actors the chance to produce five projects of their choice — offering financing and distribution independent from a movie studio. "The inmates have taken over the asylum!" exclaimed the president of another studio when he heard the news. But UA was successful, and continued to profit throughout the 1920s and 1930s. The company is still around today, and is now owned by MGM.

The news about the creation of UA also served as a handy distraction from gossip about two of its founders. Mary and Douglas Fairbanks had been friends for years, but it had turned into more. This was complicated, because they were both married when they first got together, albeit unhappily so. He filed for a divorce, and then so did she. And three and a half weeks later, Mary Pickford married Douglas Fairbanks.

There had been shock from moviegoers who disapproved of this scandalous relationship. But once they married, studio publicists managed to spin it, selling America on the idea that Mary and Douglas were Hollywood royalty. Fans became obsessed with this power couple (who were perhaps rather like the "Brangelina" of their time), with newspapers reporting on their every move. They lived in a mansion the press nicknamed "Pickfair," where they wined and dined celebrities like Charlie Chaplin and Albert Einstein. Mary and Douglas remained a source of fascination throughout their ten-year marriage, until Douglas fell in love again, this time with a British socialite.

Towards the end of the 1920s, Mary further cemented her place in film history by helping to set up the Academy of Motion Picture Arts and Sciences in 1927. She was one of only a few women among the 36 original members, and the founding of the Academy led to the introduction of the Oscars.

By this time, Mary Pickford was eager to shed her innocent persona. She cut off those famous ringlets, and in 1929 made her first sound movie, 'Coquette'. "I wanted to be free of the shackles of curls and playing little girls," said Mary, "and I thought that [sound] was one step toward it." 'Coquette' was made in the early days of talkies, where seamlessly capturing audio hadn't yet been fully mastered. Giant microphones were hidden inside furniture, forcing the cast to stand awkwardly beside the pieces of furniture to deliver their lines. But Mary worked hard on her first speaking role, and it paid off. Her performance in 'Coquette' won the second-ever Academy Award for Best Actress.

Though Mary successfully made the transition from silent to sound films, she never quite felt at ease in them. Her final appearance as a screen actress came in 1933, but throughout the next forty years she remained active in Hollywood. Mary worked behind the scenes as a producer, and mentored new female stars like Shirley Temple. In 1976, Mary was awarded an honorary Oscar for her overall contribution to film. Three years later, Mary Pickford passed away, aged 87.

My favorite images of Mary Pickford are the ones where she is posing with animals. There are quite a lot of them, including a famous picture where Mary is sitting with a cat on her shoulder. On the surface, these photos show the sweet innocence that made her famous. But I like them because I know that underneath that calm smile, Mary Pickford was a badass. Her gutsy determination pulled her family out of poverty and empowered her to become the first movie star, the highest paid actor of her time, a pioneering independent producer, and a woman who stood up for her worth before any other woman in film.

33

A 1924 edition of Photoplay magazine summed her up the best: "No role she can play on the screen is as great as the role she plays in the motion picture industry. Mary Pickford the actress is completely overshadowed by Mary Pickford the individual."

Margaret Booth: The First Film Editor

Outside of the film industry, very few people knew the name of film editor Margaret Booth. But in the industry, her name was revered, and a little feared.

Margaret's career in Hollywood spanned seven decades. She was there at the birth of editing itself, when the process involved cutting film with scissors. She worked during the transitions of silent film to sound, from black and white to color, and from studio system to New Hollywood. She was the great woman behind the great men, working with D.W. Griffith, Louis B. Mayer, and Irving Thalberg. She was also the first person to be titled Film Editor.

All of this began after a family tragedy. Margaret Booth's older brother Elmer was an actor who worked for D.W. Griffith and supported the entire family with his salary. One tragic day in 1915, Elmer was in a car with two other actors when they were hit by a train. Elmer died instantly. At his funeral, D.W. Griffith delivered a eulogy, and approached Margaret to offer her a job as a film joiner to help pay the family bills.

D.W. Griffith was the director who revolutionized the art of cutting film. At the start of cinema, this process didn't exist. Movies were one continuous shot with a single camera angle, and went straight into theaters as they were. The first cut movie was Edwin S. Porter's 'The Life Of An American Fireman' in 1903, which added a simple close-up so the audience could easily see the fireman's hand pulling an alarm.

But D.W. Griffith showed that film joining could be an important storytelling device. He realized that by cutting the film between different points of view, he could tell a larger narrative and shape the story. It was also a handy way to create tension, which he often did by cutting between hero and villain during an action scene.

The job of a film joiner or negative patcher was originally an entry-level position which didn't require any prior skills. This opened the door to Margaret, who learned how to cut films in D.W.'s studio. It was a frustrating process — joiners squinted at negatives through a magnifying glass, trying to determine where to cut with scissors and where to rejoin with tape. They couldn't watch the film as they were working on it, so their only way to see the print in action was to pull the negative quickly between their fingers. Margaret said, "Sometimes there'd be a tiny pinpoint on the negative, and then you knew you were right, but it was very tedious work. Close-ups of Lillian Gish would go on for miles, and they'd be very similar."

The process became easier with the arrival of the first cutting machine in 1919, which had foot pedals to run the film and a spy-hole to view it through. It looked similar to a sewing machine, and perhaps because of that (and because it was a low-level job), there were many women working as film cutters.

After a few years with D.W. Griffith, Margaret Booth got a job with another Hollywood legend, Louis B. Mayer. Also working at his studio was director John M. Stahl, whom Margaret would observe as he edited. He would shoot much more than he needed, and then leave the extra footage (quite literally) on the cutting room floor. At the end of each day, Margaret would gather up the excess film and stay overnight practicing cutting techniques. One day, John was frustrated that he couldn't make a scene work. When he left, Margaret gave it a try, cutting it how she thought it should go. When he saw her work, he hired her on the spot to be his personal cutting assistant.

When Louis B. Mayer's studios merged with Samuel Goldwyn's company and Metro Pictures, they became known as MGM. Louis hired the young executive Irving Thalberg to head production. Irving noticed Margaret's talent and assigned her to cut MGM's biggest movies. Irving also kept encouraging her to direct, but she wasn't interested.

By the late 1920s and early 1930s, cutting was no longer an entry-level job. These workers were highly skilled, and integral to the success of a story. Margaret continued to hone her skills and learned new techniques with the arrival of sound. She never made a cut just for the sake of it, and she had the innate ability to know exactly where one should go, and how much should be trimmed. "Rhythm counts so much," Margaret once said; "the pauses count so much."

Irving Thalberg realized the title of Cutter didn't live up to how important Margaret Booth was, so he changed her title in the credits to Film Editor. Previously, the term of Editor was only used for a position like Script Supervisor, but after this, it was adopted by the entire film industry. It was also used for the Academy Awards, who added a Best Film Editing category in 1935. Margaret Booth was nominated in 1936 for her work on 'Mutiny on the Bounty'. A year later, Irving Thalberg passed away. Margaret stayed at MGM, and Louis B. Mayer promoted her to the highly respected role of Supervising Editor, responsible for the post-production of films. Margaret stayed in this position for 30 years, overseeing classic films like 'The Wizard of Oz' and 'Ben-Hur'.

Director Sidney Lumet wrote about Margaret Booth's unique talent in his book 'Making Movies'. He recalled a moment in the 1960s when Margaret had flown to England to watch rough cuts of three MGM films in production. She screened the movies back to back; when she met with the directors, she told Sidney, "You're running two hours and two minutes, I want the picture under two hours." He and his editor got to work, but found it difficult to cut down. The next morning, Margaret came in, and when he told her of his frustration, she instructed him on the exact shots to cut and by how much. "Her film memory was phenomenal," wrote Sidney Lumet, "she named seven or eight moments, always perfect on where the shot occurred, what took place in the shot, how its beginning or end might be trimmed — and she'd seen the picture only once."

Margaret Booth received an Honorary Oscar in 1978 for her contribution to film, and died in 2002 at the age of 104.

Frances Marion:
The Award-Winning Writer

The highest paid screenwriter in the 1920s and 1930s was Frances Marion. She was also the first person to ever win two Academy Awards in the same field, worked as a battlefront correspondent during World War I and was called "the all-time best script and storywriter the motion picture world has ever produced."

With all of these accomplishments, it seems only appropriate that her name should be similar to that of a famous American Revolutionary war hero, although Frances Marion was not actually her original name.

Marion Benson Owens was born in 1887 in San Francisco. As a child she constantly wrote in her diary, and she had a gift for art. Both of these skills came in handy when she was employed as a young adult at the San Francisco Examiner. Her job was to report on theater productions, write stories and draw sketches to accompany them.

One day, Marion was given the assignment of interviewing and sketching Marie Dressler, an actress of the stage and screen. As she left, one of the head reporters called out to her that if she failed, she would be fired.

Marion didn't know if this was a joke; she raced over to the theater and went to see Marie backstage. Unbeknownst to Marion, Marie was in the middle of a huge fight with William Randolph Hearst, who owned The Examiner. So when Marion announced the paper she was from, she found the door shut in her face pretty quickly. Desperate not to lose her job, she stayed backstage, and when Marie came out, Marion told her she'd be fired if there was no interview. Marie paused and asked, "Is that what those bastards told you?" and then agreed to give Marion "the golldarndest interview I ever gave to any reporter!" They spoke for over an hour, and Marie left Marion with the words, "I'll see you again."

This came true many years later, when Marion was living in Los Angeles with her second husband. It was 1914, and she was in a park sketching. A woman sat down next to her, feeding popcorn to the birds, and Marion realized this was Marie Dressler. She didn't say anything for fear Marie wouldn't remember her, but as soon as Marie saw her, she asked, "Are you the girl who interviewed me in San Francisco?" And then, "I've often wondered what became of you. Hate to lose track of anybody I'm fond of."

They caught up over lunch, and Marie told Marion that with her good looks, she should get into acting. Marion insisted she only wanted to work behind the scenes, but promised she would visit the studio. But by the time she was able to get there, Marie Dressler had left for New York. So this wasn't to be Marion's break into Hollywood, but the two had cemented a real friendship. In the future Marion would play an important part in Marie's career.

Another chance encounter led to her meeting Mary Pickford. This came through a friend, who introduced her to actor Owen Moore at a party. Owen was married to Mary at the time, and Marion couldn't help but tell him how much she admired his wife's talent. He replied gruffly, "Mary has an expressive little talent, but hardly what one would call cerebral." Marion was shocked he would talk about his wife in this way and walked off. Later, he approached her and offered the chance to meet Mary and sketch her portrait. It was an invitation she couldn't decline.

When the two met, they hit it off, chatting easily for an hour and sharing personal stories about their unhappy marriages. This was the start of a very close friendship and eventually a working relationship, but again, this was not how Marion got her first break.

Marion's chance to work in Hollywood actually came through a different friend, journalist Adela Rogers St. Johns, who was lunching with director Lois Weber when Marion happened to walk by. Lois saw something in the young, pretty brunette, and asked Adela to arrange a meeting. This was common for Lois, who was known for hiring and mentoring young women.

Marion met Lois at Bosworth Studios with her portfolio of sketches in hand, and said she'd like to design costumes and movie sets. Impressed, Lois offered her a studio job as "one of my little starlets." Confused, Marion insisted she only wanted to be on the "dark side" of the camera, but Lois explained that at her studios, everyone did a bit of everything. She also wanted Marion to change her name. When she signed her contract, Marion Owens became Frances Marion.

Lois Weber became a huge inspiration for Frances, who watched her in admiration as she filled every role from writer to actor to director with ease. She spent a few years working for her and learned as much as she could, but when Lois got a job at Universal Pictures, Frances decided not to join her.

By 1917, her friend Mary Pickford had become the most powerful woman in Hollywood. Although Mary wasn't technically supposed to have a say in hiring, she insisted that Frances Marion be the writer of her next movie, 'The Poor Little Rich Girl'. From this success came more, with 'Rebecca of Sunnybrook Farm', 'Pollyanna' and many others. Later, Mary would call Frances, "the pillar of my career."

This is something I admire about Frances Marion. Throughout her career, she made long-lasting friendships with many women, who supported each other in work as well as their personal lives. She was a great writer with a sharp wit and a flair for complex plots. But even more remarkable than her abilities was how she became pivotal to so many careers.

39

She met Greta Garbo on the set of 'The Scarlet Letter' in 1926, and four years later wrote Greta's first speaking film, 'Anna Christie', for which Greta won an Oscar. She persuaded Marie Dressler to come back to Hollywood, writing scenarios for her when everyone else thought Marie was past her "use-by" date. Marie won an Oscar for 'Min and Bill' in 1932, was nominated for an Oscar for 'Emma' in 1933, and had a pivotal role in the classic 1934 ensemble comedy, 'Dinner at Eight'. All were written by Frances Marion.

She helped these women and many more, because she too had been helped at the beginning of her career. "I owe my greatest success to women," Frances said later, "Contrary to the assertion that women do all in their power to hinder one another's progress, I have found that it has always been one of my own sex who has given me a helping hand when I needed it."

Through hard work and a lot of determination, Frances became the highest paid screenwriter in Hollywood. She also directed films, albeit briefly: 1921's 'Just Around the Corner' and 'The Love Light' with Mary Pickford. And while others struggled with the transition from silent film to sound, Frances sailed through. Her greatest critical success came with two talkies, 1930's 'The Big House' and 1931's 'The Champ'.

'The Big House' was a realistic crime drama set inside a prison, and it won Frances Marion an Academy Award for Best Adapted Screenplay. She was the first woman to win this category, and a year later became the first writer with two Oscars when she won Best Story for 'The Champ'. This was about a washed-up boxer trying to reconnect with his son; it had a 1979 remake starring Jon Voight and Faye Dunaway.

Eventually, Frances Marion got tired of Hollywood. With the introduction of the studio system and stricter censorship, it became too restrictive to be creative. As she quipped, Hollywood was like "writing on the sand with the wind blowing." So Frances walked away from the movie business, but kept writing, and in 1937 she released the first ever guide book on screenwriting, called 'How to Write and Sell Movies.'

By the time Frances Marion ended her career, she had written over 325 films across every single genre. She produced, directed, and broke barriers for future women in screenwriting. She is an inspirational figure because of her talent, her ambition, and her support of other women.

She has also inspired contemporary writers such as Cari Beauchamp, the author of a book about Frances Marion called 'Without Lying Down'. The title is from a great quote by Frances, who once said, "I spent my life searching for a man to look up to, without lying down." Cari says Frances is someone she looks to as a reminder of what women can overcome. "Anything I'm going through, she went through," said Cari, "I spend very little time on angst, because it's been faced before, it's been overcome before. Once you know you're a link in the chain, then you're not alone, you're not battling this by yourself. You're a link in the chain, and it's tremendously empowering and liberating."

Helen Holmes: The Action Hero

During the height of her fame, actress Helen Holmes was not happy with her scripts. She was frustrated by a lack of daring stunts, and claimed the male screenwriters refused to write action for women if they weren't capable of performing it themselves. "If a photoplay actress wants to achieve real thrills," she told a magazine, "she must write them into the scenario herself."

Helen Holmes was one of the first female action stars, a courageous, independent woman who was at the center of a long-running, popular franchise. Her fearlessness in performing death-defying stunts made her a mythic hero.

Helen's own history is a bit of a myth itself. There are no official records to show exactly when or where Helen was born, but it's been estimated as being somewhere close to 1892. Around the age of 18, Helen moved to Death Valley in California, where stories say she learned to pan for gold with Native Americans. Some history books have her moving to New York and becoming a stage actress before heading to Hollywood. Others say she went straight to Los Angeles from Death Valley. Either way, Helen found herself living in Hollywood in her early twenties, where she struck up a friendship with silent film star Mabel Norman. Mabel then introduced Helen to the "King of Comedy" — director and producer Mack Sennett, who then encouraged her to become an actress.

Within a year of first being in front of the camera, Helen made twenty pictures. A year later, she had a contract with Kalem Studios, where she fell in love with director J.P. McGowan. The two were married sometime between 1912 and 1915. Again, the date remains a mystery, with no marriage certificate to be found.

Both Helen and J.P. had fathers who worked in the railroad industry, and perhaps inspired by that, they began making films which starred Helen in or around (or frequently, on top of) trains. This was at the same time that first-wave feminism was growing, and Helen was eager to prove that women could be action heroes too.

At the theaters, serials were all the rage. These were long-running series featuring a main character in different adventures across multiple episodes, usually with a cliffhanger ending. These serials screened before the feature film, with each episode lasting around 20 minutes. And it was the female-led serials which gained the biggest following; audiences loved seeing lady protagonists in action scenarios. I enjoy their titles: 'The Perils of Pauline', 'The Exploits of Elaine', and 'The Hazards of Helen'. The latter starred Helen Holmes.

Helen's character in 'The Hazards of Helen' was a railroad station telegraph operator who fought crime on the side and did indeed get herself into hazardous situations. She jumped onto moving trains, wrestled men who were holding guns, leapt between burning buildings, galloped horses down rocky mountain cliffs, and saved the railroad company from financial ruin. Many of these adventures were written by Helen herself, and she also filled in as director when her husband was hospitalized after a nasty fall on set.

After almost 50 episodes, Helen and her husband left 'The Hazards of Helen' and Kalem Studios to set up their own company. At Signal Film Productions, they made more popular serials, such as 'The Girl and the Game' and 'A Lass of the Lumberlands', featuring Helen partaking in even more exciting railroad-themed adventures.

The press had a fascination with Helen and wrote stories about her daredevil antics with breathless headlines like "Houdini Outdone by Helen Holmes!" Another article noted her strength, saying Helen liked "pretty gowns" but could "burst the sleeves of any of them by doubling her biceps." And 'Moving Picture World' magazine covered the excitement of "Helen Holmes Day," for which the California State Fair had organized Helen to perform a live stunt. In front of an audience of around 250 people, she jumped from a moving train into a moving car mere seconds before the train crashed.

For some of her more dangerous scenes, Helen was doubled by a professional stuntman. But she insisted on performing as many as she could, which led to some scary moments, such as the time the brakes on her truck failed as she was speeding downhill, or when she narrowly escaped a burning train, and that other time when her eye was punctured by cactus thorns. There's also an unconfirmed rumor that Helen's thumb was severed when she jumped from a horse onto a moving train.

But it was a broken heart that did the most damage. When her marriage to J.P. McGowan fell apart, Helen stayed off the screen for two years. The strain of working together in remote locations and performing intenswe action scenes had taken their toll on the couple. Their separation was reported in the Los Angeles Times with the headline, "Helen Holmes Principal in a Domestic Smash Up!" To make matters worse, the financial company backing Signal Film Productions went bankrupt, taking their studio down with it.

43

Helen returned to the screen a few years later and created Helen Holmes Pictures to produce her own work. She even reunited with her estranged husband briefly, both romantically and as collaborators, but they never quite reached the success of their earlier serials. As the 1920s wore on, the image of women changed. The modern flapper girl and the goth-like vamp were in, while the adventurous serial star was out – well, for women anyway, there were still serials starring male actors throughout the 1920s and 1930s. (And these characters inspired another decades later, in the form of Indiana Jones.) In 1936, a reporter for the Los Angeles Times noted the change for women, writing, "There are no more serial queens...the serials now prefer to let their menfolk wear the pants."

But in her day, Helen Holmes was a hero. Along with other serial stars, Helen showed audiences what a fearless woman looked like, right at the time when women needed to be brave and fight for their rights. Even "The Duke" had a thing for her. John Wayne admitted that as a teenager, Helen Holmes was his first crush.

STRUGGLING IN THE SYSTEM (1930s)

It's staggering to learn that in the first three years of the Great Depression, approximately one hundred thousand jobs were lost in America each and every week. The stock market crash of 1929 had a huge impact on industries; movies were not immune, and nearly a third of all theaters shut down by 1933.

Hollywood suffered, but managed to survive by adjusting the way it made films. Feature-length sound films were costly to produce, so studios relied on banks to finance their projects. Producers had to make sure they got their investment back, and the most powerful were ambitious young men like "Boy Wonder" Irving Thalberg, who was just 20 years old when he was put in charge of production at Universal. Professor Karen Ward Mahar explains that this was when women started to disappear from Hollywood. "Banking interests came to town, and defined women as unfit to handle large numbers of people or large amounts of capital." They preferred to deal with male executives.

In the 1930s, eight movie studios ended up with most of the power, and they produced two-thirds of all Hollywood feature films during the decade. There was the major "Big Five", comprised of Twentieth Century Fox, MGM, Paramount Pictures, RKO, and Warner Bros, and the minor "Little Three": Columbia Pictures, United Artists, and Universal Studios. All of these companies were run by men except United Artists, where Mary Pickford continued to work.

With this new concentration of power, the big movie studios became an oligopoly, a word I needed to look up. According to the Oxford Dictionary, it is "a state of limited competition, in which a market is shared by a small number of producers or sellers." To put it simply, a few movie studios controlled the majority share of film revenue in America. They had their own labs to print their films, and bought theaters to exclusively play their product. They mastered the art of Vertical Integration, where they controlled every part of their own production, distribution, and exhibition. This was otherwise known as the 'Studio System'.

Each studio began to have its own identity. They placed their biggest stars under contracts so they couldn't work for anyone else, and created movies based around them. There were also specific genres for each studio — for example, Warner Bros had gangster films, Universal was the home of horror, Paramount made comedies with the Marx Brothers, and MGM had "more stars than there are in heaven."

A constant across all of these studios was the type of people working for them. The images on the screen may have been black and white, but the actors were overwhelmingly one color. When non-Caucasian actors appeared in movies, they were relegated to the sidelines and given roles fraught with racist stereotypes. They also had to deal with segregation on film sets and lower pay. Sometimes white actors would replace them completely, playing different races with crude "blackface" makeup.

45

So, why would non-white actresses even want to enter a business which actively excluded them? That's what author Nancy Wang Yuen explored in her book 'Reel Inequality'. These actors were as Nancy said, "very realistic about their chances of success. But many of them saw it as activism in Hollywood, and I was surprised by how much they were interested in changing the system from within. Tiny, minuscule changes like changing out costume...to invoke authenticity. Over and over again, actors of color across different groups were able to challenge the system, and saw themselves as change agents in the system."

The few and limited opportunities for non-white actors were further restricted with the arrival of the production code, with its ruling against interracial romance. The code was a form of censorship, brought in after protests started over the content of movies. In the late 1920s and early 1930s, studios began producing riskier films full of sex and violence, hoping to get audiences into theaters by offering more "bang" for their buck. Groups like the Catholic Legion of Decency complained, and a list of rules were enforced. The subjects outlawed included many that were particular to women, such as abortion, birth control, and pretty much everything other than fashion and love.

The 1930s represents a sharp decline for women holding power in Hollywood, as they were restricted by the studio system, star contracts, and the production code. But despite numerous obstacles, several brave women stood out.

Dorothy Arzner: The Only Female Filmmaker

During the 1930s, Dorothy Arzner was the only female filmmaker who continued to work in Hollywood. She made commercial hits, wore suits, invented the boom microphone, and was the first woman to be invited into the Directors Guild of America, as well as a fierce feminist and a lesbian. She was definitely ahead of her time.

46

As a teenager, Dorothy helped her father serve customers at his restaurant in Hollywood. The clientele included several celebrities like Mary Pickford, Charlie Chaplin, and D.W. Griffith. As Dorothy wanted to study medicine, she enrolled at college. But she never finished her degree, because when America joined World War I, she dropped out to volunteer in France in the ambulance corps.

When Dorothy returned to America, a friend she had made in Europe introduced her to William C. DeMille. He was the brother of high profile Hollywood director Cecil B. DeMille, and he too worked in the movies. William gave Dorothy a job as a script typist at the Famous Players Lasky studio, which soon became Paramount.

Dorothy was a hard worker, who quickly moved up from typist to screenwriter and then to film editor. She set her sights on directing, and in the late 1920s, she told the studio if they didn't let her in the director's chair, she would go to Columbia Pictures.

In 1927 she directed her first feature, called 'Fashions for Women'. This was a silent film with a mistaken identity plot, all about a cigarette girl who pretends to be a famous fashion model and falls in love with a duke. It was a huge commercial success and proved to Paramount they had made the right choice by giving in to her demands to direct the film.

As the 20s turned into the 30s, silent films were making way for sound. Before the production code governing censorship was created, there were seven glorious years we now call 'pre-code'. More than just a time before the production code was enforced, for cinephiles these films remain a rare gift. Pre-code movies were almost defiant in their raciness, with open discussion of sex, drugs, interracial relationships, and homosexuality. All these subjects were banned once the code came in. For women, pre-code films offered interesting roles where they were more in charge of their sexuality.

One of my favorite of the pre-code films is Dorothy Arzner's 1929 work 'The Wild Party'. This was Dorothy's first sound film, and also star Clara Bow's debut speaking role. Clara was the original "It Girl," a term given to her after she starred in a film called 'It' and became the poster child for the flapper movement. Clara had had a tough life; she'd grown up with a father who had sexually abused her and a mother who tried to murder her (and was later institutionalized), and in Hollywood she'd often felt used by male directors on set. But with Dorothy, Clara was well cared for.

47

'The Wild Party' was a remake of an earlier silent film Dorothy had directed. Clara played a college student who loved to party and had a crush on her professor. It featured a largely female cast, and underneath its antics, it was really about female friendships and women choosing independence over a man.

While she was making 'The Wild Party', Dorothy noticed how Clara couldn't move freely while worrying about the microphone, which was large and had to be hidden somewhere in clothing or furniture. Having to worry about talking directly into a stationary microphone greatly restricted where an actor could move, which was a distraction to their performance. So Dorothy had a brilliant idea. She asked her crew to put the microphone on a fishing rod, and dangle it above Clara, moving the mike as she moved. This worked, and the boom microphone was born.

The common theme throughout Dorothy Arzner's work concerns the complexities of women and their relationships. Looking at her films now, they are a treasure trove of feminism, and it is absolutely astounding to think that she made them during the male-dominated studio system era.

One of the great examples of this is the 1933 film 'Christopher Strong', in which Dorothy cast Katharine Hepburn in a role that was perfect for (or perhaps, helped to create) Hepburn's persona as an adventurous, strong-willed, independent woman. In a nod to the serial queens of the silent era, Katharine plays aviator Lady Cynthia Darrington who falls in love with a married man, the titular Christopher Strong, and in a reversal of the normal gender roles, seduces him in a very direct manner. When Cynthia falls pregnant, she realizes Christopher will never leave his family and that she doesn't want to be the "other" woman. So she takes on the aviation challenge of breaking the record for flying the highest altitude, which she knows she won't survive.

In the end, Cynthia chose to keep her own independence and to not hurt the wife any further. And though the title is named after the male character, the film is told from Cynthia's perspective. This was noted by critic Pauline Kael, who wrote that 'Christopher Strong' is "one of the rare movies told from a woman's sexual point of view." The costumes are wonderful too, with Katharine wearing pants and at one point, a magnificent metallic moth evening gown (which is never quite properly explained, but which should be Googled to be believed).

Dorothy's most famous film is 'Dance, Girl, Dance' starring Lucille Ball and Maureen O'Hara. It was made in 1940, but didn't find an audience until decades later, when it was embraced by second-wave feminists in the 1970s. It was truly ahead of its time and made pointed remarks about the male gaze in entertainment, and how women are persuaded to be part of it.

Lucille and Maureen play two dancers, Bubbles and Judy, who are constantly dealing with aggressive male behavior, unwanted flirtation, and pressures to perform in a strip burlesque show. Bubbles agrees to do it, but Judy just wants to dance ballet. This causes tension between the two friends.

All of the dance scenes are shot from spectators' viewpoints — whether it is Judy's teacher watching her practice or the sleazy audience at the burlesque show.

In one remarkable scene, the crowd is heckling Judy to strip while she is dancing ballet; fed up, she walks to the edge of the stage and looks down at the audience. "I know you want me to tear my clothes off so you can look your fifty cents worth. Fifty cents for the privilege of staring at a girl the way your wives won't let you." She continues angrily, "We'd laugh right back at the lot of you, only we're paid to let you sit there and roll your eyes and make screaming clever remarks. What's it for? So you can go home and strut before your wives and sweethearts and play at being the stronger sex for a minute? I'm sure they see through you just like we do!"

In response, one of the women in the audience stands up and gives Judy a clap, and slowly, the rest of the crowd joins in. It's a triumphant moment, but as Judy leaves the stage, Bubbles slaps her in a jealous rage, claiming she stole her spotlight. Judy slaps back, and the two have a cat fight on stage, while the audience glares on.

This is a scathing message about women in film. By having Judy looking back at the audience and seeing their perspective, Dorothy reverses the power of performer and spectator, pointing out how women are seen as objects to be looked at, expected to shut up and strip. And then, Dorothy quickly returns the power to its usual place, as the two women degrade themselves and ruin their friendship in front of the crowd.

Sadly, 'Dance, Girl, Dance' was Dorothy's final film. While working on her next movie in 1943, she contracted pneumonia, and after directing sixteen feature films in total, decided to leave Hollywood. She found her place teaching film at UCLA, where she mentored a young director by the name of Francis Ford Coppola.

When she died in 1979, she had no Oscars to her name; but Dorothy Arzner nonetheless left a legacy, for when female filmmakers started to slip back into Hollywood in the 1970s, they looked to Dorothy for inspiration. She was someone who had everything working against her — a lesbian, a feminist, and a female director in the 1930s – but she was hugely successful. As Katharine Hepburn wrote to her in 1975, "Isn't it wonderful that you've had such a great career, when you had no right to have a career at all?"

Mae West: The Sex Symbol vs the Code

In 1930s Hollywood, Mae West was a terrifying prospect. Here was a woman who really owned her status as a sex symbol, and used it to make pointed remarks about America's fear of sex. And it was that fear which ruined her career.

From a young age Mae West was well aware of how she appeared. "I'd always look at myself in the reflection of the store windows to see how I'd look," said Mae, "I never wanted to be seen carrying a big, ugly package — only pretty, little ones tied with ribbons." Her father had been a boxer, and her mother was a corset model. The combination of those two things is exactly how I think of Mae: she was a fighter, dressed in a corset.

Mae performed from almost the very start of her life. At age five, she started winning amateur neighborhood talent shows, and by 13 she was being paid to act on Broadway.

After years of performing, Mae decided to write her own play, under the pen name Jane Mast. She called it simply, 'Sex', being purposely provocative to grab attention. The play centered on a prostitute in Montreal, but it went deeper than that; it was a thoughtful look at how sex is treated as taboo. As if to prove her point, newspapers refused to run print ads for the play because of its title. But Mae was a smart businesswoman, and she went public saying that this was a form of censorship, knowing that the papers would cover her protest.

They did, giving her exactly the publicity she needed to engage audiences. The show was a hit and ran for 375 performances. But bowing to growing pressure from those who thought it was obscene, the show was raided by police in 1927. Mae West and around 20 cast members were arrested on charges of indecency. She refused to shut the show down, and in court, the judge asked Mae if she was trying to show contempt. She responded, "On the contrary, your Honor. I was doing my best to conceal it."

It was that kind of witticism that made Mae West so brilliant. She was sent to prison for ten days, but as she left, she sold her story to a magazine for one thousand dollars, then used the money to set up the Mae West Memorial Library at the female prison.

51

Mae's next plays were also controversial. 'The Drag' was about gay men, and is often called the first play to show homosexuality in a sensitive light. 'Pleasure Man' featured a troupe of female impersonators. This show was also raided by police twice, and 60 cast members were arrested while still in costume. Mae bailed the actors out both times, and was acquitted in court thanks to a split jury.

Then in 1932, Paramount found itself in financial trouble and looked to Mae West for help. The studio wanted to buy the play which had been her biggest success, called 'Diamond Lil'. It was about a saloon singer and prostitute in the 1890s, and had Mae wriggling her way through her sexy starring role, resplendent in elaborate costumes. As often was the case with Mae's work, it was about sex, but actually featured nothing indecent.

Universal Pictures had tried to buy the play a few years earlier, but had been warned by the Motion Pictures Producers and Distributors of America (MPPDA), which advised on the content of films, that it had too many "vulgar dramatic situations" to be made. Paramount got around this by altering a few details, including changing the title, to 'She Done Him Wrong'. Mae chose to cast Cary Grant as her co-star, saying that she loved his voice. He wasn't yet famous, but this film helped to promote him as a sexy leading man.

Audiences around the country loved the film so much that there were reports of people sitting through multiple screenings. Photoplay magazine ran an article saying Mae was "blonde, buxom and rowdy," and that she specialized in "naughty ladies with big souls and golden hearts." The film, its star, and her body became famous.

Mae's voluptuous figure was coveted, both because it was different and because this was in the middle of the Great Depression, when many people were starving and thin. Her attitudes toward sex were also bold and new. Mae had ownership over her body, and saw sex simply as a natural act. "We can no more eliminate the primary emotion of sex-hunger from our birthright, then we can remove our hearts," said Mae. By being so open with her thoughts, Mae removed any smuttiness and shame. The New York Times said she was "the healthiest influence which has reached Hollywood in years."

When Paramount came knocking a second time, Mae was able to make some demands. She wanted final cut approval, the ability to choose her director and leading man (Cary Grant once again), and most importantly, she wanted to write a new script, one not based on a play. For 'I'm No Angel', she consulted her existing joke books for sexy one-liners to add to the film. One of the most famous was, "When I'm good, I'm good, but when I'm bad, I'm better."

At the time, censors were becoming uncomfortable with the content of movies. Despite the MPPDA making suggestions, they weren't always heeded. There was a rush of violent gangster films like 'Public Enemy' and a slew of sexual movies, including the two Mae West pictures. The Catholic Legion of Decency and some women's groups protested about the "morally corrupt" content, and the production code came into force.

With its list of strict rules, the change was dramatic. In 1933, Mae West had topped the box office, but in 1934, it was Shirley Temple.

The code restricted Mae's fierce sexuality and was the beginning of the end for her career. Mae had been working on her next film, 'I'm No Sin', but with the code it was quickly changed into a pale and unrecognizable imitation. Gone was the title, in favor of the more generic 'Belle of the Nineties'. Also out was any provocative material and witty one-liners about sex. The film was lackluster and didn't do well with audiences.

As for her image, Paramount and the publicity team worked hard to recreate Mae West. They insisted that her performances and frank interviews were complete fiction, and tried to erase her working-class background. For her next film, Mae worked with censors to make sure it was completely clean, and the ads for 'Goin' To Town' stated this was a "new, streamlined Mae West," ready to "set a new standard." But without the ability to be herself, in all her sparkling sexual glory, audiences lost interest.

53

In the end, Mae West was "too much" for Hollywood. Too sexy, too bawdy, too much herself and not a carefully created Hollywood starlet. But her legend has lived on, and as Mae herself said, "You only live once, but if you do it right, once is enough."

Hattie McDaniel: The Oscar Winner

When Hattie McDaniel attended the 12th annual Academy Awards as a nominee, producer David O. Selznick had to call in a favor just so she could sit down. The 1940 Oscars were held at the Cocoanut Grove nightclub inside the Ambassador Hotel, which had a strict segregation policy. Hattie was allowed in, but had to sit at a table hidden in the back, far away from the rest of the cast from 'Gone With The Wind'.

This is just one example of the many battles Hattie McDaniel had to face in Hollywood. From getting interesting roles to attending her own premiere, the value of her Oscar, and even where her family was allowed to bury her...it was not easy to be Hattie. Inside Hollywood, she had to deal with racism. Outside, she was criticized for playing stereotypes. But she had to play by the rules in order to break them. As Hattie famously said, "I would rather make seven hundred dollars a week playing a maid than being one."

Both of Hattie's parents were former slaves who escaped during the Civil War. They met at a "contraband camp," filled with other slaves who had managed to break free. Her father volunteered for the Union Army, and later they married. But when they started to have children, they faced heartbreak after heartbreak, with six babies dying at birth or soon after. By the time Hattie was born, the family was living in extreme poverty, and she suffered from malnutrition as a baby. And despite her father's service in the Army, the Government refused his pension several times. On one occasion, his claim was denied on the grounds he could not prove his exact age. "It is impossible for me to furnish a record of my birth," he replied, "I was a slave."

They had a hard life, but the McDaniel family was full of natural talent, so their small rented house was always filled with song and dance. Hattie's brother Otis was a particularly skilled dancer, and was determined to change his family's situation. He and his brother Sam, along with some friends, started performing as the Cakewalk Kids, hiring themselves out for community functions and white society dances. The Cakewalk was a dance move originally created by slaves poking fun at their white masters, but it had become a popular trend around the country.

Hattie would sometimes perform in their shows, and she drew praise for her singing and satirical skits. Often, she poked fun at the "Mammy" stereotype, but ironically, this was the very role which would make her famous later on.

When she was fifteen, Hattie took part in a drama competition. This is a moment she always pointed to as being life-altering. She performed an emotional rendition of the poem 'Convict Joe', a story of a husband who kills his wife during a drunken rage. As she finished, she was in tears, and the crowd erupted in applause, rising to their feet. Hattie won the Gold Medal, and said later this win gave her an indescribable feeling of happiness and the knowledge that performing was her destiny.

In the early 1930s, after a brief stint as a blues singer, Hattie moved to Los Angeles. There, she met casting agent Charles Butler, one of the few black people working behind the scenes in Hollywood. He was hired by Central Casting as "head of all Negro employment," and his job involved going into black neighborhoods to search for African-Americans who could fill small roles in Hollywood movies.

This was a conflicting prospect for many black actors, because while Butler was able to get employment and money for the community, he was seen as working for a racist structure, which would only hire actors for the background or as stereotypes.

That's what happened to Hattie, who was hired by Charles for $7.50 a week. She began to be cast in movies, always small, subservient roles. But with each and every part, Hattie found a way to make them her own. This was how she rebelled against the system. These characters were meant to be hidden in the background, but Hattie made sure she was seen.

Her success wasn't always welcomed by the black community. Some actors, like Clarence Muse, recognized her talent, but organizations like the National Association for the Advancement of Colored People (NAACP) criticized Hattie for taking on demeaning characters and being used by Hollywood to further racism.

In the mid-1930s, Hollywood was excited by the news that producer David O. Selznick was making an epic film adaptation of 'Gone with the Wind'. The racist tone of the book was a concern for the NAACP, but because of its size, the role of Mammy was seen as a good prospect for African-American actresses.

Casting was a big process, and everyone wanted a say as to who should play Mammy. Producer David O. Selznick received hundreds of letters from all different people in Hollywood, vouching for which actress they thought would make the best Mammy. One he received was from Bing Crosby, who wrote, "Being loath to go down in history as the only citizen not sticking my nose into the casting of 'Gone with the Wind', I would like to suggest a Mammy." Bing said he didn't know her name, but there was a "little lady" who he had worked with on 'Showboat' who "would be a cinch," and suggested David ask the casting office for her name. He was referring to Hattie McDaniel, and David wrote back, "thanks for the suggestion, and also for not wanting to play Scarlett." Soon Hattie was called in to test for the role of Mammy and when her audition was over, David knew he had found the one.

Prior to shooting 'Gone with the Wind', Hattie and Clark Gable had become friends. He was the dashing actor who had had great success a few years earlier with his film 'It Happened One Night'. During the filming of 'Gone with the Wind' he was a friend to the black actors on set, determined to use his power to make sure there was no discrimination or segregation. Once, he saw a row of toilets for the cast labeled "Whites" and "Coloreds" and got incredibly upset, saying if the signs were not taken down, they would need to find a new Rhett Butler.

On set, Hattie was known for entertaining the cast with jokes and songs, but as soon as the camera rolled, Hattie transformed. There's one pivotal scene towards the end of the movie where Mammy is telling the character of Melanie about Rhett's grief after losing his child. It's a short scene, but extremely powerful and Hattie shows the kind of dramatic emotion that black actors almost never had the chance to play in their small roles at this time.

After that scene, the cast and crew were in awe. Olivia de Havilland had hoped to win Best Supporting Actress for her role as Melanie, but later said that at that moment, she knew it would belong to Hattie. "That scene probably won Hattie her Oscar," she said, "and almost broke my heart too — at least at the time."

When production had wrapped, David O. Selznick wrote a letter to thank Hattie for her work, saying, "I think you will find it is universally acclaimed as one of the finest performances of this or any other year." The press agreed, with Variety pointing to that emotional scene, saying, "Time will set a mark on this moment in the picture as one of those inspirational bits of histrionics long remembered." And the Los Angeles Times praised Hattie as "worthy of academy supporting awards."

The film held its big premiere in Atlanta, Georgia, in 1939, but Hattie McDaniel and her co-star Butterfly McQueen were not allowed to attend. The city enforced the Jim Crow rule of segregation on the theater, and they even deleted her image from the program, so it only showed pictures of the white cast.

All the positive reviews for Hattie McDaniel in 'Gone with the Wind' led to David O. Selznick pushing for a Best Supporting Actress nomination. The win was historic, with Hattie McDaniel becoming the first African-American to get an Academy Award. She was proud of her achievement and genuinely thought this win would change things. Hattie was sure this would lead to more substantial roles, but unfortunately, she was never offered the breakthrough part she hoped for. "It was as if I had done something wrong," Hattie said in 1944.

Overall, Hattie had roles in an estimated 300 movies, but only received screen credit for about 80 of them. And 74 of those were subservient roles. She gave her Oscar to Howard University, but it was deemed "valueless" by appraisers and went missing in the early 1970s, never to be recovered.

Hattie McDaniel had another moment of success in 1947 as the voice of 'Beulah' in a popular radio play. This turned into a TV show in the early 1950s, but Hattie was only able to shoot six episodes before she fell ill from cancer. When she died, Hattie's final wish was to be buried at the Hollywood Forever Cemetery, where many celebrities were laid to rest. She was denied, once again due to segregation.

There were seventy years between the Oscar wins of Hattie McDaniel and actress Mo'Nique. Mo'Nique took the stage in a blue dress and gardenias, as an homage to Hattie's outfit from the 1940 ceremony. In her speech, Mo'Nique thanked Hattie for "enduring all that she had to, so that I would not have to."

In her own Oscar speech, Hattie McDaniel said her greatest hope was to "always be a credit to my race and the motion picture industry." She was supposed to be subservient, but she refused. Hollywood gave her an inch, and she made it an award-winning mile. And in doing so, she made that hope come true.

Anna May Wong: Erasure and Exoticism

For many American audiences watching movies in the 1920s, their first experience seeing an Asian-American star was through the work of Anna May Wong. She was a silent film actress who defied expectations by making the transition to talking pictures, and along the way, became a popular star in Europe.

Anna May was born Liu Tsong Wong in 1905, which translates to "frosted yellow willow." She was a third generation Chinese-American, speaking Cantonese at home, and English at school. Her childhood was very American and her neighborhood was a cultural mix, with hers being the only Chinese family in their local block. Their neighborhood was also a popular spot for filming movies, and young Liu loved to watch them being made. Crew members nicknamed her "C.C.C." for "Curious Chinese Child," because she used to hang around on each of the sets watching the filming process intently. Liu would also save her lunch money to attend the small nickelodeon theaters that had started to spring up around Los Angeles. And by age 11, she had decided she wanted a career in the movies, and combined her English and Chinese names to call herself Anna May Wong.

At 14 years old, Anna was playing in her neighborhood when she was approached by James Wang, a casting director whose job was to recruit Chinese actors and extras for Hollywood movies. He offered her a small part in a film called 'The Red Lantern', playing a young Chinese girl. Anna said later that she was "flattered, until I learned that he had just had an order for 600 Chinese actors in a hurry and hadn't been able to find but fifty." Still, she prepared to shine in her tiny role by using makeup as she had seen the actors do on sets. When she arrived with brightly rouged cheeks, the director told her to wash her face immediately, because she was supposed to be playing a peasant. The film was released in 1919, and Anna and her friends excitedly went to the premiere to see her big debut. But her moment on screen was too quick, and even Anna couldn't tell which of the girls was her.

After more roles as extras, Anna was sure that acting was the profession for her. This became even more clear after she suffered through a rare illness called Saint Vitus's Dance. The disorder causes the body to jerk uncontrollably, and the Chinese medicinal cure for it was just as painful. After surviving this ordeal, Anna decided she wanted to concentrate fully on her passion for acting. She dropped out of school and started to look for bigger roles. And she felt she had nothing to lose. "I was so young when I began," Anna later told Motion Picture Magazine, "that I knew I still had youth if I failed, so I determined to give myself 10 years to succeed as an actress." Anna May was just 16 years old, so her father made the rule that she should have an adult chaperone at all times.

Anna's first big role came that very year, in 'Bits of Life', which is considered to be the first anthology film ever made, telling four separate stories. Though she was still just 16, Anna's role was to play a mother in one of the segments, the wife of a man played by Lon Chaney, who was 22 years older than she was. 'Bits of Life' was well-received, and the following year, in 1922, Anna was cast in a movie which made her the first Chinese-American film star.

'Toll of the Sea' was the second feature film shot using Technicolor, and the first color film that was able to be screened in regular movie theaters. The fascination of this new process made the movie a huge hit. The script was written by Frances Marion, and her brief was to create a movie which would showcase the use of color in movies. Frances said, "The story itself was of little importance compared to the widespread interest in the potential of color." She decided on a story set in China, using a plot similar to the opera 'Madama Butterfly'. The lead role, a Hong Kong girl named Lotus Flower was won by Anna May Wong. In the story, Lotus falls for an American man, but their interracial relationship causes scandal. When she becomes pregnant he fears it will hurt his career, so he leaves her to go back to America. Four years later he returns, now with a new American wife, and insists on taking their child back to the U.S. to have a better life. In the end, Lotus throws herself off the side of a rocky cliff.

It was quite a demanding part for a 17-year-old who had only been in bit roles, but Anna rose to the challenge, and along with the movie, she was a hit. The New York Times praised her skill in a review, writing, "Completely unconscious of the camera, with a fine sense of proportion and remarkable pantomimic accuracy...She should be seen again and often on the screen." With this, Anna became a rarity in Hollywood. Asian-American actresses were not often seen on screen, and definitely weren't given prominent, complex roles to shine in. And apart from Japanese actor Sessue Hayakawa, no other Asian actor had yet broken through to become a star.

But of course, the very structure of Hollywood restricted the type of roles Anna May Wong could play. The production code in force at the time forbade non-white actresses to play serious love interests with white actors. You could hint at interracial relationships, but the attraction would then need to be punished by the death of the non-white character, lest the film send the message that mixing of cultures was ok. "No film lovers can ever marry me [on screen]," said Anna, "If they got an American actress to slant her eyes and eyebrows and wear a stiff black wig and dress in Chinese culture, it would be alright. But me? I am really Chinese. So I must always die in the movies, so that the white girl with the yellow hair may get the man."

As author Nancy Wang Yuen explains, the production code even prevented Asian actors from starring with white actors who were playing Asian. "They couldn't star opposite a white man, and they couldn't even star opposite white actors who were playing Asians, because that counted as anti-miscegenation as well. There were those kind of structural codes in place that prevented them from ever even being considered. Anna May Wong did want to audition for bigger roles, but she was told that she couldn't because they had already cast a white man as the Chinese lead."

The roles she was offered consisted of racist stereotypes. They were either the subservient Asian slave girl, the exotic siren or the villainous "Dragon Lady." In this way, Anna May Wong's career reflects what many Asian-American actors still have to go through today. Be exoticized, play "Oriental" stereotypes, or don't exist at all. Orientalism is a racist way of seeing a variety of cultures from The East as one - from Japanese to Arabic to African and Chinese - all labeled exotic, mystic, uncivilized and often, barbaric. Asian actors also have to deal with the practice of whitewashing in Hollywood, where roles meant for actors of color are played by white actors. This still happens now, and back in Anna May Wong's day, it was even more common, with white actors donning "yellowface" to play Asian characters. So white people could play whatever role they wanted, but everyone else had to take the scraps.

To counter this, Anna tried to make good use of every opportunity given to her. Hollywood heavyweight Douglas Fairbanks had spotted her in 'Toll of the Sea', and sought her out to star next to him in 1924s 'The Thief of Baghdad'. In the swashbuckling film, Anna played a scheming slave, and the movie made over two million dollars at the box office. Audiences loved her, but Anna's career didn't please everyone. The Chinese government had tried to shut down 'The Thief of Baghdad', saying Anna's role was too erotic, and her parents constantly repeated the old Chinese proverb to her, saying, "a good man will not be a soldier and a good girl will not be an actress." Anna's parents were also sad that she was still single, but Anna found it hard, with Chinese-American men preferring Chinese women who were more "traditional," and American men preferring American women. Tabloid magazines also reported on her single status, with headlines like "Oriental Beauty Compelled to Choose Between Heritage of Race and Her Preference for an American Husband."

Over the next few years Anna had roles playing a variety of "exotic" nationalities. She was an Eskimo in 'The Alaskan' and the Indian princess Tiger Lily in 'Peter Pan'. But her parts continued to be of the small, supporting variety. By 1928, Anna May Wong was fed up with the roles given to her by Hollywood, and the extra pressures placed on her, so she decided to move to Europe, following in the footsteps of African-American actors Josephine Baker and Paul Robeson. "I was so tired of the parts I had to play," said Anna. "Why is it that the screen Chinese is nearly always the villain of the piece, and so cruel, a murderous, treacherous snake in the grass. We are not like that. We have our own virtues. We have our rigid code of behavior, of honor. Why do they never show these on the screen? Why should we always scheme, rob, kill? I got so weary of it all."

She found big success in Europe, where she made films in English, French and German, surprising audiences by speaking multiple languages. Her speaking voice was honed through speech lessons at Cambridge University, for which she spent a lot of her own money. This was a worthwhile investment, with talking pictures becoming increasingly popular around the world. She had a beautiful speaking voice, and her American accent was a shock for people not used to seeing Asian-Americans on screen. Fellow actress Katharine DeMille said Anna had "the world's most beautiful figure and face...and when she opens her mouth out comes Los Angeles Chinatown sing-sing girl and every syllable is a fresh shock."

Anna spent two years in Europe, but was so homesick, she returned to Hollywood in 1930. And nothing had changed. Her first role back was in the crime drama 'Daughter of the Dragon', where she played another dragon lady, a Princess living next door to the villain, Dr. Fu Manchu, who wants to take over the world. Fu Manchu was a character created by author Sax Rohmer, and one of the worst examples of how Hollywood portrayed Asian characters as "evil." Seeing villainous Asian characters and anti-Asian images on screen furthered the racist idea of "yellow peril" - the thought that the people of East Asia proposed a danger to the Western world. Fu Manchu was called "the yellow peril incarnate in one man," and was solely focused on bringing down Western civilization. The character appeared in a series of books, five movies and a radio serial. In the films, Fu Manchu was played by Swedish-American actor Warner Oland, who made a career of portraying characters in "yellowface" makeup. As well as Fu Manchu, Warner portrayed the detective Charlie Chan in 16 movies.

Despite her starring role in 'Daughter of the Dragon' and an increased profile after her work in Europe, Anna May Wong received half the amount of pay that her co-stars Warner Oland and Sessue Hayakawa were paid. But a better role came for her in 1932, next to Marlene Dietrich in 'Shanghai Express', directed by the legendary Josef von Sternberg. The film was a big success at the box office, and received Oscar nominations for Best Picture and Best Director, winning one for Best Black and White Cinematography.

Critics hailed Anna in 'Shanghai Express', but her success wasn't celebrated in China, with one headline claiming "Paramount Utilizes Anna May Wong to Produce Picture to Disgrace China." The press in that country had never supported her career, with articles describing her work as being "more than enough to disgrace the Chinese race." On her first trip to China in 1936, Anna was repeatedly questioned about her roles. She didn't write the characters, she had to insist, and these were the only parts offered to her. This is an extra pressure that many Asian-American actors have to face. It is not enough to simply have a career in Hollywood, you also have to think of how an entire race is being portrayed. Anna wasn't "American" enough for Hollywood, or "Chinese" enough for China. "It's a pretty sad situation," she once said, "to be rejected by the Chinese because I am too American."

Anna May Wong's career as an actress slowly faded over the 1940s and 1950s, and she was never able to get the type of lead roles and true stardom she craved. Her story remains another example of a talented actress held back by racism and sexism in Hollywood. But just by existing, by trying to be seen, Anna was able to begin to humanize early Asian characters on screen. And through her international recognition, through her interviews and appearances, Anna managed to educate audiences on the extra pressures she faced being an Asian actress in Hollywood.

Anna May Wong passed away in 1961 at the age of 56, after suffering a heart attack. And though her obituary in Time magazine called her "the screen's foremost Oriental villainess" her legacy stands for so much more. Her struggles are still being felt by Asian-American actors today, but her persistence encourages many to keep fighting.

The Woman's Picture

During the Great Depression, women started working. For the first time, they had a small income, and many would save up 25 cents to take themselves to the movies. There, they could escape the harsh realities of Depression-era life and watch their favorite movie actresses on screen.

In Hollywood, women continued to be successful screenwriters. These ladies had forged careers in the 1920s, and wanted to write stories in the 1930s which reflected their own independent spirits. Female screenwriters wanted to deliver films that the growing female audience inside the theaters would enjoy watching.

These films were called "The Woman's Picture," and they were incredibly popular between the 1930s and the early 1960s. It was a genre of its own, though it encompassed action, drama, screwball comedy, film noir, epics, and romance. The defining aspect of a woman's picture, as Professor Jeanine Basinger writes in 'A Woman's View' was that "it had a woman in the center of the story, a temporary liberation from her life of some kind, a tough choice between that liberation and love, and at the end, the reaffirmation that finding a man to love them is the most important thing, and that she absolutely cannot have both."

This was the interesting paradox of the woman's picture - these films perpetuated the idea of women needing men, but at the same time they empowered audiences by showing the character's independence. In order for the choice at the end to be suitably dramatic, what she was giving up had to be really exciting. For their 25 cents, women could go the movies and see characters who were on the verge of breaking free. The majority of the film showed a woman in power, and while it usually reversed that in the final five minutes, this didn't negate its overall impact. As Jeanine said, "when morality has to dramatize its own opposite to make its point, the opposite takes on a life of its own."

Here are some of my favorite examples. In 1933's 'Mary Stevens, M.D.', Kay Francis plays a doctor. A whole lot of melodrama ensues, including unrequited love, a baby out of wedlock, then the death of that baby... but in the end she saves another child's life (by using her hair pin); and female audiences loved the character's courage. 'The Great Lie' from 1941 starred Mary Astor as a woman more interested in being a concert pianist than a mother. 'Now Voyager' from 1942 had Bette Davis transforming from ugly duckling to beautiful swan, but gave her so many great qualities that audiences loved her character at every stage. She was already the hero at the beginning, despite the lack of makeup, eyebrow grooming, or fancy clothes.

The 1943 film 'Ladies Courageous' is all about female pilots. There's a lovely flashback scene, where a young girl at school is looking out the window, dreaming of flying a plane in the sky. Suddenly, a plane comes down and lands on the school's grounds. When the pilot gets out... it's a woman! And the girl knows it's a sign that she can do anything she dreams of.

I asked Jeanine Basinger for her favorite woman's picture, and she said she loved 'Mildred Pierce' from 1945, starring Joan Crawford. "I saw it as a child with my mother," said Jeanine. "When we came out of the theater, my mother reported that I said, 'Mom, why doesn't Mildred just get a new and better husband?' And then I said, 'Or maybe she doesn't need to have one,' and my mother thought she would never worry about me again, ever."

The Woman's Picture grew during the 1930s and thrived in the 1940s. The genre started to die in the 1950s, with television taking over, and by the 1960s, these films and most of their stars had been retired.

But in their day, these movies were star vehicles, offering meaty roles to their actresses where they were the lead and the men were in the background. These characters had clearly defined personalities, took charge, and were allowed to be unlikable and flawed. And though the situations were highly dramatic, the characters were women — not women with male characteristics, or otherworldly beings like superheroes or aliens. As Jeanine Basinger said, "Now, we have fewer positive female role models in terms of showing the ability to take action, to think for yourself, and to hold a very important high-level job or fly an airplane. Am I crazy here? I wouldn't mind seeing that!"

 # WAGING THEIR OWN WAR (1940s)

We all know that famous image of 'Rosie the Riveter'. She is an iconic piece of World War II imagery, with her knotted scarf in her hair, her sleeves rolled up, biceps flexed, gritted teeth, and the slogan, "We Can Do It!" emblazoned over her head. It's a poster still used and referenced today, and it shows how the image of women changed during World War II.

Propaganda icons like Rosie were used to encourage women to get out and work. With men required to fight on the front lines, women were needed to fill their places in the workforce. And quite suddenly, ladies who had been told their entire lives that home was where they should be were seeing images in advertising and messages in movies telling them they were just as capable at labor as men. The work was definitely tough for women at this time and the workplaces were full of sexism, but for some women, World War II actually offered career fulfillment unlike anything they had ever experienced.

The power of promoting women as war workers was also reflected on the big screen. Of course, female characters were still required to look glamorous and ultimately find love, but they were shown performing empowering tasks. There was 1943's 'Women Like Us', about female factory workers. And 1942's multi-Oscar winning 'Mrs. Miniver,' where Greer Garson played a housewife who transforms into the ultimate "wartime Madonna." She was a woman who was beautiful, courageous, and selfless in her nurturing of family and orphans.

I particularly love 'So Proudly We Hail', also made in 1943. This movie starred Claudette Colbert, Veronica Lake, and Paulette Goddard as a group of nurses on the front lines. The ending in particular is extremely powerful. Veronica Lake's character realizes the only way to save her unit from enemy attack is to sacrifice herself. And so, she shakes her long, blonde locks free from her helmet, takes the pin out of a single grenade, hides it under the lapel of her uniform, and walks purposely towards the opposing battalion.

The next example is problematic, because it's simultaneously empowering for women and completely racist. 'Dragon Seed' from 1944 featured Katharine Hepburn in the biggest budget movie she'd made up until then. Hepburn played a strong, feminist character living in a small village during the war who preferred attending political meetings to doing housework. When she has a child, she gives up her baby to fight alongside the men. She is also the one who kills the "evil" Japanese army by poisoning their duck soup. The problem? Katharine Hepburn, a white woman from Connecticut, played a Chinese woman, complete with extremely offensive yellowface makeup. Several of the other Japanese and Chinese characters were also portrayed by white actors.

The war raged on, and inside cinemas around America, audiences were increasingly female. Women's pictures continued in popularity, and the newsreels playing before the films showed women working in factories and female celebrities doing their part for the war effort. Such as Bette Davis, who ran the Hollywood Canteen in an old nightclub on Sunset Boulevard. If you were a soldier wearing a uniform, the food was free and the service was often provided by a star, such as Shirley Temple, Lana Turner, Lauren Bacall, Katharine Hepburn, Lucille Ball, Loretta Young, and many more.

The first Hollywood tragedy of World War II was a woman — actor Carole Lombard. She was known for her comedies and was dubbed "America's Screwball Queen" by Life magazine, and she became one of the highest paid stars of the late 1930s. Her fame grew even more when she married Clark Gable, "the King of Hollywood."

After World War II broke out, Carole focused her celebrity status on promoting the war effort. She actively participated in selling bonds, and in 1942 Lombard traveled to Indiana, where she, her mother, and MGM publicist Otto Winkler sold over $2 million worth in one day. Carole was due to take a train home to Los Angeles, but wanted to catch a plane in order to get back to Los Angeles faster and work on her rocky marriage, which was suffering after reports of Clark's infidelity. Both Carole's mother and Otto tried to talk her out of this idea, so she challenged them to a coin toss — if they won, she'd take the train; if she won, she'd get the plane. Carole won the coin toss, and tragically, her plane crashed into a mountain on its way to L.A., instantly killing everyone on board. Clark Gable was so distraught after her death, he signed up to serve in the U.S. Army Air Corps, just as Carole had been encouraging him to do.

After World War II, the film industry boomed, and 1946 ended up being the best year at the box office yet. During the Depression and the war, the government had largely let the big studios get away with monopolizing the industry, with the studio system, star contracts, studio ownership of theaters, and control over every part of the filmmaking process. But in 1938, the U.S. Justice Department sued all of the studios in a huge antitrust case. Paramount, as the largest of the bunch, was the primary defendant, and the case became known as the Paramount Decision.

The studios were let off the hook with an understanding that they would change their ways. But a decade later, nothing had really changed, so the Justice Department brought the lawsuit back into play, and this time they took it all the way to the Supreme Court. The Court found them guilty of violating the Antitrust Act by completely controlling the distribution system, and ordered them to sell their theaters.

This led to the crumbling of the power of the big studios, but it didn't open any new doors for women to return to Hollywood. So several brave women sought to change the industry themselves and waged their own personal wars.

Hedy Lamarr: The Pin-Up with the Patent

That old cliché that you should never judge a book by its cover applied perfectly to Hedy Lamarr. Her beautiful looks made her a movie star, but she was constantly fighting to be recognized for her brain. It was her intelligence that gave us an invention we all use every single day.

69

Born Hedwig Kiesler in 1914, she dropped out of school when she was sixteen, and at eighteen was cast in a movie which catapulted her to fame. The film was called 'Ecstasy' and required Hedy to be naked and simulate sex. It was the first movie to ever show a female orgasm on screen, with the camera staying on Hedy's face during the pivotal moment. Later, Hedy said her facial expressions were caused by the director poking her with a pin. At the film's premiere, Hedy's parents were shocked. She had warned them the movie was "artistic" but didn't mention the sex scenes. "I wanted to run and hide," Hedy said, "and my father solved the predicament. He simply rose and said grimly, 'We will go.' I gathered my belongings in one grab." The film gave Hedy her first taste of notoriety, but its reputation would come back to haunt her later.

A few years after, Hedy was performing on stage in Austria when she began to be wooed by Friedrich "Fritz" Mandl. Fritz was a wealthy and famous arms manufacturer with ties to powerful and terrifying people. They married when Hedy was just nineteen, she quickly began to realize how controlling he could be. She gave up her career in acting at his request, and then watched as he spent a fortune trying to destroy every single copy of 'Ecstasy' because he didn't want anyone to see his wife in that way. Over the years, Fritz became more paranoid, instructing his servants to listen in on Hedy's phone conversations and keep her inside the house when he was out. He also restricted her money to a small allowance and kept the key to her jewelry box.

One of Hedy's duties as his good wife was to attend his business dinners. Their guests included Mussolini and members of the Nazi party, who Fritz did deals with despite being Jewish himself. They spoke freely, with top-secret conversations about complex weapons systems including remote-control torpedoes and submarines, not thinking that Fritz's beautiful young wife, who was sitting there smiling, would be following along. As would be the case throughout her life, Hedy was much smarter than anyone appreciated.

At the time Hedy was secretly planning how to escape from her marriage and from the house, which she called a "prison of gold." There are many conflicting stories about how Hedy finally managed to leave Fritz. She told different versions over the years. As she once said, "I am sure that not in any motion picture would an escape scene be more dramatic," and the stories do seem like something straight out of a movie. My favorite story involves her drugging a servant, stealing a maid's uniform, and sneaking out of the house to catch a train to Paris. Other stories say she simply snuck out when her husband was away.

However she did it, Hedy managed to escape Vienna, "veiled and incognito and with all the trappings of a melodrama mystery," and ended up in London. As it happened, this was where Hollywood mogul Louis B. Mayer was taking a look at new studios built for MGM. How these two came to cross paths is another story that is hard to confirm, but whether they met at a party or through an agent who made the introduction, Louis ended up offering her a contract to come to America and act for MGM, which she promptly turned down because it didn't pay enough.

Hedy knew she could persuade Louis to offer a better deal if they spent more time together, so she arranged to be on his boat from London to New York. Her smart plan worked and she managed to completely charm Louis and his wife, and by the time they docked at Ellis Island, she had a star contract with MGM and a new last name of Lamarr.

Hedy Lamarr arrived in Los Angeles in late 1937, and spent six months working on speaking English and losing weight. Two things required of a successful starlet. At a party in 1938, she met the famous French actor Charles Boyer, who thought she was beautiful and gave her a role in a film called 'Algiers'. This was a remake of the French film 'Pépé le Moko', about a jewel thief who falls for a gorgeous woman and by doing so brings about his own capture. The movie was one of the biggest hits of 1938, a rare highlight during a particularly bad year for the box office.

Hedy got rave reviews, with the press heralding the arrival of a new Hollywood star. The only negative comment she received was that her breasts had to be padded because they were small as the result of losing weight. This was something she was already self-conscious about, having allegedly overheard producer Walter Wanger saying she had "small tits but a magnificent face." That sexist comment would end up influencing her life in an unforeseen way.

Though Hedy was a new star in Hollywood and was invited to many fancy parties, she didn't drink or attend any of those events. Instead, she stayed at home and took up the hobby of inventing.

She played around with creating a bouillon cube which would transform water into soda and an attachment to a tissue-box to get rid of used tissues. Those weren't successful, but soon, World War II gave her a brilliant idea.

Hedy had been keeping up with the news from Europe, and had heard about several tragedies where innocent civilians traveling by ship were killed by enemy torpedoes from submarines. At this same time, George Antheil, a composer and inventor was writing about endocrinology for Esquire magazine, claiming to be an expert on women and their glands. Hedy had read his articles and decided she had to meet George to see if he could make those two glands in her chest bigger. He remembered later that she was "the most beautiful woman on earth" and agreed to help her. As she left, Hedy reportedly wrote her number on his car windshield in lipstick.

The next day, he called Hedy to invite her to dinner. Along with the conversation about glands, they spoke about the war and their inventions. George had created a way to synchronize multiple player pianos using radio frequency. It turns out this was exactly the answer Hedy had been looking for. Taking all the knowledge she had gathered from those dinner parties with her former husband, she wanted to invent a new type of remote control torpedo which could hit those German submarines. Hedy had learned that the radio frequencies used between transmitters and torpedoes could be easily jammed, so her idea was to synchronize the signals so they could both change to random frequencies at the same time and thus go undetected. She called it "frequency hopping." And so, with Hedy's inside knowledge and George's previous experience with radio synchronization, they got to work.

At this time, Hedy Lamarr was considering leaving Hollywood, but continued to act. After 'Algiers' she was a hot property, but she had only had small parts since making it, which all focused on her appearance. In 1941, Hedy appeared in the flashy Busby Berkeley musical 'Ziegfeld Girl' next to Judy Garland, Jimmy Stewart, and Lana Turner, but the big takeaway to the press was how she looked in the elaborate headdress which was part of her costume.

During that same year, George and Hedy finalized their invention; they called it the "Secret Communication System" and submitted it to the U.S. Patent Office for approval. The office saw enough promise in their plans to pass it on to the Navy for consideration. But the Navy refused to implement the device, on the basis that it was "too bulky to be incorporated in the average torpedo." This confused George and Hedy, as the mechanisms were actually tiny. They figured the Navy might have misread their explanation about using technology from George's invention and thought they were proposing a radio frequency device as big as a piano. There's also the thought that they knew Hedy was involved, and dismissed it on the basis that she was a movie star. But despite the Navy's refusal to use it, eventually the patent office did accept their invention, and in August 1942, Hedy Lamarr and George Antheil received an official patent number.

During World War II, Hedy was determined to help out the cause in whatever way she could. She traveled the country to sell War Bonds and helped out at the Hollywood Canteen, where she served food and danced with soldiers. She continued to look for good roles; she had wanted to star in 'Casablanca' but MGM had refused to lend her out, and she lost the role to Ingrid Bergman. Later on, she turned down two roles which could have helped her career, 'Gaslight' (which also went to Ingrid Bergman) and the film noir 'Laura'.

Still, Hedy had a few popular roles in the 1940s, such as 'Tortilla Flat' with John Garfield and 'White Cargo', though worryingly, in this one, she played a bi-racial African woman. This was what the 1940s were like. Actresses of color lost roles to white actresses in blackface. But Hedy's biggest hits during the 1940s were radio plays, which broadcasted her voice straight into listener's living rooms and kept her a household name, and had nothing to do with her looks.

73

After the 1940s, Hedy's life took a sad turn. Over the next few decades she suffered from mental illness, was caught shoplifting twice, and had a lot of plastic surgery to hold on to her beauty. She also began to sue anyone and everyone she believed was trying to defame her, such as Mel Brooks in 'Blazing Saddles', who had named

Harvey Korman's character Hedley Lamarr, with jokes about her lawsuits. Hedy was not amused, so she sued Mel and Warner Bros.

Hedy also took her book publisher to court in 1966 over her autobiography, 'Ecstasy and Me'. Hedy claimed that she had given a ghost writer hours of interviews and dictation to tell the story of her life. When she received the manuscript, she signed off without reading it, desperate for the money. Her lawsuit claimed that the resulting book was a complete work of fiction, and she asked for $9.6 million in damages. She didn't win.

While all of this was going on, unbeknownst to her, Hedy's patent was being used. Parts of the invention that she and George devised were tweaked and put into action during the Cuban Missile Crisis in the 1950s and again during the Vietnam War in the 1960s. Decades later it was declassified, making it available to people outside of the military. Inventors who were tinkering with cell phone technology announced in the 1990s that they had been using the patent created by movie star Hedy Lamarr.

And so fifty years after Hedy Lamarr and George Antheil had their patent approved, Hedy was finally recognized as an inventor. This came as a shock to many people, who assumed she was just a pretty face to be revered on the screen. Instead, she had a vision for a futuristic technology each of us use today, in Wi-Fi, Bluetooth, GPS and more. Beauty is fleeting, but Hedy's legacy is enduring and gives women a role model in science. This is worthwhile, because as Hedy famously said, "Any girl can be glamorous. All you have to do is stand still and look stupid." But to be an inventor in the 1940s took much more.

Olivia de Havilland: The Lawmaker

Actress Olivia de Havilland became famous as the love interest cast opposite Errol Flynn. He was the dashing Australian star of the Robin Hood movies, always playing the hero role. But it was his beautiful sidekick Olivia who would end up being a real hero, fighting constrictive contracts which had kept actors locked in as possessions of the movie studios.

During the 1940s, every big star in Hollywood was essentially seen as currency. They were placed under a tight contract with one of the studios, and their main purpose was to make as much profit for the producers as possible. These contracts worked more in the favor of the studios than the stars, and they were able to be tweaked and extended as the studio wished. Each individual contract was supposed to be for seven years. Under these terms, actors didn't necessarily choose their own projects; instead they were assigned films of varying quality to star in. If they didn't want to do the project, they were put on "suspension" until another role could be found; basically it was a form of punishment where they weren't able to work and didn't get paid. And this time spent not working was added to the end of their contract. The studios got away with these extensions by claiming the cumulative working time would still be seven years... just spread out a little.

Stars could be "lent out" to other studios, but the negotiations (and compensation) were all done without the actor's involvement. And sometimes, the actor was purposely offered a role the studio knew they would turn down so the studio could keep them for longer. During these suspensions, a star also could not renegotiate their contract or terminate it to work with anyone else. It was all a way to prevent their biggest stars from leaving and keep overall studio costs down. But this restrictive practice ended when Olivia de Havilland fought back.

Olivia was just 18 when she was given her first contract with Warner Bros. She acted in a couple of small movies, but became a star at 19 when she was cast in a role opposite Errol Flynn. When Olivia first met Errol, he asked her, "What do you want out of life?" And Olivia's answer was very revealing of her personality; she said, "I want respect for difficult work well done."

She didn't get much difficult work, because her roles opposite Errol were supposed to be simple love interests. But these were well done, because Olivia gave every character she played an edge of fierce intelligence. Their most famous pairing was 'The Adventures of Robin Hood', where Errol played Robin and Olivia was a sassy Maid Marian. Despite her attempts to show what she was capable of, Warner Bros kept casting her as simple objects of lust for leading men.

On the surface, she let Warner Bros believe she was happy to do whatever they wanted. But behind the scenes, Olivia figured out a way to play the system. She had received a phone call from director George Cukor telling her that David O. Selznick had seen 'Robin Hood' and wanted Olivia to test for a role in 'Gone with the Wind'. George knew this needed to be done quietly because of her contract. "Would you consider doing something illegal?" he asked, whispering over the phone.

They arranged for Olivia to sneak into an office on the MGM studio lot to meet George Cukor and read for the part of Melanie, Scarlett O'Hara's sweet friend. When she was done, George called David O. Selznick and told him he had to meet her. That weekend Olivia drove to David's house, where she auditioned by acting out a scene between Scarlett O'Hara and Melanie. The role of Scarlett for this test was performed by David O. Selznick. "With his kinky hair and his rotund body and his thick spectacles, he was the most ridiculous Scarlett you could imagine," said Olivia, "and he read with such drama, clutching the curtains. It was so comical. I found it hard to keep a straight face." But she did, and as soon as it was over, David realized he had to cast her. "I guess we have to talk to Jack Warner," he said.

Selznick did, but Jack Warner refused, and then Olivia talked to him as well, but Jack still refused. He didn't want to lend her out, especially not for a supporting role. "If you want to play anything, why Melanie and not Scarlett?" he asked.

So Olivia took matters into her own hands, asking Jack Warner's wife Ann out for tea. She convinced Ann that any success she had with MGM would be beneficial for future roles at Warner Bros. Ann understood, and managed to turn her husband around.

'Gone with the Wind' became Olivia's chance to show a new side to her acting. As Melanie, she was the down-to-earth opposite of Scarlett O'Hara, and her performance won her an Oscar nomination.

When she went back to Warner Bros, Olivia expected to be met with substantial material — she was now an Oscar nominee, after all. But the studio kept assigning her the same type of simple love interest parts she was playing before 'Gone with the Wind'. She turned these roles down, and Warner Bros added suspension time to the end of her contract. When her seven sequential years were almost up, Olivia was ready to leave, but because of those suspensions, Warner Bros had her locked in for a further six months. So she took charge.

A few years earlier, another woman had attempted to fight back against these contracts. In 1936, Bette Davis had taken Warner Bros to court after being denied a role she really wanted to play — 'Mary of Scotland' for RKO. Jack Warner refused to lend her out, so she kicked up a fuss. Bette tried to request changes to her contract, but these were all denied, so in retaliation, she turned down the movie they wanted her to do, 1937's 'God's Country and the Woman', and was suspended without pay.

Upset, Bette flew to London to work with another studio, but Warner Bros sued her for breach of contract. Bette wanted to fight back, but it was difficult to do this from another country. In court, she referred to her contract as a form of slavery. The judge replied, "But this slavery has a silver lining, because the slave was...well remunerated." The court voted in favor of Warner Bros, forcing Bette Davis to return sheepishly to Hollywood, but her case set the ball rolling for Olivia de Havilland.

77

Olivia's lawyer had advised her to look into California state law and what it said about lengths of contracts. "It was quite short," said Olivia, "and very clear that no term of employment could exceed seven years without being classed as servitude. I thought about it and I was told the case was good, though judges might not be honest, I was a woman, after all. So I said, if I'm going to do it, I'm going all the way..." Olivia knew this case was risky; if she failed, she might never work again. Or she could end up locked in her contract with Warner Bros for as long as they decided, with suspension after suspension meaning she couldn't leave. But she had to try, so in 1943, Olivia de Havilland took Warner Bros to the California Supreme Court.

In this landmark case, lawyers for Warner Bros tried to argue that it was Olivia who had the problem. After 'Gone with the Wind', they said, she thought she was too good for the studio and had made their lives difficult by turning down perfectly good movies. But the Supreme Court ruled in Olivia's favor, saying studios were not allowed to extend their seven year contracts by adding suspension time. Olivia was overjoyed, but her fight wasn't over. Warner Bros appealed, and for the next three years, Olivia de Havilland was prohibited from working.

But her fight was worth it. The studio's appeal failed, and the court upheld the original judgement. It was unanimous, Olivia had won, and Warner Bros, as well as the rest of the studios, could no longer have stars for more than seven years. This became known as the "de Havilland Decision," and it is still used as precedent today. In fact, more than half a century later, actor and musician Jared Leto used the de Havilland Decision to win a court case against his music label.

The de Havilland Decision put a big crack in the studio system, which continued to crumble towards the end of the 1940s. As for Olivia de Havilland, she went on to win two Academy Awards for the type of complex, strong female characters she had always wanted to play, finally getting her original dream of "respect for difficult work well done."

Rita Hayworth: The Illusion

When you hear the name Rita Hayworth, the first thing that probably comes to mind is a self-confident flip of red hair from 'Gilda'. Maybe that black dress too, barely staying on as she shimmied and sang in front of swooning men. Or perhaps you think of her as the striking pinup in 'The Shawshank Redemption', seen on a poster hanging on

the prison wall of Andy Dufresne, concealing the escape
route underneath.

But Rita Hayworth was not what she seemed. She was an illusion.
Her all-American looks were a creation, a carefully orchestrated
transformation which involved removing any trace of her Hispanic
heritage. And the sad thing is, it doesn't seem like it was her choice.
She didn't manipulate men, she was manipulated by them. Rita
wasn't the confident sex goddess movie star she projected, she was
a former sexual abuse victim who was painfully shy and wanted out
of the film business. Rita kept the truth about her identity a secret,
and in the end, perhaps she didn't even know who she truly was.

Before she became Rita Hayworth, she was Margarita Cansino. As
a child she was a little overweight and incredibly shy. She learned
to dance at a young age because her father Eduardo was a dancer
from Madrid, and her mother Volga was a former showgirl from the
Ziegfeld Follies. The family moved to Los Angeles in the 1930s,
where Eduardo worked as a choreographer for Warner Bros and had
his own small dance studio.

The Great Depression saw the closure of most businesses like
Eduardo's, so to pay the bills he started performing again. He was
the first man in Margarita's life to control her, deciding his twelve
year-old daughter would be his new dance partner, taking her out
of school to perform in casinos. "Here was a girl, my own daughter,"
he said, "with whom I could build a whole new dance act." To get
around any age restrictions, Eduardo pretended his daughter was
his wife, and sadder still, he allegedly sexually abused her behind
closed doors. It got so bad, Volga started to share a bed with her
daughter in order to protect her.

In between performances, Eduardo and Volga would lock Margarita
in her dressing room while they went to gamble. When they took
her out, Margarita was paraded around in nightclubs frequented by
Hollywood types in the hope she would be discovered. In 1933 this
came true when Max Arno, a casting director at Warner Bros, spotted
young Margarita and a year later, he brought her in for a photo-test.

"She didn't say much, and we thought she couldn't speak English," Max said. "In the end we didn't sign her because of certain hair problems she had." These so-called "hair problems" were a coded way of saying she was too Hispanic-looking. She had beautiful thick hair, it was dark and curly with a low hairline — and not Anglo enough for 1930s Hollywood.

The next man to try to change Margarita was Winfield Sheehan, a film executive who signed her to her first contract and put her in drama class and elocution lessons to get rid of her accent. He also shortened her name to Rita, and placed her in small roles playing Spanish dancers in tiny movies. Rita didn't actually want to be a star, but she went along with all of it, playing her assigned role of wannabe actress.

One of the directors of her early movies noticed the difference between her personalities on camera and off camera. This was a disparity which would increase as her career progressed. "She was very nervous, terribly emotional," said director Allan Dwan, "She was probably just some innocent little virgin, but on the screen she was always a woman. She looks as if she had the knowledge of everything, when in fact she didn't know a damn thing."

When producer Darryl Zanuck was hired at Twentieth Century Fox, he fired Winfield, and Rita's contract was suddenly terminated. She freelanced for a little while, but then soon came along another man with his sights set on using her.

Eddie Judson was a 41 year old former car salesman who had met Rita briefly and decided he wanted to make her a star, and his lover. He was the same age as her father, and although Eduardo was suspicious of Eddie, he let him take his 18-year-old daughter out on the town. On these dates, Eddie coached Rita on what to wear, what to say, and how to present herself in front of people from Hollywood. He also convinced Harry Cohn, the President of Columbia Pictures, to sign her to a contract. Harry Cohn reluctantly agreed, saying he'd take her on if Rita would change her last name. They decided on Hayworth, a variation on her mother's maiden name that was suitably American sounding.

Rita's hair was still a "problem," so Eddie took Rita to the hairstylist at Columbia to see what they could do. Her black hair became auburn, and the stylist suggested that Rita get electrolysis to change her hairline. She was subjected to two years of this painful treatment; it zapped every single hair from her forehead, one by one.

Throughout this transformation, Eddie continued to take Rita out. He made her wear expensive dresses and jewelry and seated her in prominent booths at Hollywood nightclubs where he thought directors like Howard Hawks might notice her. To pay for all of this, he insisted that her parents give them the money Rita had earned when she was a teenage dancer. Then, despite the age difference, they got married. It wasn't until after she said, "I do" that Rita learned Eddie had been married twice before.

The new Rita Hayworth started getting roles, with a part in the 1939 movie 'Only Angels Have Wings' and the lead in 'The Strawberry Blonde' in 1941. For this role, playing a glamorous local girl in a small town, Rita's hair was dyed bright red, and now, any semblance of her true ethnic background was gone.

The irony was, now that she was a convincing Anglo woman, she started to get parts playing Spanish ladies. Back in those days, if a role was big, only white actors got to play it, no matter the race of the character. People of color were only used in small roles, placed in the background or pushed to the sidelines. Rita played a Spanish socialite in the 1941 movie 'Blood and Sand', and it was a hit. Producer Darryl Zanuck, the same man who had fired Rita years earlier, was so pleased with the movie that he didn't screen any previews. "It's the greatest film I've ever seen," he said, "ship it as is."

81

Meanwhile, Rita's husband Eddie continued to be a controlling, terrifying presence in her life. He would cheat on her, threaten to throw lye in her face, and even pimp her out to producers such as Harry Cohn. Eddie ordered Rita to have sex with the powerful movie mogul, organizing a weekend away on Harry's yacht and then "falling ill" at the last minute so Rita would have to go solo. In a rare moment of strength, Rita refused Harry's sexual advances. Harry was furious, and never forgot it.

After all of this, Rita was determined to leave Eddie, and eventually he agreed to a divorce after she promised to give him all of her money, plus a share of her earnings every single month. After he took her life savings, Rita couldn't even afford to eat and had to rely on being invited to friend's houses for dinner. "Ruining my career was his only concern," said Rita; "He gave everything he had, and his efforts paid off."

Slowly, she started to again make money by getting bigger roles, such as 'You'll Never Get Rich' opposite Fred Astaire, who said Rita was "sometimes inert" in person, but in front of the camera was "as bright as a dollar." She worked with Fred again in 'You Were Never Lovelier' and then was cast in 'Cover Girl' opposite Gene Kelly, a musical about a dancer who wins a contest to be a magazine cover girl. Her win takes her to Broadway, but in the end, she chooses love over a career. Rita was perfectly charming in the role, but seems to struggle during the more dramatic scenes. Her singing voice also had to be dubbed, as it was her entire career, but she really shone in the dance scenes. It's in these moments where she seems to lose any pretense and genuinely appears to be enjoying herself.

One scene in 'Cover Girl' required a wedding dress costume. While wearing it, Rita couldn't contain her excitement. "Rita sat there with her hands in her lap," said co-star Lee Bowman, "and a lovely big smile on her face. When any of us asked, 'What is it, Rita?' she'd just shake her head and say, 'Mmm, I've got a secret'." Her secret? She was to marry director Orson Welles that very day.

Rita's most iconic role came in 1946, playing the title character in 'Gilda'. She shone as the femme fatale who masked her insecurity by pretending to be confident and sleeping with men, something Rita could definitely relate to. Secretly, she wanted out of the movie business, preferring to stay at home and not continue to play the part of a movie star. But the success of 'Gilda' made her more than famous, turning her into an icon and a worldwide phenomenon. With 'Gilda' the persona of "Rita Hayworth" took on a life of its own. She'd never been in charge of her identity, but now, it was completely out of her control. Later that year, her sex bomb image was turned into an actual bomb. The "Gilda Bomb" was the fourth atom bomb ever detonated; it was dropped on Bikini Atoll as part of a test, with an image of Rita as Gilda painted on it. When she heard the news, Rita was incredibly upset, and once again, wanted to leave Hollywood.

Orson Welles persuaded her to stay, and though the two split within the year, they made a movie together the next year. Her casting in 'The Lady From Shanghai' partly came from Harry Cohn trying to take his revenge by making Rita work with her ex-husband. Meanwhile, Orson wanted to explode the image of Rita Hayworth, movie star. So he took Gilda, chopped off her famous red hair, dyed it blonde and turned her into a cold, deceptive murderer. Rita went along with it, hoping she too could show a different side of herself.

Throughout filming Orson sent all the footage back to his editor in Hollywood without viewing any of it, and when Harry Cohn saw a rough cut he was angry. It was a complete mess, and Harry offered to pay a thousand dollars to anyone who could explain the plot to him. Nobody could. But thanks to Orson's incredible skill, the final cut came together, and 'The Lady From Shanghai' went on to be a classic film noir.

Rita Hayworth continued to make movies, including the musical 'Pal Joey' with Frank Sinatra. She also continued to have more husbands; and throughout it all, she seemed to get further away from who she really was. During the 1960s, Rita began to forget her lines; this was chalked up to her excessive drinking. In the 1970s she was spotted in public looking disheveled and confused. This was all caught on camera and spread around the world, prompting fans to wonder what had happened to Gilda. A decade later, Rita was finally diagnosed as suffering from Alzheimer's disease, becoming the first public face of this illness. She passed away in 1987 at age 69.

Reading about Rita Hayworth makes me incredibly sad. On screen she was luminous and seemed like the perfect pin-up girl of the 1940s. But she was abused and manipulated throughout her entire life. All she wanted, she said, "was to be loved, like anyone else."

The only way she knew how to relate to men and love was through sex. And the only thing people knew about her was the false image created for her, which she struggled to live up to. In the end, she lost her war. "Every man I knew went to bed with Gilda," she said, "and woke up with me."

The Femme Fatales

The effects of World War II left many feelings percolating in America. There was elation and relief of course, but also anxiety, suspicion, and a fair bit of confusion over changing gender roles. Soldiers had come home to independent women who had jobs and were the heads of the household. Things had changed, and interestingly, while birth rates soared, so too did divorces.

Film noir was a new genre of film which was symbolic of the darker side of post-war America. They were often detective mysteries involving broken male heroes who were tricked by sexually powerful women called femmes fatales. This translates to "fatal women," and was representative of the suspicion surrounding these new, powerful post-war ladies.

It was all about darkness. Film noir had stories set in dark alleys at night. They were full of shadows cast by everyday objects such as horizontal blinds, which played on the characters' faces as if they were trapped behind bars. And the characters were usually trapped in some way, caught in a web of lies, deceit, and a messy search for the truth. Good and evil weren't so black and white in film noir. The stories were usually told from the male character's perspective through narration and flashbacks, and the audience had to put together the puzzle at the same time as the hero.

The key to the mystery always included a woman, and while they sometimes appeared helpless, they usually knew more about the situation than anyone else. Underneath their beautiful exteriors, which made them appear to just want love, lay an ulterior motive, luring "good" men into an underground world of danger.

Even if the crime involved another man, the femme fatale was often the biggest threat, and had to be dealt with accordingly. Femmes fatales were most often punished by death. Still, it was liberating to watch these women in their power, and these films sparked rare conversations about female sexuality.

Film noir also gave several actresses complex roles to sink their teeth into. Mary Astor played one of the first femmes fatales in 1941's 'The Maltese Falcon'. This was the role for which she became best known. Her Brigid O'Shaughnessy was fascinating — she had a submissive outer layer which masked her danger, intelligence, and pain. This was a lethal combination, and it served to send Humphrey Bogart's Sam Spade on a wildly thrilling goose chase. As Sam says to Brigid, "if you actually were as innocent as you pretend to be, we'd never get anywhere." Neither would the film.

Sometimes film noir crossed over with the Woman's Picture, as it did in 'Mildred Pierce' from 1945. You may automatically associate this movie with Joan Crawford, who starred in the title role, but it was Ann Blythe who played the wicked femme fatale. Veda Pierce trapped her mother in an intricate series of lies, manipulation, and murder. And this character showed that it wasn't just the men who could be brought down by a deadly woman.

Perhaps the most iconic femme fatale was Barbara Stanwyck in 'Double Indemnity'. As Phyllis Dietrichson, she was many things at once: a damsel in distress, a fed-up housewife, and a cruel woman who wanted her husband dead. It's a testament to Barbara's ability that she was able to portray that whole range, from vulnerable to villainous — often at the same time.

That sums up Barbara Stanwyck herself. She wasn't as famous as some of her female peers, probably because she could do everything. There was no one distinct persona, no simple category to place Barbara in. You look at her photos, and she is so different from one to the next. She starred in screwball comedies, westerns, women's pictures, and film noir. And in her own story, Barbara seemed to live nine lives.

She began as Ruby Stevens, and was only four years old when her life changed abruptly. Her pregnant mother was pushed out of a moving trolley car by a drunk and died of septicemia. Just a few months later, her father abandoned the family, and Ruby was separated from her brother when they were taken to different foster homes.

So she had to be tough from a young age, and went from performing in burlesque shows and the theater in New York in the 1920s, to Hollywood in the 1930s and 1940s. As she began to act, Barbara was often told by male producers that she had "no sex appeal," which was cruel, but she proved her audience appeal with hits like 'Stella Dallas' and 'The Lady Eve'. By the time the role in 'Double Indemnity' came around, Barbara Stanwyck was the highest paid actress in America.

At first, she was nervous about playing an evil woman. She went to director Billy Wilder's office to share her fear. "I love the script and I love you," she said, "but I am a little afraid after all these years of playing heroines to go into an out-and-out killer." According to Barbara, Billy looked at her and asked, "Well, are you a mouse or an actress?" She gave her answer by deciding to do the role.

He wanted the character to have a "sleazy phoniness" about her, but realized as they began to shoot that the stiff blonde wig he had placed on Barbara's head wasn't working. "We hired Barbara Stanwyck," he said, "and here we get George Washington." Yet, underneath that terrible wig, Barbara gave her character an intelligence and depth.

Later, in director Cameron Crowe's book, 'Conversations with Wilder', Billy talked about the fierce intelligence that Barbara possessed. "With Stanwyck," he said, "I had absolutely no difficulties at all. She knew the script, everybody's lines. You could wake her up in the middle of the night and she'd know the scene. Never a fault, never a mistake — just a wonderful brain she had."

Barbara Stanwyck took the femme fatale, that symbol of the dangerous new woman of the 1940s, and infused her with empathy.

Behind that villainous exterior, she was troubled and vulnerable. Her Phyllis was much more than a disposable object, and though the production code forbade sympathy for criminals, with 'Double Indemnity', the audience rooted for the femme fatale, the woman, to finally win.

 # THE DREAM FACTORY (1950s)

Growing up watching classic films, it was always the movies of 1950s Hollywood that particularly appealed to me. It just all looked so glamorous. The beautiful women, the dashing men... all smiling faces and wholesome values, a picture-perfect escapist ideal. This was the dream Hollywood was selling to the world, churning out movies one after another in a factory-style assembly line of fantasy. There was immense pressure to maintain this output, and Hollywood had a habit of eating up the weak. The stress of this perfectionism brought out the deepest insecurities of actors as they attempted to live up to the image they had been prescribed. And so, the dream became a nightmare for many stars trapped inside it.

Women of 1950s America were also caught between two worlds. After the war, women who held jobs filling in for men were either demoted, fired, or expected to return to their previous positions as housewives – and to be happy about it. The "We Can Do It!" messages of 1940s films reverted back to promoting traditional gender roles, complete with smiling "Stepford Wives," who would be happy to give without asking for anything in return. The female stars of Hollywood further reinforced this, such as the cheery housewife persona seen in Debbie Reynolds and Doris Day as well as sex goddesses like Marilyn Monroe and Jayne Mansfield.

87

The Woman's Picture was also slowly disappearing from the screen, heading to television in the form of soap operas. Television was the biggest blow to the movie industry in the 1950s, with Americans purchasing five million TV sets over the decade and choosing to stay home over going to the theater. To tempt audiences back out, movies started experimenting with new technologies, which all promised big spectacle. This included color film, a wide-screen format called CinemaScope, and a brief 3-D trend. Meanwhile studios were refusing to license their movies to these television channels, so the airwaves were flooded with foreign films and B movies. But in the late 1950s, studios started letting the networks run their pre-1948 catalog, and the two mediums finally began to work together.

Aside from the threat of television, there was a darker fear running through Hollywood with the rise of paranoia about Communism. A witch hunt for members of the Communist Party "secretly" working in Hollywood had begun; and as more and more people were accused, named, and blacklisted, this paranoia turned into frenzied panic. It seems ironic that the group leading the charge called themselves the "House Un-American Activities Committee" (HUAC), when the very activity of hunting people down and blacklisting them seemed very un-American.

Some stars buckled under the pressure of HUAC, naming names during the hearings in order to get them off their backs. But others refused, setting up their own groups in retaliation, like The Committee for the First Amendment. The actresses involved in this group included Lauren Bacall, Lucille Ball, Dorothy Dandridge, Bette Davis, Judy Garland, Katharine Hepburn, Lena Horne, and Myrna Loy, who was one of the original founders.

This was a dark time in Hollywood history, a time when everyday citizens could call up a hotline and claim that any film star, writer, or director was a Communist and have them blacklisted, even without substantial evidence. Producers were terrified of offending anyone with their content, so the movies suffered, and audiences had to put up with watered-down, cautious content. The focus on these safe "American" ideals made it even more difficult for women and non-white actors to get interesting roles.

In stark contrast to these Hollywood movies were the risky foreign films, where directors involved in new cinematic movements like the French New Wave and Italian NeoRealism were experimenting with avant-garde techniques and pushing boundaries with stories addressing real issues. With more international movies being exported to America, audiences in the U.S. started to be exposed to this challenging material, which cracked the veneer of perfect glamor that Hollywood was trying so desperately to project.

In 1948, Italian director Roberto Rossellini created the two-part anthology film 'Ways Of Love'. The second part of the movie, 'The Miracle', centered on a mentally unstable peasant woman who had an affair with a man she believed to be Joseph; and when she gave birth to his child, she called him The Messiah. Though the film provoked some negative reaction in Italy, there were no real censorship issues until it reached the United States. In 1950, 'Ways Of Love' was released in a single theater in New York; and the American Catholic Church was offended. They wanted the film banned on the grounds of being sacrilegious, and New York authorities gave in to the pressure and revoked the film's license to play in theaters.

The U.S. distributor of the film appealed via a lawsuit, which ended up reaching the Supreme Court. In 1952, the Court ruled in favor of the distributor; it also overturned an old 1915 ruling which had denied movies protection under the First Amendment. This was huge. This lawsuit, called the "Miracle Decision," paved the way for the destruction of the Hays Production Code, which would change American cinema forever.

89

Before all that happened, Hollywood was determined to hold on to its classic glamor. Movies were an escape, a way for audiences to see an ideal life, the American Dream, lit up large on a big screen. But for many actresses stuck playing these roles, life was anything but a dream.

Dorothy Dandridge:
Fighting Against Stereotype

For a brief moment, it looked as if Dorothy Dandridge might just make it in Hollywood. She had great success in the early 1950s, and the hope was that she would get a rare opportunity to change the game, a chance to be an actress whose roles were not racially stereotyped, or even an African-American female icon who wasn't overly sexualized and didn't have her beauty defined by the tone of her skin. Maybe she'd even be able to navigate the business without being torn down for an alleged scandal. But this was 1950s Hollywood, so no matter how hard she tried to do all of this, it was impossible. In the end, her personal demons were exacerbated by the system, and she didn't live long enough to see the impact she had on the world.

"Dottie," as she was affectionately known, was born to entertain. It ran in her blood — her mother was an actress, and her sister was a natural singer. The two sisters started performing from a young age; eventually they went on the road in the 1930s, singing in nightclubs as The Dandridge Sisters. By the 1940s, they went their separate ways, and Dottie moved to Hollywood, where she started to pick up tiny roles in B pictures. They were small, but enough to convince Dorothy that she wanted to make acting her career; and more than that, she dreamed of being a star.

In 1942, Dottie married dancer Harold Nicholas, and a year later they had a child called Harolyn, or Lynn for short. Over the first five years of Lynn's life, Dorothy noticed that Lynn wasn't developed enough for her age. Concerned, she took her daughter to the doctor, where it was discovered she had severe brain damage, caused by a loss of oxygen during birth. This would prevent Lynn from developing any further, meaning she would never be able to speak or look after herself in the future. Dorothy was devastated, and while it certainly wasn't her fault, she never forgave herself.

By now, the offers for bit parts in Hollywood had started to wane, so Dorothy decided to work on her live act. She saw this as a way to get the attention of Hollywood producers, and she enlisted band leader Phil Moore to help hone her performance. Quite quickly, Dorothy became a sensation. She had a knack for anticipating what a crowd wanted and transforming herself into it. And audiences, particularly men and the press, fell in love with her. Life magazine wrote an article about Dorothy, saying she was "the most beautiful Negro singer to make her mark in nightclubs since Lena Horne." This was the first of many comparisons Dorothy would get to fellow actress/singer Lena Horne.

Dorothy's plan had worked; the studios took notice, and in 1952 she was cast in MGM's all African-American production of 'Bright Road'. The film starred Harry Belafonte, and Dorothy played a teacher struggling to help a difficult student. This was exactly the type of role she had wanted, as it was modern and had none of the damaging racial stereotypes normally assigned to characters of color. Despite positive reviews, MGM didn't promote the film, as they would for movies with all-white casts, and its box office receipts were very low.

Dorothy's next opportunity to break into Hollywood came in 1954 with another African-American production, an adaptation of the opera 'Carmen'. Dottie knew she could do a great job playing the sexy title character, but director Otto Preminger had a different idea. After watching her in 'Bright Road' as the sweet schoolteacher, he told Dorothy to learn the role of good girl Cindy Lou and come back to audition the following day. But that only made Dorothy even more determined to win the part of Carmen; she knew she could do it if she treated it like a performance. All she needed to do was figure out what Otto was looking for, and transform herself into it.

The next day, Dorothy sauntered into Otto's office, with tousled hair and vixen makeup, wearing a low-cut blouse and a tight skirt. The director couldn't believe what he saw. "It's Carmen!" Otto declared, and with that, Dorothy had her big break. This movie made her a star.

'Carmen' proved a film with an all-black cast could make millions. It inspired rave reviews and think pieces on what the success might mean for African-American actors. Audiences were excited, but Harry Belafonte, who had also starred in 'Carmen', was tentative in his optimism. He pointed out how far Hollywood still had to go before black characters were allowed to exist as fully realized characters within white movies.

Much of the focus in the press following the release of 'Carmen' was on Dorothy Dandridge. She had the makings of a star and showed true talent as an actress. This was confirmed when the 1955 Oscar nominations were announced - Dorothy Dandridge had been nominated for Best Actress alongside Grace Kelly, Judy Garland, and Audrey Hepburn. She had arrived.

Although she lost her category to Grace Kelly for 'The Country Girl', Dorothy did make history that night. She announced the Academy Award winner for Best Editing and so became the first African-American actor to ever present an award at the Oscars.

Afterwards, there were more milestones, with a performance at the famed Waldorf Astoria in New York — a first for a black singer — and a three picture contract with 20th Century Fox. All signs pointed to Dorothy Dandridge being a major star. She just needed her next role. So, she waited. And waited. And waited some more.

Offers did come Dorothy's way, like a role in the 1956 epic 'The King and I', but this was not what she had been waiting for. Against all the advice from studio producers and agents who told her she should grab the chance to be in such a big film, Dorothy turned the role down. The part was a slave, and Dorothy refused to play any stereotypes. She also turned down the comedy 'The Lieutenant Wore Skirts' because the part was too small. Dorothy was sure the right role was on its way, one that would be a lead part and a positive image for African-Americans. But the right role never materialized.

She held out for three long years, until she realized all of that buzz about Dorothy Dandridge being the "next big thing" had gone away. If she wanted to continue working as an actress, she couldn't afford to keep saying no. Dorothy made her return to the screen in the ensemble film 'Island in the Sun' in 1957. It had a diverse cast, starring Harry Belafonte, Joan Fontaine, James Mason, and herself. She and Harry were paired up with the white characters as love interests, though the production code at this time prohibited them from actually kissing.

Dorothy's next few roles were not what she wanted to do, but she felt she had no choice. In 'Tamango', she played a slave who was the mistress of a white man. The film sat on a shelf for years, and when it was eventually released, it was slaughtered by critics. 'The Decks Ran Red' was a B-picture, and 'Malaga' was a low budget crime film made in Europe. She also started to receive negative press for her supposed haughty attitude on set and rumors of relationships with white men.

Part of that story was true, Dorothy had a secret affair with director Otto Preminger while he was still married. But by 1959, their relationship had ended, and Dorothy had been the one to call it off. This decision came back to haunt her when she was making her next movie, the all African-American production of 'Porgy and Bess'. On the surface, the film had appeared to be a good opportunity for Dorothy. It was going to be a big-budget extravaganza with top-notch talent, and it had already been both a successful book and an opera. The director of the opera was set to direct the film adaptation, and it was being produced by Samuel Goldwyn, who had a good reputation for quality material. He promised to be sensitive, but the way the characters had been depicted in the book troubled the black community. Bess was a drug-addicted prostitute, and the rest of the roles were rapists, murderers, and drug dealers. The fight for African-American civil rights was starting to take form, and this seemed like a significant step backwards.

Harry Belafonte and Sidney Poitier had turned down the movie, but Dorothy needed the money. "I decided that if Goldwyn was that bent on doing the picture, he might as well do it with me," she said.

It was a disaster from the beginning. First, a fire ripped through the set, destroying valuable costumes and props. Then, the director and Samuel Goldwyn clashed, and the director was fired. A replacement filmmaker was called in, and it was Dorothy's ex, Otto Preminger. He was bitter towards her for ending their affair and made the shoot absolute hell. "He treated her like a dog," said co-star Ivan Dixon. "She would cry. It was terrible to see."

'Porgy and Bess' opened to lukewarm reviews. Dorothy had given the role her all, and watching now, you can't help but see parallels between her character, who was desperately trying to find her way, and how Dorothy herself felt about Hollywood. But this was 1959, and the movie was too old-fashioned to be a hit with audiences.

By the time the 1960s came along, Dorothy's Hollywood roles had dried up. "I hurled myself in front of another white man," said Dorothy, who had married nightclub owner Jack Denison and performed at his fledging club. They split four years later with Dorothy citing physical abuse, stating in their divorce papers that her husband had struck her face on several occasions.

Soon after the divorce, Dorothy Dandridge declared bankruptcy and had to place her child Lynn in a state-run mental home. And then, on September 8, 1965, Dorothy's manager arrived at her house and found her dead in the bathroom, naked but for a blue scarf around her neck. She had overdosed on depression medication; when she passed away, she had only two dollars in her bank account.

It's not known whether this was a suicide or an accidental overdose, but it's hard not to wonder what Dorothy Dandridge might have gone on to achieve if she had survived. To me, she represents a missed opportunity. If she had only been born later, she might have received the kind of success she craved. She certainly had the talent, and the drive. But 1950s Hollywood was not ready for her, and soon they forgot all about Dorothy Dandridge. Decades later, she has become a role model for African-American actors like Halle Berry, who thanked Dorothy in her Oscar speech, saying, "This moment is for Dorothy Dandridge."

Dorothy had the ability, she showed promise, she was a sex symbol and an icon. She had everything going for her, but due to the color of her skin, Hollywood wouldn't give her the stardom she deserved. "If I were Betty Grable," Dorothy once said, "I would capture the world."

Marilyn Monroe: The Myth

The first time I remember seeing Marilyn Monroe was in a movie called 'Gentlemen Prefer Blondes'. It was a favorite for me and my two sisters; we knew all of the songs, dances, and dialogue, and would perform them frequently, much to the chagrin of my parents. Marilyn was luminous in Technicolor, her platinum hair shining as she sauntered in sparkling costumes while singing about diamonds. Her character Lorelei was not very bright, but she didn't need to be, with the ability to attract wealthy men who would look after her. It was a terrible message to be getting as a young girl, but I was drawn to the glamorous look of Marilyn. My deeper fascination started when I was given a book about her life and I realized that entire image was a complete mirage.

The character of Marilyn Monroe is the ultimate piece of 1950s fiction. She was a cartoonish version of a sexy woman — platinum blonde, wide-eyed, childlike, speaking in a whisper, always seemingly ready to fulfill a man's needs without asking for anything in return. During her life, she was easy to ridicule. But in her death, the real Marilyn Monroe came into the spotlight. Marilyn's overdose shocked the world, revealing that underneath her glamorous veneer was a fragile, needy, abused child who never got the kind of real love she craved. She'd had a dream of Hollywood, but becoming that dream destroyed her.

95

Most of us know her backstory. Norma Jeane Baker was born in 1926; and from the very start of her life, she felt as if she had nobody to depend on. She was shuttled between foster homes, and as a young child was sexually abused. To make matters worse, no adult believed that the assault had taken place. So, early on, Norma Jeane learned that her only worth was her body, which men were allowed to use as they pleased.

After doing some modeling, she broke into Hollywood in the late 1940s; by that stage, upon getting advice, she had colored her hair platinum blonde, had plastic surgery, and taken the new name of Marilyn Monroe. The myth was born. After small parts in movies like 'All About Eve', where she appropriately played a naive young actress, the gossip columnist Hedda Hopper announced in 1952 that Marilyn Monroe was the new "It Girl" of Hollywood.

Marilyn's fame grew, thanks to 'Gentleman Prefer Blondes', 'How To Marry A Millionaire', 'Bus Stop', 'Some Like It Hot', and that iconic upskirt moment as The Girl in 'The Seven Year Itch'. But she absolutely despised these "dumb blonde" roles and longed for something more serious. Speaking about her character in 'Some Like It Hot', Marilyn had rolled her eyes and said, "No woman on earth would be so dumb as not to see that the two drag artists, Tony Curtis and Jack Lemmon, were men."

But directors refused to look past the fantasy of Marilyn, because as we know, sex sells, so they continued to objectify her. This made her feel empty inside, and Marilyn desperately searched for credibility, studying with two of the top acting coaches in America. It didn't matter, she was never going to be given the opportunity to show any other side of herself. Audiences, in particular women, continued to ridicule her characters. And as Marilyn became more famous, she was more alone than ever.

She was also never taken seriously by the men in her personal life, though she had sought out intellectual icons for exactly this reason. These men, much like Hollywood, weren't interested in her brain. They wanted Marilyn for how she looked and how she made them feel, not how they made her feel. She suffered from deep depression and insomnia, which she treated with an endless supply of pills, given to her by a doctor who slowly entrenched himself more and more in her life.

These pills caused her to oversleep and be scattered during filming. She also began to get a reputation for throwing tantrums, though these were usually a result of her deep insecurities. If she felt she wasn't good enough, Marilyn would burst into nervous tears. This slowed down production; filming would halt until she stopped crying, and the entire movie crew would wait in frustration.

As the decade progressed, the image of Marilyn Monroe became even more exaggerated, an over-the-top expression of sexuality and womanhood. This was near the start of second wave feminism in the 1960s, so her look and attitude were becoming quite outdated. And Marilyn was slowly losing her true self in this persona, though she seemed hopeful that she could turn things around.

Then suddenly, on August 5th, 1962, Marilyn Monroe was found dead. Her death, like most of her life, was surrounded by myth and inspired many conspiracy theories. It also led to a deeper understanding of who she was. Her tragic death at 36 years old hinted there may have been more going on under the surface than people thought. Film critic Molly Haskell explains this perfectly in her book, 'From Reverence to Rape', writing, "Our feelings about Marilyn Monroe have been so colored by her death and not simply, as the uncharitable would have us think, because she is no longer an irritation or a threat, but because her suicide, as all suicides do, casts a retrospective light on her life. Her 'ending' gives her a beginning and middle, turns her into a work of art with a message and a meaning."

97

Today, seeing Marilyn's image is unavoidable. If you take a quick walk down Hollywood Boulevard you will see her face displayed on everything from t-shirts to magnets to tins of mints. This always makes me quite sad. Here was someone who just wanted to be loved for who she truly was, and now she's infamous for who she projected herself to be. I can't help wondering, do people worship her image because it is a reminder of that little girl lost? That there is more to beautiful women than we give them credit for? Is it a comment on Hollywood's commodification of sex? Or is it because she is a woman who will never age, who will remain frozen and beautiful, always available for our consumption and capitalism whenever we want?

Ida Lupino: Mother of Us All

Looking back, the 1950s were a particularly interesting time in world cinema. In France, there was the French New Wave movement, which reworked old genres to create bold new styles. In Poland, directors such as Andrzej Wajda tackled confronting stories about his country in the post-World War II era. In Japan, Akira Kurosawa and Yasujirō Ozu played with story form and camera movement. And in Italy there was Neorealism, with socially relevant topics filmed in a realistic documentary style.

Hollywood was much slower to take on this trend toward realistic cinema, held back by the production code and the studio system. One of the few people determined to try and tell real stories on the big screen was also one of the most unlikely. A petite English actress who had once been dubbed "the English Jean Harlow," Ida Lupino. But when you dig into her story, you find she always had the type of strong will, persistence, and self-confidence needed to be a female filmmaker in the 1950s.

Ida Lupino was born in 1918 into a family of entertainers, "seven generations" of them, as she liked to remind people. Her father Stanley was an actor in musical comedies, and her mother Connie was a tap dancer once called "the fastest tap dancer alive." Ida knew from a young age what her destiny would be; her father told her, "you're a strange, interesting girl. Your mother and I, to be honest with you, prayed when she was pregnant we would have a son. I think you're going to end up doing what my son would have done. You will write, direct, and produce."

It was also a given that Ida would be an actress. With her parents working long hours and often away on theater tours, her grandmother would keep her occupied by giving young Ida access to her mother's costumes, makeup, tap shoes, and a mirror, where she would spend hours dressing up and watching herself. Her parents often came home to find her curled up asleep on the floor, still in costume. Ida also loved to act out cheeky little scenes, like ripping up her clothes and going door to door in her English neighborhood claiming she was starving. And whenever she put on performances at home, her father would instruct her to take it very seriously. The Lupinos' job was to entertain, and Ida knew that was what she must do.

When she was thirteen, Ida begged her father for a walk-on role in one of his movies. To do this, she had to skip school. He was determined that she should receive an education, but eventually allowed it. Ida loved every minute of being on set, and decided then and there to become a full-time actress. She went to her parents and told them she wouldn't be returning to school. They were hesitant, but eventually agreed on one condition: Ida had to keep herself in acting work. If she couldn't get roles, she had to go back to her education.

This was a challenge Ida gladly accepted, and she was determined to make it happen without using her family name. She called herself Ida Ray, and managed to get an agent and a small part in a movie. In the end, Ida was dropped from the film because she was deemed "too attractive" to appear next to the leading lady. Ida wasn't upset. This experience confirmed she had the looks to be an actress, so now she just needed to work on her craft.

Ida enrolled in the Royal Academy of Dramatic Arts in 1931, where she studied classical theater technique and performed in many plays. One day, the students had the chance to audition for famed playwright George Bernard Shaw. It was a particularly hot day, and while Ida was waiting, she had to keep fixing her hair and makeup. When she was summoned to his office, George looked her up and down before saying she was "obviously an eccentric," and that if she "wanted to go to all that trouble to attract attention, I suppose it's all right...I suppose an exhibitionist like you would be good in the part. You can have it." Ida was confused by his comments, until she looked in the mirror and realized her hair and face were covered in red lipstick. The heat had made the lipstick melt all over the comb she had used to brush her hair and the handkerchief she had dabbed her sweat with.

Her film debut came a few years later at age fifteen. The movie was 'Her First Affaire', and the role called for a Lolita-like young girl who falls for a married author of romance books. She loved the part and gave it her all. "My agent had told me that he was going to make me the Janet Gaynor of England," said Ida, "I was going to play all the sweet roles. Whereupon, at the tender age of 13, I set upon the path of playing nothing but hookers." The movie and its star were well received, and the director made a prediction that Ida wouldn't be in England for much longer. She made five more movies in her country, with each part furthering her reputation for playing young vixens, and soon, she was a star.

Offers from Hollywood had been coming in ever since 'Her First Affaire'. Ida had been reluctant, but when Paramount said they would give her a high-paying contract, Ida's father advised her to go. The studio wanted her for the lead in 'Alice in Wonderland', but Ida already knew she didn't want that role. "You cannot play naive if you're not," she said. Regardless, in 1933, she and her mother set sail for New York City.

Representatives from Paramount Pictures met them with much fanfare, giving Ida a big reception at their hotel, with press lined up to talk to this new English star. As she walked in to meet them, a publicist whispered in her ear, "You're now sixteen." This wasn't a stretch, Ida handled herself with much more confidence than your average fifteen year old.

A week later, Ida and her mother arrived in Hollywood, and her picture appeared on the front page of the Los Angeles Times. The article announced her as being one of the hopefuls to audition for the lead in 'Alice in Wonderland'. Ida loved the attention, but still didn't want the role. This was solved when she did the screen test, and shocked the producers with her maturity. She was tough, sophisticated and feisty, and it was obvious she was not suited to play the innocent Alice. Instead, Paramount decided they would make her the "English Jean Harlow" and set about dying her hair platinum blonde and molding her into a teenage sexpot.

Over the next couple of years, she starred in a variety of films, but struggled to get the type of meaty roles she wanted to play. Her contract with Paramount forced her to take on movies of lesser quality, and Ida longed for parts where she could show her acting ability in real stories.

And then in 1934, Ida Lupino contracted polio. She was terrified, and in a lot of pain. The disease paralyzed her right arm, and rendered her unable to walk. Ida was devastated at the thought she might be stuck in a wheelchair for the rest of her life. But her internal strength got her through, and she managed to beat the disease, regaining feeling in her arms and getting up to walk again.

She was back to her determined self. And when Ida heard director William Wellman was set to direct 'The Light That Failed' in 1939, she knew she had to play the role of Bessie. She'd dreamed of playing the street girl with the "marvelous eyes" ever since she'd read the Rudyard Kipling classic. Ida had met William at a party a few years earlier, and decided to take matters into her own hands. She went to his office on the Paramount lot, burst through the door and declared, "You're doing Kipling's 'The Light That Failed', and this is my part. You have got to give me a chance. I know it right now. I know the whole script!" Ida impressed William with her boldness, and the movie was a hit. After that, she had roles in the gangster film 'High Sierra' with Humphrey Bogart, the film noir 'Moontide', and by 1941 Ida Lupino was one of the biggest stars in Hollywood.

But her world changed when her father died a year later, and Ida remembered what he had predicted about her future as a writer and director. She spent the next few years closely observing directors on set; then, a chance meeting made Ida realize what she needed to do.

In the late 1940s, Ida was at a party when she met director Roberto Rossellini. He was one of the originators of the Italian Neorealism style, and had won great acclaim with his 1943 film 'Rome, Open City'. The movie was an emotional and confrontational look at Nazi occupied Rome. At the party, Roberto talked to Ida about the difference between European and American cinema. "In Hollywood movies, the star is going crazy, or drinks too much, or he wants to kill his wife," he said. "When are you going to make pictures about ordinary people in ordinary situations?"

This question stuck with Ida, and she decided she wanted to be the one to make these realistic movies. Along with her husband, she set up her own production company, called The Filmmakers. Their first project was a movie about an unwed mother, titled 'Not Wanted'. She didn't feel ready to direct, so had hired another filmmaker to helm the movie, but a few days before the cameras started rolling, he suffered a mild heart attack and had to pull out. Ida stepped up to take over, and she was a natural. A reporter who had been on set observing her work wrote that he was impressed with her speed and efficiency in giving orders.

Ida hoped 'Not Wanted' would "show the public the heartbreak of the unwed mother;" but when the film was released, reviews were mixed, though The Hollywood Reporter said the story was "done with taste, dignity and compassion." Ida Lupino had arrived as a director.

Between 1949 and 1954, Ida wrote and directed six feature films based on socially realistic topics like polio and rape. She wasn't scared to tackle controversial stories and found her strong personality was well suited to the role of director. Ida was decisive, but not "the kind of woman who can bark orders." It was the 1950s, and she had to be pragmatic as to how she treated the men on set. "Often, I pretended to a cameraman to know less than I did," admitted Ida. "That way, I got more cooperation." In reality, she knew more than most of the crew. On set, Ida Lupino referred to herself as "Mother," and her director's chair had "Mother of Us All" embroidered on the back.

Ida also juggled her career as a star actor, making seven films during those five years. But as the 1950s went on and Ida entered her thirties, offers for movie roles became less interesting. She moved to television, where she acted and directed for series like 'The Untouchables', 'Alfred Hitchcock Presents', 'The Fugitive' and most famously, an episode of 'The Twilight Zone' which seemed to be self-referential. The episode aired in 1959; Ida played an aging actress who locks herself inside a screening room to watch her old movies over and over again.

Ida Lupino directed her last television episode in 1968, and acted in small parts until 1978. She passed away from cancer in 1995 in Los Angeles.

To succeed as a female director today, it takes incredible persistence, courage and confidence. Ida Lupino had all of that and then some and ended up as a rare filmmaker in 1950s Hollywood. She made movies that talked about real issues which were in direct contrast to the dream factory products of the studios. She was a woman with entertainment in her blood, who always stood up for herself and didn't care what anyone said. And she was successful as a female director at a time when there were none.

Ida Lupino's good friend Joan Fontaine described her best, as "the nearest thing to a caged tiger I ever saw outside a zoo, I don't think she has ever been still a whole minute of her life...Ida isn't normal. No one ever accused her of that. One of her peculiarities is that she does everything well."

 # NEW HOLLYWOOD (1960s & 1970s)

The 1960s in America was a decade of contrasts. There was hope and fear, peace and rebellion, idealism and cynicism. In Hollywood, there was death and rebirth. The studio system collapsed, the icons of classic Hollywood were cast aside, the production code was abolished, and a new wave of young filmmakers began to take over.

The movie studios had lost much of their power during the Paramount Decision anti-trust lawsuit, which had forced the studios' divestment of their theaters. Without being able to guarantee a release for each of their movies, the banks started losing confidence in funneling money into Hollywood. The rise of television also saw a sharp decline in audiences going to theaters, and some big financial flops hurt the bottom line even further.

The 1963 'Cleopatra' was a grand-scale historical epic starring Elizabeth Taylor. It remains one of the biggest financial failures in movie history. The film was plagued with a series of disasters, from reshoots to changing locations and an on-set scandal involving a love affair between Elizabeth and Richard Burton, both of whom were married at the time. The budget bloated to the equivalent of roughly $320 million today, making it the most expensive film ever made up to that point. It was the biggest hit of 1963, but that year was a particularly rough one at the box office. Thanks to its exorbitant budget, 'Cleopatra' failed to make a profit. Because of this, 20th Century Fox was pushed to the brink of bankruptcy, and had to sell part of its studio lot to developers.

The failure of 'Cleopatra' signaled the end of an era. These type of large budget historical epics with big stars were a legacy of classic Hollywood, but the old ways of making films just weren't working anymore. Studios also realized they could no longer filter decisions about their entire film production through just one man at the top, and those old movie moguls from classic Hollywood were aging out and retiring.

Gone too were the star contracts, which had bound actors to work for one studio. Now, producers had to negotiate with agents on a per film basis, and movies with "package deals" became more attractive options to fund — projects with stars, producers, writers and directors already attached. Agents became the new gatekeepers of Hollywood, and the key to a movie going ahead. This represented a significant shift in the balance of power in Hollywood.

With movie revenue continuing to decline, movie studios became targets for acquisition. They were absorbed into huge conglomerate companies; Gulf & Western bought Paramount, MGM was purchased by a hotel tycoon, Kinney took over Warner Bros and so forth. And a new generation of young men were hired to run them.

During all of this, a feeling of unrest grew in America. African-American people were tired of being treated like second-class citizens, and protests which had begun in the mid-1950s took shape as a civil rights movement throughout the 1960s. Of course Hollywood was slow to change in terms of racial equality, and on film the same old stereotypes existed. But offscreen, many stars used their voices to stand up for their rights. Actors like Ruby Dee, Sidney Poitier, Harry Belafonte, Ossie Davis, Dick Gregory, and Sammy Davis Jr. lent their support to the movement and were crucial in raising funds and bringing wider attention to race issues. These stars provided a model for the type of celebrity activism we still see today.

Among women in the 1960s, there was also a feeling of unrest. Writer Betty Friedan called this "the problem that has no name," and it was keenly felt amongst housewives. Women had everything society told them they needed — a husband, children, a home, fancy new appliances — but they were just not happy. Betty's book 'The Feminine Mystique' articulated a feeling that had been growing amongst women since the end of World War II. Women wanted to be educated, to be able to work, to be independent financially and emotionally. They wanted equal opportunities in all aspects of their lives, both private and political.

'The Feminine Mystique', along with Simone de Beauvoir's 'Second Sex' and the work of journalist Gloria Steinem gave rise to the second wave of feminism. Women had been important in the other political and social activism groups, but many felt that the protests were still about the equality and freedom of men. To counter this, new groups were formed with the sole interest of fighting for the rights of women. But as happens with much of feminism, the group focused primarily on white women. It wasn't until 1973, with the formation of the National Black Feminist Organization, that women of color were able to express their unique experiences of dealing with racism, sexism, and inequality.

A slight change for female characters in the 1960s came with the depiction of a more sexualized woman in Hollywood. She was a new version of the 1920s flapper — a woman who had love affairs without being married, and had control over her sex life, such as Audrey Hepburn's Holly Golightly in 'Breakfast at Tiffany's' and Natalie Wood in 'Sex and the Single Girl'. But with the production code still in place, sex still could only be hinted at, and these hints remained the only type of liberation during the 1960s for women in film.

Not much was done to encourage female filmmakers during the 1960s, or to attempt to change the male-driven narratives of mainstream movies. It's interesting that the few films which did touch on the subject of feminism, such as Mrs Banks and her song 'Sister Suffragette' in 'Mary Poppins', or Debbie Reynolds as the 'Titanic' heroine Molly Brown in 'The Unsinkable Molly Brown', were all set during the early part of the twentieth century. Modern women's stories were perhaps too scary; and it would take until the 1970s before they would start to be explored in Hollywood movies.

Film historians now point to 1966 and 1967 as being the watershed years which changed Hollywood forever. This began when the Motion Pictures Producers Association (MPAA) appointed Jack Valenti as their new leader. One of his first assignments was to reevaluate the old Production Code. By this point, the code was severely outdated, and barely heeded. Producers constantly found inventive ways around it, as they did for Italian director Michelangelo Antonioni's 'Blowup', which was so full of profanity, full-frontal female nudity, and drug use that even with severe cuts it wouldn't have been approved for release. To get around this, MGM created a front company to distribute the movie; the new shell company was not a signatory to the code, so it wasn't required to stick to it.

Around this time, the "baby boom" generation of Postwar America was starting to come of age, and there was a call for movies that reflected their growing feeling of alienation and confusion. Two films in 1967 showed how this could be done in new ways — 'Bonnie and Clyde' was inspired by the French New Wave, and used its visual styles in ways not really seen in American cinema before; and the success of 'The Graduate' forced studios to think about younger audiences as a form of revenue for the first time.

In 1968, Jack Valenti decided to scrap the Production Code by changing to a ratings system similar to the type used in England. This change helped usher in a new artistic freedom not seen in Hollywood for many decades. Along came the "Movie Brats," a new kind of male director so nicknamed by authors Michael Pye and Lynda Myles. The "brats" were Martin Scorsese, Francis Ford Coppola, Steven Spielberg, George Lucas, Dennis Hopper, Brian DePalma, Peter Bogdanovich, Robert Altman, Hal Ashby, and Terrence Malick. These filmmakers were born in the 1940s and grew up watching classic Hollywood cinema, but were also influenced by the fresh style used in foreign films. They didn't work their way through the studio system or come from a theater background, instead they studied at film schools, often helping each other throughout their careers.

Their work paid homage to other filmmakers, but these new men threw out the rules of old Hollywood. Their movies changed American cinema, and are still studied today. But an unfortunate side effect of the rise of these movie brats was the decline of interesting roles for women. These directors largely focused on telling stories about complex men, with ladies relegated to the sidelines.

Film critic Molly Haskell was writing for the 'Village Voice at the time, and she noticed how there was a rise of male buddy movies where male stars had all the roles, like 'Midnight Cowboy', 'The Sting', and 'Butch Cassidy and the Sundance Kid'. She realized that though this was the age of feminism, there had actually been better parts for women during the studio system. "What struck me was the irony of women having had so much more power when they were under the studio," Molly said; "They were, in a sense, chattel to the studio system, owned by the studios, and their power was restricted, they were typecast, and women rebelled. But most of the parts really were good, and they were featured, and they were nurtured. They were built up into stars whose personae carried over from film to film so that viewers could identify with them and feel a borrowed autonomy and independence. Certain women in particular, like Bette Davis, Rosalind Russell, Katharine Hepburn, represented a thrilling kind of outspokenness."

Molly wrote about this in her book 'From Reverence to Rape', and her theories at the time didn't sit well with second wave feminism. "When I wrote this, it seemed counterintuitive, because at this time, it was about the women's movement. The assumption was that things were now much better off for women, when in fact, they weren't." Molly said. "To look back now, you tend to see the women who rose to the surface, like Ellen Burstyn, Cloris Leachman, Jane Fonda, and Vanessa Redgrave. There were interesting things going on. It's just that if you look, compared to the earlier studio films, where women were 50% of what was going out, and certainly had equal salaries, then it didn't look very good. It didn't look as if women had the leverage anymore, and that was a big thing."

But there was the rise of what Molly Haskell calls the "neo-woman's film," with movies like Martin Scorsese's 'Alice Doesn't Live Here Anymore', and 'A Woman Under the Influence' by John Cassavetes, which commented on the despondent feeling women had during the 50s, 60s and 70s. "Women were frustrated at being housewives," Molly said, "and this was the kind of moment of consciousness raising, and rejection of traditional roles, but without any sure ideas about what came next. That feeling of uncertainty is in those movies. They're not about heroic women marching out and saving the day. They're about women who are baffled and disgruntled."

Meanwhile, another important section of the community was fighting for representation on screen. Since the beginning of cinema, Native American characters had been depicted as stereotypes such as bloodthirsty savages, stoic and serious characters, or magical medicine men. One of the first people to publicly stand up and speak out against these stereotypes was actress and activist Sacheen Littlefeather, at the 1973 Academy Awards.

Sacheen had met actor Marlon Brando through one of her neighbors, director Francis Ford Coppola. As president of the National Native American Affirmative Image Committee, she wrote Brando a series of letters where she explained the harmful representations of Native Americans in Hollywood films. After the Wounded Knee Incident of 1973, during which members of the American Indian Movement made headlines by taking back a South Dakota town, Marlon Brando decided to take action to support them.

Brando was nominated for Best Actor at the 1973 Oscars for his role in 'The Godfather', but instead of attending the award show, Marlon asked Sacheen Littlefeather to go in his place, and if he won, to use that time to speak out against Hollywood racism. He had written an entire speech, but Sacheen was told she would be arrested if she went over 60 seconds. When Marlon won, Sacheen took to the podium, politely declining to take the award from Roger Moore. She explained calmly that Marlon was not going to accept his Oscar win due to the treatment of Native American people in Hollywood movies. Sacheen received a smattering of boos, but generally gained support for speaking out. Her gracious and brave speech was applauded by activist Coretta Scott King, who called her personally to thank her.

Another group in dire need of representation on film was the LGBTQ community. The production code made filmmakers too scared to have gay characters, though there were a few winks and nods hidden within certain movie scripts. Until 1974, homosexuality was still listed as a mental disorder by the American Psychiatric Association, so there was a lot of fear from non-straight actors about losing their jobs if they came out of the closet.

The very notion of "coming out" didn't become commonplace until after the gay rights movement of the late 1960s. This new type of activism had been slowly building alongside the women's rights movement and other civil rights struggles, but exploded into action with the riots at the Stonewall nightclub in 1969. Coincidentally, these riots happened on the same day as the funeral for icon Judy Garland. Once the production code was removed, Hollywood gradually started to include gay and lesbian characters, but progress was still very slow and stereotypes abounded.

In the 1960s and 1970s, Classic Hollywood gave way to New Hollywood, as American filmmakers started to make European-style auteur films. This was vitally important for the art of filmmaking, but still largely left women out of the equation. "It was a peculiar time," said Molly Haskell; "In the old days, one thing that gave women ascendancy was the fact that it was good marketing — women were the ones who decided who went to the movies, among couples. So there were women's films, and the female audience was crucial. Suddenly that didn't matter. These male directors were getting Hollywood money to make personal movies, and they didn't have to worry about it."

As Hollywood weathered these tumultuous decades, there were a few female filmmakers who managed to push through the crowd and be heard. Sadly, classic movie stars like Joan Crawford and Bette Davis were edged out, but new actresses made an impact and pushed forward the conversation of equality on and off the screen.

Joan Crawford & Bette Davis: The Famous Feud

When the studio system crumbled and the idea of star contracts had dissolved, it meant the end for many classic film actresses in Hollywood. Some careers were tragically cut short by overdoses, suicides, and accidents, while others began to wane as younger, more modern actresses stepped up to take the spotlight away from older stars. But there were two classic Hollywood icons who refused to go quietly, and who weren't about to accept the idea that they were past their use-by date - Joan Crawford and Bette Davis. By teaming up with each other (as well as occasionally by fighting against each other), these two stars had a career renaissance and earned themselves a notorious place in Hollywood history.

Joan and Bette had reportedly been feuding for decades, going after the same roles and the same men. It's difficult to tell how much of this hatred for one another was real and how much was exaggerated by the press. Competition between women has always been a particularly exciting topic for gossip columnists and audiences. There's something about two powerful women fighting that holds a kind of macabre fascination for people – we still see this played out today in tabloid magazines and reality television shows.

In Joan and Bette's case, people loved to hear about these two Hollywood icons because they were so similar and yet so different. They both had been stars in the 1930s, where they were given roles which reflected their larger-than-life personas. Joan Crawford was the glamorous movie star, the type of woman that ladies wanted to be and men wanted to be with. Bette Davis was the actress, with an unconventional beauty that intrigued men and a persona that women found relatable. And through hard work and an incredible force of will, Joan and Bette remained in Hollywood a lot longer than anyone thought they would.

By the 1960s, both Bette Davis and Joan Crawford were in their fifties. The types of roles they had previously been offered were starting to dry up, and they were both tired of being passed over for younger stars. Joan had worked with director Robert Aldrich on a film called 'Autumn Leaves' in 1956, and when she got the script for 'What Ever Happened to Baby Jane?', she persuaded Robert to direct the film. Then Joan got to work on selling the idea to Bette Davis, knowing she would be perfect to play her sister. Bette said yes, but only if she could be assured that Joan and Robert were not sleeping together, because she didn't want Joan to receive any special treatment or extra close-ups. But the fact that Joan had asked Bette to be in the film in the first place, and had repeatedly stated that she "always wanted to work with Bette Davis," suggested there was no unworkable rivalry between them when they started filming.

111

In 'What Ever Happened to Baby Jane?', these two powerhouses played sisters, both former stars living in isolation in Hollywood. The characters needed each other as much as they hated each other, and the roles couldn't have been more perfect, or more meta, for the way the audience thought about Bette and Joan.

The studio aimed to maximize its profit from any publicity surrounding these two by purposely exaggerating the story of their feud. There are rumors about Bette actually kicking Joan during a fight sequence, and of Joan hiding weights in her costume before a scene where Bette had to lift her. Throughout the shoot, the ladies insisted these stories were pure fiction. "There is no feud," Bette Davis told a reporter at the time, "we wouldn't have one. A man and a woman, yes, but never two women – they'd be too clever for that."

Joan and Bette were professionals, but their acting styles were very different, and their big personalities sometimes clashed. This was encouraged by the studio and Robert Aldrich, who knew more explosive chemistry offscreen would help the acting feel real onscreen. And though their methods were cruel, the resulting press and PR campaign about the feud helped to bring audiences into theaters, and the film was really good. As a result, 'What Ever Happened to Baby Jane?' became a big commercial and critical success.

The movie was nominated for five Oscars, including Best Actress for Bette Davis. It is true that Joan Crawford wasn't happy about being left out, and she approached the other nominated actresses, offering to accept their award if they couldn't make the ceremony. At first, Bette wasn't too bothered by this, and the other nominees took Joan's offer as a sincere gesture of solidarity. Anne Bancroft was thankful, and asked Joan to accept for her if she won for 'The Miracle Worker'. When she did, a smiling Joan pushed past Bette to walk onstage. It was at that moment Bette realized this had been a ruthless move by Joan; it was revenge for not being nominated herself. From then on, it definitely was a feud between them, and Bette Davis vowed never to forgive Joan Crawford.

Even though the film had garnered Oscar nominations and made its budget back in just 11 days, it still wasn't enough to keep Bette and Joan employed in the type of roles they wanted. This was

Hollywood, and if you were a woman, you were only as good as your last birthday, not your last movie. Bette Davis even posted an advertisement looking for work in the trade magazines, saying, "Mother of three. Divorcee. American. Thirty years experience as an actress in motion pictures. Mobile still and more affable than rumor would have it. Wants steady employment in Hollywood (has had Broadway)." The tone was tongue-in-cheek but the message was genuine. Bette didn't want to give up working as an actress just yet.

So Bette and Joan reluctantly agreed to work together once more, on a follow-up to 'What Ever Happened To Baby Jane?' The film was called 'Hush... Hush, Sweet Charlotte'. This time, Joan would be in the villain role, with Bette as the victim. But it was the opposite on set. Tensions were high from the beginning. Bette hadn't forgotten about the Oscars, and Joan was paranoid she would take revenge. Joan's fears were exacerbated when she arrived at the airport for the shoot and found nobody there to pick her up. Also, Bette held parties at her cabin where she purposely invited everyone except Joan, trying to win over crew members. On another shoot day, the entire crew packed up and left the location without taking Joan. It's likely this was an accident, but Joan was convinced Bette was behind it. She was humiliated.

Joan's contract dictated she had to finish the picture, but she'd had enough. She decided the money simply wasn't worth all of this fighting, so she left, flew back to Los Angeles and checked herself into a hospital, citing exhaustion. Multiple meetings, conversations with lawyers, and tense talks with the studios followed. In the end Robert Aldrich got permission to replace Joan, and flew to Switzerland to convince Olivia de Havilland, who happened to be Bette's good friend, to take the part. Joan was outraged, claiming in a round of interviews done from her hospital bed that nobody had told her she was being replaced. "I wept for nine hours," she said to one reporter. "Aldrich knew where to long distance me all over the world when he needed me, but he made no effort to reach me here to say that he had signed Olivia. He let me hear it for the first time in a radio release...and, frankly, I think it stinks."

Following 'Hush... Hush, Sweet Charlotte', Bette Davis continued to work, moving to television, where she stayed right until the end of the 1980s. Joan Crawford made a couple of B movies, but then started to drink heavily. She'd had a reliance on alcohol for a long time, but now, living alone in a New York apartment, she sank deeper into it.

The feud between Bette Davis and Joan Crawford may have been fun to watch, but the stories of these two iconic women were proof of ageism and sexism in Hollywood. They stand as stark examples of how the classic stars of old Hollywood were quite brutally pushed aside for the new. And it's sobering to think how they might have helped each other through this changing Hollywood, if only they hadn't been pressured into viewing each other as competition.

Even if they were never going to be good friends, there is something quite sad about the idea of Joan dying alone from a heart attack, and Bette Davis using the opportunity to make one last quip about her. "You should never say bad things about the dead, you should only say good. Joan Crawford is dead. Good."

Jane Fonda: New Hollywood Icon

At the moment Jane Fonda was born, her father, actor Henry Fonda, took out his camera and started snapping photos. He took so many of them that eventually the nurses asked him to stop. Then, he ran down the hallway to write a telegram to director William Wyler, who had just directed Fonda in 'Jezebel' with Bette Davis. He wrote, "I admire your pictures and would like to work for you. I am eighteen minutes old. Blonde hair and blue eyes, weight: eight pounds... and I have been called beautiful. My father was an actor. Signed, Jayne Seymour Fonda." She was less than half an hour old, but already Jane Fonda's destiny had been written, by a father who would be a commanding and difficult presence in her life.

Her parents divorced when Jane was young, and her mother Frances was constantly battling with severe episodes of depression and eventually ended up in a mental hospital. When Jane was twelve, her father sat her and her brother Peter down to tell them their mother had died from a heart attack. A few weeks later, a school friend gave Jane a magazine which had an article about Frances. That was how she learned that her mother had committed suicide by slitting her own throat with a razor.

Not long after this, Jane developed an eating disorder, which was further exacerbated by Henry's criticism. "Once I hit adolescence," Jane wrote in her memoir, "the only time my father ever referred to how I looked was when he thought I was too fat or wanted me to wear a different, less revealing bathing suit, a looser belt, or a longer dress." Growing up, she was so scared of him that when she fractured her spine in a swimming accident, she didn't tell Henry about it for a week.

After school, Jane attended Vassar College, but soon dropped out. She went to Paris to study art, and then came back to the States to do some modeling. By the age of 20, Jane was living with her father in Los Angeles and battling depression and anxiety about what to do with her life. It was her friend Susan Strasberg who encouraged her to try acting. She was the daughter of the famous acting coach Lee Strasberg, and she set up a meeting between Lee and Jane to talk about his classes at the Actors Studio in New York. Jane was invited to join the summer program and decided to give it a shot. Henry didn't approve of these classes; he believed acting was something that couldn't be taught, and ridiculed the method acting exercises. Jane was dubious too, but was determined to try. This ended up being a life-changing experience.

Jane volunteered to perform one of Lee's sense-memory exercises on stage, which involved pretending to drink a glass of cold orange juice. She had practiced at home with a real glass of juice, ignoring Henry as he scoffed at her. When she walked on stage, Jane tried to imagine how that glass had felt in her hands. And it worked. "For the first time I was experiencing something unique to actors," Jane wrote, "I knew I was on stage before an audience, pretending – yet at the same time I was alone and totally in the moment." Her performance had surprised Lee Strasberg, who watched, enthralled, and then said, "I see a lot of people go through here, Jane, but you have real talent." On her way out of class, Jane was ecstatic; "Lee Strasberg told me I was talented," she thought, "he isn't my father or an employee of my father's. He didn't have to say this."

With that, Jane Fonda decided to pursue a career in acting, and vowed to work hard on her craft. "Instead of the usual two classes a week that everyone took, I took four. Instead of one scene every few months, I'd do double," she wrote. "I knew there would be those who'd say I'd gotten my breaks because I was Henry Fonda's daughter. At those times I needed to be able to say to myself, 'I'm studying hard...I don't take this for granted.'"

All of that work led to her first film role in 1960, the romantic comedy 'Tall Story' with Anthony Perkins. She was nervous and insecure, and described the filming experience as a "Kafkaesque nightmare," which brought about intense anxiety. "My bulimia soared out of control and I began sleepwalking again," she wrote. "It was summertime and hot, so I often slept nude. On one occasion I woke up on the sidewalk in front of my apartment building: cold, naked, searching in vain for where, and who, I was supposed to be."

She was especially nervous about being compared to her father, and had begged the film publicists not to mention his name. But of course, this ended up being the sole focus of both the advance press and the reviews which followed. "Nothing could possibly save the picture," said Time Magazine, "not even a second-generation Fonda with a smile like her father's and legs like a chorus girl."

After a brief moment where she decided to quit acting, Jane picked herself up again, and decided to work even harder. Throughout the 1960s she averaged two movies every year, including the western 'Cat Ballou' with Lee Marvin, which did pretty well. But her first bona fide hit came in 1967 with the charming screwball comedy 'Barefoot in the Park'. Her co-star was Robert Redford, with whom she'd previously worked on a film called 'The Chase', but on this shoot they became close friends. Jane called making this film "a joy," saying how in between takes, she and Robert would share stories about living in Los Angeles and their mutual love of horses. At this time they couldn't have guessed how important they'd each be to the film industry. Jane later wrote, "I remember Bob describing with great passion a piece of property he had bought in Utah...little did either of us imagine this property would become the Sundance ski resort, and later the Sundance Institute, which has made such significant contributions to independent filmmaking."

Robert had starred in the Broadway stage version of 'Barefoot in the Park', and with his knowledge of the text, he helped Jane find confidence with her character. Their genuine chemistry made the movie a huge success. 'Barefoot in the Park' was their biggest box office hit to date, and Jane's best reviewed role to that point. After 'Barefoot' came 'Barbarella', which remains one of Jane's most iconic roles. The sci-fi sex comedy was directed by Roger Vadim, the man who had made Brigette Bardot an icon in France, and Jane's husband at the time. In 'Barbarella', she played a wide-eyed sex kitten, which seems so at odds with her feminist sensibilities when viewed now. Being half naked in so many of her scenes brought back Jane's body insecurities. "Every morning I was sure Roger would wake up and realize he had made a terrible mistake – 'Oh my God! She's not Bardot!'" But the movie went on to become a cult classic.

'Barbarella' established her as a sex symbol, but 1969's 'They Shoot Horses, Don't They?' made her an Oscar contender. The film was directed by Sydney Pollack, and Jane sank deep into playing Gloria, a suicidal Depression era character. She gave a brilliant performance, impressing critics like Pauline Kael, who wrote in the New Yorker, "Fonda goes all the way with it, as screen actresses rarely do once they become stars...Jane Fonda stands a good chance of personifying American tensions and dominating our movies in the seventies..."

And that is exactly what Jane did, with a rush of wonderful performances throughout the 1970s, winning her two Best Actress Academy Awards. The first was for 'Klute' in 1971, and the second was for the Vietnam war film 'Coming Home' in 1978. 'Klute' was directed by Alan J. Pakula, and was one of the first films of the 1970s which addressed modern women's issues. Jane had a complex role, playing prostitute Bree Daniels, a woman living in fear for her life. The movie looked at female sexuality, male paranoia about women, and how much women need or don't need a man's approval. "In retrospect I see the parallels between myself and Bree," Jane wrote, "a woman who felt safer hooking than facing true intimacy."

'Klute' also marked the beginning of Jane's focus on films with a strong feminist point of view, which included 'Coming Home', the nuclear disaster thriller 'The China Syndrome', and 'Nine to Five'. This empowering comedy commented on women wanting respect in the workplace. The characters played by Jane, Lily Tomlin, and Dolly Parton stood up to their sexist manager and challenged the idea that women should just be secretaries and not the boss themselves. Jane also used her voice outside of cinema as an outspoken critic of the Vietnam War. She took part in many protests which admonished the U.S. government for being involved in the war, and in 1972 took a controversial trip to North Vietnam. Jane posed for photos with the Vietnamese army, sitting on an anti-aircraft gun used against American troops. These pictures caused a lot of anger back in the States, where she was given the nickname "Hanoi Jane" and called a traitor to her own country. There were even death threats when she returned, from a group calling themselves the American Liberty League.

The anger leveled towards her came from a complex place. First, here was an American who was laughing with a war enemy while sitting on a weapon of destruction. And second, the person doing the laughing was a Hollywood sex symbol, an actress, a famous person, and a woman. "I am Henry Fonda's privileged daughter who appears to be thumbing my nose at the country that has provided me these privileges," Jane wrote in her autobiography; "More than that, I am a woman, which makes my sitting there even more of a betrayal...And I am a woman who is seen as 'Barbarella', a character existing on some subliminal level as an embodiment of men's fantasies. Barbarella has become their enemy." But she does regret taking that photo in the first place, calling it, "my biggest lapse of judgement in my life. I'm glad I did everything I did, except that."

Adding to this stress was her strained relationship with her father. As Jane's career success grew, Henry became more competitive. When asked for his thoughts on her first Oscar win, he said, "How in hell would you like to have been in this business as long as I, and have one of your kids win an Oscar before you do?"

Ironically, Henry's first and only Oscar win came from a film where he co-starred with Jane. 'On Golden Pond' played on their difficult relationship, starring Henry as a terse father and Jane as a free-spirited daughter. Playing the wife and mother was the legendary Katharine Hepburn. The film was produced by Jane, who saw the screenplay and knew this could be the role to finally give her father an Oscar. Henry was sick, his health failing from heart disease, so this was also her last chance to act opposite him. But he was gruff, just like the character, and you can feel this tension when you watch the movie. In Katharine Hepburn's biography, she spoke about making 'On Golden Pond', saying, "There was certainly a whole layer of drama going on in the scenes between her and Hank, and I think she came by to watch every scene he and I had together. There was a feeling of longing about her."

That was true. Jane had always longed for her father's love. Their work together was tough, but ultimately cathartic, and was rewarded in 1982 when Henry Fonda won the Best Actor Oscar. He was too unwell to attend the ceremony and Jane accepted the award on his behalf. She wrote in her memoir that this was "the happiest moment of my life." Henry Fonda died just a few months later. Jane Fonda was born in the shadow of her famous father, but she managed to step out to forge her own unique path. She showed how actresses didn't need to be defined by any one thing – she was a sex goddess and a serious actress, an activist and an aerobics queen, a feminist and a fearless leader. Henry Fonda was an icon of Old Hollywood, but Jane Fonda became a symbol of New Hollywood.

Female Filmmakers, Finally

In the early 1970s, it remained almost impossible for a female director to get an opportunity in studio movies. Nonetheless, comedian Elaine May managed to do that and more, becoming the first woman to have a major studio release as a director, writer, and star.

Elaine was born in Philadelphia to a theater director father and an actress mother. With that pedigree, it's no surprise that after she finished school, Elaine headed west to Los Angeles to study acting. In 1955, she moved to Chicago to continue her studies, and it was here that she met Mike Nichols. They both were part of an improvisation troupe, but quickly realized how well they worked together. So, they created an improv comedy duo and started performing at the university, before going on to nightclubs, then bigger venues, followed by television appearances, radio spots, and a run on Broadway plus three best-selling comedy albums. It was a whirlwind transformation from students to famous comedians, and they made a huge impact, despite their partnership only lasting four years.

In 1961, Mike and Elaine disbanded their duo at the very height of their popularity. Mike Nichols went onto a career as a director, most notably directing 1967's 'The Graduate', and Elaine May began writing plays, and then eventually screenplays.

When Elaine became frustrated by the changes directors made to her scripts, she decided she wanted more control. Her directorial debut was with a film she had written called 'New Leaf' in 1971. She also starred in the film as a clumsy botanist who meets a gold digger and encourages him to change his ways. With this film, Elaine May joined the exclusive group of director-writer-performers in Hollywood films, alongside names such as Charlie Chaplin and Orson Welles.

Her final cut of 'New Leaf' was reportedly 180 minutes long; so Paramount edited out 80 of those minutes. Elaine was upset at the studio tinkering with her movie and took them to court. She lost the case and publicly disowned her movie, saying this was not the cut she wanted audiences to see. But despite that conflict, Elaine continued to work with the studio, and her follow-up was a big success, 1972's 'The Heartbreak Kid'. This time around, she decided not to star, instead focusing on directing this romantic love triangle story based on a screenplay by Neil Simon.

Elaine tried something different for her next movie, a crime drama she wrote and directed called 'Mikey and Nicky' starring Peter Falk and indie director John Cassavetes. Making the film cost more than twice the original budget, and Elaine was fired from Paramount Pictures. But there was no way Elaine was going to let them finish it without her. Before she left, she took two reels of her movie and told the studio she was holding them hostage until she was rehired. It worked, but the film failed at the box office, and she wasn't hired to direct again for more than a decade. This is a common trend for female filmmakers, they are sent to "directing jail" if they make a misstep.

Warren Beatty decided Elaine should get another chance, and he persuaded Columbia Pictures to let her direct 'Ishtar', his big budget adventure, in 1987. The film starred Warren and Dustin Hoffman as two struggling singer/songwriters who take a gig in Morocco and end up getting involved with a group of guerilla rebels. From the start, the film had many things working against it, from creative differences to a difficult shoot; particularly the many press accounts of the problems the film was having. With so much negative publicity, 'Ishtar' struggled to find an audience and quickly became a commercial and critical flop. Elaine May never directed another feature film, but she was nominated for two Academy Awards for her work as a writer. The first nomination was for 'Heaven Can Wait' in 1978, starring Warren Beatty; the second was for 'Primary Colors' in 1998, directed by her old partner Mike Nichols. The two friends had also worked together just before this on the screenplay for 'The Birdcage'.

There were very few chances given to female filmmakers to work for Hollywood studios, so many women turned to low budget independent films to help start their careers.

One of the all-time feminist indie films was made by Barbara Loden, a Tony-award-winning theater actress. Barbara wrote the screenplay for 'Wanda' nine years before she was able to make it; it had taken her six years to gather up the money for the production. She was shy about directing as well as acting in a starring role, but her husband, director Elia Kazan, managed to convince her to try both.

'Wanda' was a gritty, brilliant look at a female wanderer who drifted between jobs and men. It felt very truthful, very real to the plight of women, perhaps because Barbara strongly resembled the character. Elia Kazan said, "She once told me a very sad thing. She told me: 'I have always needed a man to protect me.' I will say that most women in our society are familiar with this, understand this, need this, but are not honest enough to say it. And she was saying it sadly."

The film was made for $160,000 and shot in only seven weeks. It found a small overseas audience of what Elia called "English intellectuals" and won an award at the Venice Film Festival, but didn't make enough money for Barbara to continue her career as a director; "She always had the feeling of knocking on doors that remained closed," Elia said of it.

This was the only film Barbara Loden would ever direct. She passed away in 1980 from cancer at only 48 years old, and 'Wanda' remained obscure in the United States. This changed in 2003 thanks to French actress Isabelle Huppert. She loved the movie and pushed for the film to be released on DVD in the United States, where it found a cult audience among women.

Claudia Weill was one of the most successful indie female filmmakers of the 1970s. She was born in New York City and made a short film and a small documentary before 'Girlfriends', her 1977 feature film debut. It was produced independently and shot over a few years, whenever Claudia could get the money. The comedy-drama follows two female roommates living in New York whose close friendship ends when one moves out to get married. It's a highly relatable story, because whether you're the first of your friends to get married or the last, we all feel the pressure of being stuck between young adult and proper grown-up.

'Girlfriends' was inspired by a line from the book 'Advancing Paul Newman' by Eleanor Bergstein. The line reads, "This is a story of two girls, each of whom suspected the other of a more passionate connection with life." Warner Bros had seen a cut and liked it so much that they bought it from Claudia Weill. It went on to be a critical success, winning the People's Choice award at the Toronto International Film Festival. The great Stanley Kubrick gave 'Girlfriends' his blessing, saying, "I think one of the most interesting Hollywood films, well not Hollywood, American films, that I've seen in a long time is Claudia Weill's 'Girlfriends'. That film, I thought, was one of the very rare American films that I would compare with the serious, intelligent, sensitive writing and filmmaking that you find in the best directors in Europe."

The success of one female director encouraged more women to try directing; and it's estimated that between 1967 and 1980, there were sixteen female filmmakers who made at least one narrative film in the studio or independent world. They were: Karen Arthur, Anne Bancroft, Joan Darling, Lee Grant, Joanna Lee, Barbara Loden, Elaine May, Barbara Peeters, Joan Rivers, Stephanie Rothman, Beverly Sebastian, Joan Micklin Silver, Joan Tewkesbury, Jane Wagner, Nancy Walker, and Claudia Weill.

123

In the experimental world, there was Shirley Clarke. She was nominated for an Oscar in 1960 for her short film 'Skyscraper', and in 1962, she directed the landmark indie feature 'The Connection'. Based on a play by Jack Gelber, the story centered on a group of jazz musicians waiting for their heroin dealer "connections" to come to their apartment. The film dealt with this socially relevant problem in a realistic way, using the style of handheld camera to give a raw quality. Shirley was also one of the signatories to the manifesto of the New American Cinema Group, which called for an end to censorship, a stop to interference from distributors, and a new way of financing low-budget films.

Exploitation movies were a popular form of low-budget film in the 1960s and 1970s, but they were very male-dominated, both in terms of on-screen content and the people who made them. There were two female directors at Roger Corman's production company, but they both struggled with the misogynistic films. Barbara Peeters directed several B movies produced by Roger Corman, but left his company after he reportedly took control of 'Humanoids from the Deep', changing her monster movie into a violent sexploitation flick. Stephanie Rothman worked as a director at Corman's New World Pictures, but she ultimately found the content unfulfilling. She left to set up the company Dimension Films with her husband, where she turned the idea of exploitation on its head. Instead of using women as objects, she began to show female stories, female desires, and female struggle.

There were also women working in the documentary world; leading the way was filmmaker Barbara Kopple. She is a two-time Academy Award winning director for her documentaries 'Harlan County, U.S.A.' in 1976 and 'American Dream' in 1990. Both of these films dealt with worker strikes, one about coal miners and one about a meatpacking plant. With her Oscar for 'Harlan County, U.S.A.' Barbara Kopple was the first female director to ever win a solo Academy Award.

She has tackled many subjects in her documentaries, but among her recurring themes are stories about women. 'Defending Our Daughters: The Rights of Women in the World', examined gender equality in various countries; 'Bearing Witness' was about five female war reporters working in Iraq; and 'Shut Up And Sing' followed the pushback that country group the Dixie Chicks experienced after criticizing President George W. Bush. 'Miss Sharon Jones!' was also about music, following singer Sharon Jones through a tough year in her life. Most recently, 'This Is Everything: Gigi Gorgeous' looked at the rise of the transgender YouTube star. Barbara Kopple has never shied away from documenting underrepresented subjects, and remains an extremely respected filmmaker in the industry.

These names are important to note, because each of these careers helped to create a path for future female filmmakers to follow.

These women of the 1960s and 1970s knocked on that glass ceiling, and though it was tough to break through it, they ended up inspiring a whole new generation waiting in the wings, ready for their shot.

Pam Grier: The Blaxploitation Hero

When director Melvin Van Peebles released 'Sweet Sweetback's Baadasssss Song' in 1971, he had no idea he was essentially launching a new film movement. This movie, along with the equally groundbreaking 'Shaft', began the short but sharp blaxploitation era. This movement saw new kinds of action heroes taking over the big screen, and the biggest of them all was one tough woman, Pam Grier.

She was a military brat, and her family moved to various bases around the country for her father's job as a mechanic in the U.S. Air Force. When her dad left the military, the family settled into a tough neighborhood in Colorado. Pam describes her family as "half-military and half-rural" because on the weekends they would visit her grandparents' farm, where she was taught how to camp, fish, and grow crops. Pam also learned how to be an independent woman by watching her mother and grandmother take charge during the women's movement of the 1950s and 1960s.

And she had to be strong at an early age. At just six years old, Pam was raped by two local boys while playing at her aunt's house. This changed her deeply and left her "lonely and traumatized," no longer the happy, precocious child she had been before. Pam started to stammer and became extremely shy, preferring to be alone and escape by reading her fantasy books. "It took so long to deal with the pain of that," Pam wrote in her memoir; "You try to deal with it, but you never really get over it...My family endured so much guilt and anger."

125

When she was older, in an attempt to boost Pam's confidence, her mother encouraged her to enter beauty pageants. At one of her competitions, she was approached by an agent who invited her to come to Hollywood and try acting. Pam said no; she hadn't ever wanted to act. "Not too many sisters at that time dreamed about becoming actresses," Pam said in one interview; "you're still a member of the Black Panthers, you're still trying to vote, you're still trying not to get run off the road or stopped or frisked." But her mother convinced her that this could be a good opportunity, and told Pam she could always come home if it didn't work out. Pam moved to Los Angeles and enrolled at UCLA Film School; she was interested in directing. "I started meeting these film students," Pam said; "I thought, 'I love this. This is why I am here. I want to get into film school.'"

To make money on the side, she took a small role in the 1970 cult classic 'Beyond the Valley of the Dolls'; she also had a job as a switchboard operator at American International Pictures, a company owned by Roger Corman, the iconic director and producer of low-budget indie horrors and B movies.

At the time, Roger Corman was looking for "an in-your-face, radical kind of natural actress who hadn't been pampered and frosted with wigs and blue eye-shadow," and Pam's colleagues persuaded her to go and see him. She finally agreed when she learned the job would pay $600. Roger Corman instantly liked her personality and paired her with writer/director Jack Hill to make a movie. Suddenly, this formerly shy girl found herself in the Philippines playing an inmate of a women's prison and doing all of her own stunts. Roger Corman had given her the method acting book 'An Actor Prepares' by Konstantin Stanislavski, and she decided to take her role in 1971's 'The Big Doll House' very seriously. "Even though I was doing what was considered a B movie," Pam said, "I thought it was *'Gone with the Wind.'" And her commitment to her role and ability to give emotion to even the thinnest of characters made her stand out.*

Pam starred in a few more films with different directors but teamed up with Jack Hill once again in 1973 to make her first blaxploitation movie, 'Coffy'. This was right at the time when blaxploitation was having its moment. By the end of the civil rights movement in the 1960s, there was a huge section of the movie-going audience that wanted to see their stories told on the big screen. Hollywood saw dollar signs and a way to help their struggling industry, so studios started putting money towards these blaxploitation films, and they turned huge profits. There were around 90 blaxploitation films released in the early 70s, and their popularity saw lines forming around the block in black neighborhoods. They were exploitation films that featured sex and violence, but they were also empowering to audiences. For the first time, African-American viewers saw issues they could relate to and black stars who were heroes.

'Coffy' became Pam Grier's breakthrough role. With a tag-line that read, "the baddest one-chick hit-squad that ever hit town," the film mixed sex, violence, and social commentary about drugs. Pam played the title role of Coffy, a nurse who seeks revenge on the dealers who got her sister hooked on drugs. With this film, Pam launched a whole new type of woman in cinema history – one who was sexy but could also kick a man's butt in a variety of ways, with many different weapons. As Pam told one interviewer, "People had only seen African-American women depicted a certain way in film, and it was about time that changed."

Audiences felt liberated seeing a black woman fight the bad guys, and this low budget movie ended up making millions. After Pam Grier in 'Coffy' came Tamara Dobson in 'Cleopatra Jones', another successful African-American action heroine. 'Coffy' and 'Cleopatra Jones' dealt with similar themes and often played as a double feature in local cinemas.

127

Following the success of 'Coffy' came one of Pam Grier's most famous roles, 'Foxy Brown' in 1974. This made Pam an icon, the undisputed Queen of Blaxploitation. Foxy was a high-class prostitute out for revenge after her boyfriend was murdered. The tagline read, "She's brown sugar and spice, but if you don't treat her nice, she'll put you on ice," and the film was a hit with both black and white audiences. Pam Grier became a major cross-over star. This was huge for the time, since non-white women still weren't visible on the big screen. If they were, it was on the sidelines and definitely not fighting bad guys.

'Foxy Brown' and Pam Grier were criticized for representing an overly sexualized black woman and playing into stereotypes of violence and drug abuse. Many critics thought that by the 1970s, films should be depicting more progress for non-white characters. Pam saw it in a different way; these movies purposely showed the dark side of the community in order to start conversations about changing it. She pointed out how her characters were progressive, in that they were funny, sexy, tough, and protected their families at all costs. "It makes sense that strong women would come out of black films," said Pam. "The woman has always been the strength of our family. Because if one thing has always been true, it is that black boys are terrified of their mamas." The box office totals of these movies proved that African-American actresses could sell tickets just as well as male stars.

Towards the mid-1970s, the blaxploitation era started to fade, and many actors had trouble finding other roles. But Pam Grier kept working. She starred in 20 films between 1971 and 1981 and did television and theater throughout the 80s and 90s. And in 1995, she met Quentin Tarantino. He was a big fan of the blaxploitation genre, and when Pam went to his office to meet him, there were posters of 'Foxy Brown' all over his wall. She asked him if he'd put those up knowing she was visiting, and he replied, "No, I meant to take those down because you were coming!"

In 1997, Quentin offered Pam 'Jackie Brown', his homage to her 1970s action films. By that stage, Pam thought she had finished working in film, because she wasn't getting many offers for roles. "Spike Lee wasn't writing roles for me, John Singleton and other black directors weren't writing roles with me in mind – I was just doing other things until Quentin asked me." 'Jackie Brown' ended up being her comeback, and she was nominated for Best Actress at both the Golden Globes and the Screen Actors Guild awards. She hasn't stopped working since.

Pam Grier has faced a lot in her life. From sexual assault to a battle with cancer in 1988 to surviving Hollywood for more than four decades, throughout it all, she has been tough, and today, she stands as an icon both as a female star and a breakthrough African-American actress who showed that women of all colors can be heroes.

MODERN HOLLYWOOD (1980s - 2000s)

The 1980s ushered in several new technologies that had a huge impact on the film industry. The biggest were the videocassette recorder and consumer video cameras. The VCR came to the United States in 1977 and quickly became the must-have appliance in every household. After some initial resistance to the idea of recording movies straight from television, the film industry realized how to capitalize on the idea of home entertainment by selling their movies on cassette tapes. And independent cinema got a huge boost from video recorders giving easier access to cheap filmmaking.

To showcase the results of this new indie movement, Robert Redford set up the Sundance Film Festival. There were a couple of big breakout indie hits in the late 80s and 90s, which were made for very little money but had box office success, like Steven Soderbergh's 'Sex, Lives, and Videotape', and Quentin Tarantino's 'Reservoir Dogs'.

Without having to rely on movie studios for opportunities, several female directors broke out as stars in the independent world. There was Penelope Spheeris, who made her debut with a trio of punk rock documentaries called 'The Decline of Western Civilization'. As a woman, she was able to get these young punk kids to open up, and it's incredible to see her hanging out with tough bands like Black Flag. Penelope went on to have a huge hit with the rock n' roll comedy 'Wayne's World' in 1992. Amy Heckerling became the first female director to work at Universal Pictures in 63 years, when she made 'Fast Times At Ridgemont High' in 1982. She also had a commercial hit in 1995 with 'Clueless' starring Alicia Silverstone. Meanwhile Bette Gordon directed 'Variety' in 1983, a rare film which explored female sexuality, and feminist icon Allison Anders made indie movies with stories about women not usually seen in Hollywood films.

As a student in the late 1980s, Allison made a movie about the LA punk rock scene; she was quite punk rock herself, breaking into the UCLA edit bays at night to cut it. A few years later she sent a letter and a mixtape to her directing idol, Wim Wenders, which led to Allison working on his movie, 'Paris, Texas'. Then she became a star of the indie film world with her second movie, 'Gas, Food, Lodging', about a single mother. The film was selected to screen at the Sundance Film Festival and the Berlin Film Festival, where it gathered rave reviews. And her third movie, 'Mi Vida Loca', was chosen for competition at the Cannes Film Festival.

Another indie trailblazer was Martha Coolidge, who made the cult classic 'Valley Girl' in 1983, starring a young Nicolas Cage in his first lead role. In 2002, Martha became the first woman to be elected President of the Directors Guild of America, where she was vocal in her efforts to expose the gender inequality of the industry. Other important indie milestones included Nancy Savoca winning the Grand Prize at the 1989 Sundance Film Festival with 'True Love' and Susan Siedelman's 'Smithereens', which was the first American independent movie to play at the Cannes Film Festival. Susan was also nominated for an Oscar for her short film 'The Dutch Master', but is probably best known for 'Desperately Seeking Susan', which featured Madonna in her first film role. And Patty Jenkins made a splash with 'Monster' in 2003, the film that turned Charlize Theron into an Oscar winning actress. She had to wait fourteen years before getting another chance to make a movie, but her second feature was a huge success, 2017s 'Wonder Woman'.

The indie scene was thriving, but inside Hollywood, movies stopped encouraging risk-taking and creativity. Gone was the New American Wave of the 1970s, because in the 1980s it was all about making money without risking box office failure. Blockbusters with mass appeal were the name of the game, and this was partly thanks to the disastrous 'Heaven's Gate'.

In 1980, United Artists had given Oscar-winning director Michael Cimino free rein to make the epic Western 'Heaven's Gate'. The film went way over budget, ballooning to $44 million, but it made just $3.5 million domestically. This was one of the biggest box office bombs of all time, and it completely tanked United Artists. After this disaster, other studios became increasingly reluctant to try anything new. And with more multiplex cinemas popping up all over the country, the objective became how to reach the largest portion of the viewing audience at one time. They needed films with broad commercial appeal that would be easy to sell and began consulting their marketing departments for movie ideas.

So instead of the director being the author of the movie, now the marketplace was in control, and studios focused on genres which consistently made the most money, namely, franchises with special effects, comic book characters, space travel, and a lot of action. Steven Spielberg and George Lucas were the masters of the blockbuster, and they rose to the top of the "movie brats" pile, while Francis Ford Coppola, Martin Scorsese, and others struggled to get their films made.

By the 1990s and 2000s, Hollywood's business plan had succeeded, and cinema attendance was up. In 1997, 'Titanic' set a new benchmark as the biggest box office success in history. Interestingly, the most powerful section of the 'Titanic' audience was teenage girls and women, who bought 60% of all tickets sold. Traditionally, action-adventure films were pitched at male audiences, but thanks to its strong female character, tragic love story, and star Leonardo DiCaprio, 'Titanic' particularly appealed to young women. This section of the audience came out to see the movie again and again, in an impressive display of repeat business. The other studios took notice. Robert Levin of Sony told The New York Times, "A while ago everyone was really focusing on the young male audience: young male action movies, young male comedies. Now we're saying, 'Wow, there's really a young female audience out there that we must be attentive to.'" In fact, that audience was always there, just underserved. Every couple of years Hollywood seems to forget how powerful female audiences can be at the box office.

The success of 'Titanic' led to a rise in films aimed at tween girls that featured women at the center of the story, films like 'Bring It On' with Kirsten Dunst, 'The Princess Diaries' starring Anne Hathaway, the comedy 'Mean Girls', and the romance 'The Notebook'. The biggest hit of all of these was the 'Twilight' film series, which was based on popular young adult novels and catered to women's tastes. By the time the franchise got to its penultimate film, 'Twilight: Breaking Dawn Part 1', 80% of its audience was female.

The first 'Twilight' film was directed by Catherine Hardwicke. She had started her career as a production designer before directing and co-writing her first indie movie, the gritty teen drama 'Thirteen'. The film was a big success and scored a Best Supporting Actress Oscar nomination for Holly Hunter. 'Lords of Dogtown' became a second indie hit for Catherine, and then she moved to bigger films. The success of 'Twilight' gave her the biggest opening weekend for a film directed by a woman in history. But inexplicably, she was replaced by a male director for the sequel.

The numbers of female filmmakers working for mainstream Hollywood in the 80s, 90s and 2000s were low, but there were a few standouts. Nora Ephron was a brilliant essayist and novelist who moved into screenwriting and directing. Her screenplays for 'Silkwood', 'When Harry Met Sally', and 'Sleepless in Seattle' were all nominated for Oscars. Nora also directed 'Sleepless in Seattle', as well as 'You've Got Mail', and 'Julie & Julia' before passing away in 2012 from pneumonia brought on by leukemia.

Nancy Meyers is another successful writer/director working in the world of romantic comedies. Her career has spanned more than three decades, and her commercially successful movies focus on a variety of women's issues, from older love affairs in 'Something's Gotta Give' to divorce in 'It's Complicated' and young career women with 'The Intern'. She's one of the few directors who creates love stories involving older women. As Diane Keaton told The New York Times Magazine, "she's the only one delivering the fantasy for women over 55."

But even with a combined box office of over $600 million, Nancy still struggles to get her films made, she revealed in an interview with The Guardian: "My kind of movie is not the kind of film that studios have wanted to make for a while now. Instead, it's been all comic-book movies, gigantic action movies and guy comedies... and, for whatever reason, they think a man would be better at directing dinosaurs, or flying people, or whatever. But I know there are plenty of super-game women who would want to make those films."

Meanwhile, other female directors made their way behind the lens after starring in front of it. Penny Marshall began her career on the hit TV show 'Laverne and Shirley' and later directed iconic films such as 'Big' and 'A League of Their Own'. Barbra Streisand made history when she directed 'Yentl', becoming the first person to produce, write, star, and sing in a movie. She followed it up with the Oscar-nominated 'The Prince of Tides' and 'The Mirror Has Two Faces'. Jodie Foster gained critical acclaim in the 90s with her film 'Little Man Tate', and Diane Keaton directed the indie film 'Unstrung Heroes' as well as the studio film 'Hanging Up', in which she starred alongside Meg Ryan and Lisa Kudrow.

Two female directors in particular have proven women could make box office hits in different genres. Mimi Ledger directed the big budget blockbusters 'The Peacemaker' and 'Deep Impact'. 'Deep Impact' held the record for the highest-grossing opening weekend for a female director until 'Twilight' broke it a decade later, and 'Wonder Woman' a decade after that. And Betty Thomas worked solidly with films such as 'Doctor Dolittle' and '28 Days'; then in 2009, she directed 'Alvin and the Chipmunks: The Squeakquel', which has grossed over $200 million in the U.S.

In front of the camera, there were several prominent female actresses who chipped away at the glass ceiling throughout these decades, especially Halle Berry, the first African-American Best Lead Actress Oscar winner, and Julia Roberts, the first woman to receive a $20 million pay check for a movie. This happened after she proved her box office draw several times over, including 'Pretty Woman', 'Steel Magnolias', 'My Best Friend's Wedding', and 'Notting Hill'.

With her Oscar-winning role in 'Erin Brockovich', she negotiated the highest pay ever seen for a woman. Then she went on to break her own record with her pay for her next movie, 'Mona Lisa Smile'. This represented a big step forward in pay equality for actresses, though it was still less than many of her male counterparts.

The focus of modern Hollywood was making money. The successes for female stars and female directors were seen as the exception, not the rule. Studios stuck to the type of content and the people they believed would bring in the biggest audiences, and this led to a calcification of what was considered a "risk" – including employing female directors, female stars, and women of color in general. It was a struggle to get work, to get movies made, and to pay the rent, but women were not ready to give up without a fight.

The Original Six

After years of being denied work in Hollywood, six female directors got together; and in 1979, they decided it was time to take matters into their own hands. Dubbed the "Original Six," they were Nell Cox, Joelle Dobrow, Dolores Ferraro, Victoria Hochberg, Lynne Littman, and Susan Bay Nimoy. Together, they proved how mighty women can be, taking two of the biggest studios to court over gender discrimination.

They began their fight by forming a group to push for gender equality. They called it the Women's Steering Committee (WSC), attached to the Director's Guild of America (DGA). With the blessing of the DGA, they launched an investigation involving a year of intense research to discover the percentage of women working as directors in Hollywood. What they found was truly shocking. Between 1939 and 1979, women directed 0.5% of all feature films and episodic television shows – half of one percent. Armed with this research, the Original Six began a campaign to challenge and expose studio hiring practices.

These ladies had put their careers on the line, and over the next three years they held meetings with boardrooms full of male studio executives – showing their research, asking tough questions, and urging companies to allocate a certain number of positions for women. They even leaked their findings to the media, hoping to spur the studios into action. But they were met with resistance, and in 1983 they experienced a particularly hopeless day that they dubbed "The Danish Debacle." The DGA had ordered a lot of danish pastries for studio executives to snack on during a big meeting, but the executives never showed up. With that, the DGA decided it was time to take legal action, and they had enough evidence from the Original Six to sue Warner Bros and Columbia Pictures for discrimination. By then, many of the six women had moved on to other projects or given up on having a career as a director, but they got together once more to select a lawyer and disseminate the outcomes of their research findings.

This lawsuit was important for several reasons. Firstly, its aim was to shine a light on the massive gender inequality within Hollywood. Secondly, it was to fight for women's right to work. The third aim was to hopefully get access to pension funds. The DGA works on a points system, where a film industry worker has to get a certain number of points to qualify for health insurance and pension. The only way to get those points is to work. So, by not being given equal employment, these women were also losing their ability to look after themselves in their old age.

The lawsuit was expanded to include discrimination towards people of color. While that research was taking place, President Ronald Reagan slashed budgets at the Equal Employment Opportunity Commission (EEOC) and also appointed a new judge, who took over the case.

135

In 1985, Judge Pamela Rymer dismissed the lawsuit. This decision was based on counterclaims filed by Warner Bros and Paramount Pictures, who argued that the DGA was part of the problem. The studios hired the directors, but the rules of the Director's Guild gave those directors the right to choose their first assistant, then the first assistant could choose their second assistant, and so forth. The studios argued they couldn't be held accountable for discrimination when they weren't responsible for all of the hiring. They claimed the DGA promoted the exact word-of-mouth hiring they were suing against. Whether or not that was true, for the Original Six, the loss of this case was heartbreaking. They felt by losing on a technicality, the point of their case – to prove discrimination was taking place in Hollywood – had been missed entirely.

But the lawsuit did make a difference in the world of television; the number of women hired to direct rose to 16% between 1985 and 1995. This was a huge increase of 15.5%, which made 1995 a landmark year for female directors in television. Unfortunately, that percentage hasn't continued to increase, even with the influx of new television shows and channels. In the years since 1995, the percentage of female directors in TV has dropped again, with the research data indicating it is stagnant at about 12%.

The story of these six ladies may not be widely known, but has served to inspire a new breed of Hollywood revolutionary. Filmmaker Maria Giese has spent years studying the details of the Original Six in preparation for her own case against Hollywood, a case that could end up being the answer.

Today, the Original Six are still continuing their own fight; mentoring other women, consulting, and persisting to get their ideas made. Their story is worth telling and their bravery worth sharing; it shows how even a few raised voices speaking out can make a huge difference.

The Female Executives

During the 1970s, Hollywood was still very much a man's world. But a handful of strong-willed ladies was quietly moving up the ranks, working their way towards the top executive positions of the movie studios. It was not an easy task, but thanks to their hard work there were more women in executive positions in the 1980s and 1990s than ever before. And for the first time, there were two major movie

studios run by women – Dawn Steel at Columbia Pictures, and
Sherry Lansing at Paramount.

Being the most powerful woman in Hollywood was not actually
Sherry Lansing's plan. When she and her husband had moved to
Los Angeles in 1966, they made the move for his career in medicine.
Sherry thought she might be able to get some work on the side
as an actress, and she picked up a few roles, one in a drama
called 'Loving' and another in 'Rio Lobo' with John Wayne, but she
didn't think she was good enough to continue. Her producer from
'Loving' suggested she should be a script reader, so she found a
job reading scripts for $5 an hour. Sherry loved it. Her enthusiasm
was noticed by an executive at MGM, who then hired her as a story
editor responsible for working on drafts of scripts to get them ready
for production. Sherry also began developing her own material,
including a sequel to 'Gone with the Wind'. And she watched as
many classic movies as she could to teach herself film history.
Of course, like any young, attractive woman in Hollywood, she had
to put up with a lot of sexism, like an encounter with director Don
Siegel, who was furious at being given script notes by a woman. "I
dealt with sexism by denying it," Sherry said in her biography; "Did
I hold grudges? Absolutely. But I felt I had two choices. Either I was
going to quit my job, stand on a picket line, and burn my bra, or I was
going to have to find a way to navigate the system until I reached
a position where my opinions would be heard." She chose to stay
the course, and after working at MGM, she was picked by Columbia
Pictures to be its senior vice president of production, where she
oversaw films such as 'The China Syndrome' and 'Kramer vs Kramer'.
Then in 1980, she was enticed over to 20th Century Fox.

She'd worked with Alan Hirschfield at Columbia, and now he was
chairman at Fox and was looking for someone to fill the head
position. He thought Sherry would be perfect. "I knew she was
experienced and I knew she was smart," Alan said, "I needed
someone who would reestablish our credibility as quickly as
possible." So, he offered Sherry the job of president.

This was a first for any woman in Hollywood history, and came at a time when women had to navigate unwanted sexual advances, inappropriate jokes, and sexism on a daily basis. Alan also made sure Sherry was well paid, saying, "No one will take her seriously unless she gets the same salary as a man." So not only did Sherry make history as the first woman to be president of a studio, she did it with equal pay. When the news broke a few days later, articles were written about what this promotion might mean for the advancement of women, while The New York Times ran a story with the headline, "Sherry Lansing, Former Model, Named Head of Fox Productions." Sherry had been a model, but it feels unnecessary to mention it in a headline about a history-making job.

A year later, Fox was bought by Texas oilman Marvin Davis, and when he made a visit to Los Angeles, he asked to meet the head of the studio. Sherry went to his office to introduce herself.

"No, no, no, honey," Marvin said, waving her away "I don't want any coffee." Sherry replied that she was Sherry Lansing and she was here to see him. "I want Jerry Lansing," Marvin replied, "the person who is running the studio." When Sherry told him that she was the person who was running the studio, Marvin was taken aback. "A girl?" he said, and then with an "Okay," he accepted it and moved on., though he did continue to call her "dollface" throughout their entire working relationship.

In 1992, Sherry moved to the hugely powerful position of CEO at Paramount Pictures, where she cultivated such mega-hits as 'Forrest Gump', 'Saving Private Ryan', 'Braveheart', and the biggest of them all, 'Titanic'. She was also the first female executive to get her own star on the Hollywood Walk of Fame and to have her hands and feet imprinted in cement outside Grauman's Chinese Theater in Los Angeles.

Beyond all of her achievements for the studio, Sherry had a reputation for deeply caring for each of her staff members, taking a personal interest in their lives, and encouraging the female members on her team. This fostered a positive working environment, and everyone worked extra hard hoping to please her. Sherry held the CEO position at Paramount for 12 years and developed over 200 movies. But as she neared 60 years of age, Sherry realized she wanted more in her life than just working in Hollywood. The film business was changing, with more focus on profits over artistic decisions, and she had a nagging feeling it was time for her to leave. These feelings crystalized into a plan after a meeting with former President Jimmy Carter. When he gave her a tour of his Carter Center and explained his charity work to Sherry, she knew this was what she wanted to do.

In 2005, Sherry turned her back on Hollywood and dedicated herself to giving back. In particular she wanted to raise funds for cancer research after losing her mother and several of her closest friends to the disease. She set up the Sherry Lansing Foundation and helped to found the charity Stand Up To Cancer, which has raised hundreds of millions of dollars.

Another history-making woman was Dawn Steel, who became president of Columbia Pictures in 1987. Remarkably, she rose to this position less than ten years after arriving in Los Angeles from New York. She began her career at Paramount Pictures, and worked in the merchandising department until Don Simpson picked her to help him out in production. Paramount at this time was run by four men known as the "Killer Dillers" - Barry Diller was CEO, Michael Eisner was COO, Don Simpson was head of production, and Jeffrey Katzenberg ran DreamWorks.

Dawn took to her new job and loved working in a creative field, but found it hard to deal with the sexism built into the industry. She was supposed to work closely with the men in charge, but found herself shut out of meetings and not invited on work trips. When Dawn persuaded the studio to take on 'Flashdance', she was told she wasn't allowed to look at the screen tests for the female lead. These special screenings were for men only. "There was a lot of pain and humiliation in those years," Dawn wrote in her memoir. "I would walk into my office and I would close the door and I would say, 'I won't cry, I won't cry, I won't cry.' At least, I wasn't going to let them see me cry."

'Flashdance' was a huge hit in 1983, and two years later Don Simpson left, and Dawn became head of production at Paramount Pictures. Finally able to take charge, she fostered the success of hits such as 'Top Gun' and 'Fatal Attraction'. But in 1987, she was let go from the studio in a particularly brutal fashion. She was in the hospital, having just given birth to her daughter Rebecca, when her husband showed her a story in a film trade newspaper. The article stated that she had been replaced as head of production.

Dawn was devastated, but within six months was snapped up by Columbia to be its president. One thing she was determined to do in her new job was to hire more women. Dawn wanted women to surround her, as producers, writers, and especially as directors. She gave Nora Ephron her first ever directing gig and gave producer Lynda Obst some of her early film credits.

Sadly, Dawn Steel passed away in 1997 at age 51, after battling a brain tumor. In her obituary, Nora Ephron wrote, "She hired women as executives, women as producers and directors, women as marketing people. The situation we have today, with a huge number of women in powerful positions, is largely because of Dawn Steel."

The other women in those top positions included Marcia Nasatir, a book editor in New York who went on to become the first female vice president of production at United Artists. Rosilyn Heller was an activist and executive who was the first female vice president of Columbia Pictures. And Paula Weinstein worked as an executive at nearly every studio before becoming the vice president of Warner Bros. Paula wanted to change the Hollywood tradition of women fighting each other rather than working together. "There was no feminism in Hollywood," Paula said. "And because we were competitive with each other, there wasn't the atmosphere that I saw in New York, where you could draw on women from other businesses to be your support group." Under Paula's guidance, Warner Bros slowly gathered an amazing group of female executives, nicknamed the "Warner Sisters."

These women at the top of Hollywood were great role models for future female executives, such as the co-head of Fox, Stacey Snider, who has said she looked up to women like Sherry, Dawn and Paula. And by the early 2000s, half of the six major Hollywood studios were run by women. So the old boys' club had a lot of new girls, thanks largely to the leadership of women in the 1980s.

The Firsts: Female Filmmakers of Color

Because Hollywood shut out female filmmakers of color for so many decades, it wasn't until the late 1980s and 1990s and the rise of independent cinema that many started to be able to work. But as soon they got their chance, these fierce women seized opportunities and made history with a series of firsts for female directors.

Take Euzhan Palcy for example; when she directed a film called 'A Dry White Season' in 1989, she became the first female director ever to work with Marlon Brando and the first black female filmmaker to have a feature-length movie produced by a major Hollywood studio. Born on the Caribbean Island of Martinique, as a teenager Euzhan noticed the huge lack of representation of people of color in American movies. Later, she said she became a director precisely because she was so angry about the way black people were portrayed in films.

At just nineteen, she directed the first film ever made in Martinique, and shortly after made her way to France to study. Here she met famed French New Wave director Francois Truffaut via his daughter Laura. Euzhan gave Truffaut a script she had been working on called 'Sugar Cane Alley', based on a novel by Joseph Zobel. He was impressed and encouraged Euzhan to turn her script into a film. This was just the push she needed, and 'Sugar Cane Alley' went on to win the Silver Lion at the Venice Film Festival and the French Cesar Award for Best Picture. This gave Euzhan another first to add to her list of accomplishments; she was the first black person of any gender to win a Cesar.

She made her way to Hollywood in the mid-1980s and shopped around her script, 'A Dry White Season'. Based on a book by André Brink, the story was about apartheid in South Africa. Paula Weinstein jumped on board as producer, and the two took it to MGM. They got the script into Marlon Brando's hands, and he was so moved by the story that he came out of acting retirement just for this movie.

In the independent world, Leslie Harris was the first African American female director/writer/producer to win the top prize at the Sundance Film Festival. She won in 1992 with her film 'Just Another Girl on the I.R.T.' which focused on a young African-American girl in a poor neighborhood. Leslie told Charlie Rose in an interview that she was "getting very frustrated in seeing a lot of films dealing with the coming of age of males," and that she "didn't see the coming of age of young females." Leslie felt that "a lot of the female characters were on the arm of the guy or in the background, and I actually wanted to bring the female characters to the foreground and deal with issues that really deal with young women coming of age in the 90s." To raise money for the film, she started her own production company, and later negotiated a huge deal with Miramax to distribute the movie.

Other pioneers include Ruby Oliver; she didn't start working as a filmmaker until she was 48, but when she did begin to make films, she became the first African-American woman to direct, write, produce, and sing in a feature film, in 1990's 'Love Your Mama'. Elsewhere, Chinese-Korean director Christine Choy was the first non-white member of her filmmaking group, and soon established herself as a strong voice in Asian-American cinema. And Chinese-American actress Joan Chen also broke barriers when she switched to directing by making a film which was banned in China. After roles in 'The Last Emperor' and 'Twin Peaks', Joan became a filmmaker with 'Xiu Xiu: The Sent-Down Girl' in 1998. Set during the Cultural Revolution in China, the film was about a young girl who was separated from her family and sent to live in a rural area and learn traditional Chinese values. The film was banned in China for its sexual content, but was well-received in the U.S. After that success, Joan went on to direct Richard Gere and Winona Ryder in the rom-com 'Autumn in New York' in 2000.

And then there's Julie Dash. Julie is the very definition of a trailblazing woman. While studying at UCLA in the late 60s and 70s, she was part of the legendary "L.A. Rebellion." This was a nickname given later to a talented group of students of color who were determined to create cinema which reflected their backgrounds and the issues they were facing in America at that time. The students worked on each other's films, training in different areas and creating a body of work which is still being shown in museums like the Tate Modern in London.

In 1991, Julie Dash made history with her feature film 'Daughters of the Dust', the first full-length movie to be written and directed by an African-American woman and given a wide theatrical release. It is a lyrical, beautiful film about a family living off the coast of South Carolina in 1902. Her achievement led the way for other filmmakers like Kasi Lemmons, who released 'Eve's Bayou' theatrically in 1997, and legendary writer Maya Angelou, who directed and released 'Down in the Delta' in 1998.

While these significant first achievements are important to recognize, it's equally important to note that they came decades later than the first opportunities for white filmmakers. Sociologist and author Nancy Wang Yuen agrees. "I think you do have to celebrate, in order to uplift, to provide role models for audiences of color. But at the same time, the more important thing is to critique the system and not take this one person and say, 'Oh, you know, racism is obviously gone, because we have this person of color.' Because that is exactly what people do," Nancy said; "We can still count on only one hand the amount of African-American, Latinas, Asian-American female directors. To celebrate is important, to say, 'Yes, there's excellence here.' But to have that stand in for the fact that it has been exclusionary forever is dangerous."

Meryl Streep: Oscar Queen

When it comes to the Oscars, no actor – male or female – has been nominated as many times as Meryl Streep. At the time of writing, she has twenty nominations to her name, eight more than the next nearest record holders, Katharine Hepburn and Jack Nicholson. Sixteen of those twenty were for Best Actress, and four were for Best Supporting Actress. She received her first nomination, in the supporting actress category, at age 30 for her second ever movie role, in 1978's 'The Deer Hunter'.

In the late 1970s, Meryl Streep was a theater actress and not yet known in the film community. She grew up in New Jersey, then studied music and drama at Vassar and Yale. Straight out of school, Meryl took to the stage in New York, performing in plays on Broadway and in Shakespearian productions in Central Park. That was where she met actor John Cazale, while working together in a production of 'Measure for Measure'. John was a theater and film actor, made famous by his roles in 'The Godfather' Parts One and Two, 'The Conversation', and 'Dog Day Afternoon'. Meryl and John fell deeply in love and were engaged to be married when he was diagnosed with aggressive lung cancer in 1977. Meryl decided to take up the offer of a role in 'The Deer Hunter' so she could be close to John, who was starring in the film with Robert De Niro. Sadly, John Cazale passed away before the film was released.

Meryl was with John in his hospital room when he died, and she suffered from deep grief in the aftermath. Right then, she heard about a possible offer for a role in 'Kramer vs Kramer', an adaptation of the book by Avery Corman. The novel was supposedly written in response to what the author termed "toxic" feminists in America, who he felt lumped men together as "a whole bunch of bad guys." The novel followed a father who becomes a single parent when his wife suddenly leaves him and their son. When the wife returns, she demands sole custody, and the two end up in a bitter courtroom battle.

Meryl thought the book portrayed the wife as an "ogre, a princess, [and] an ass," and said exactly that in a meeting with Dustin Hoffman, director Robert Benton, and producer Stanley R. Jaffe. If they wanted her for Joanna, Meryl said, they would need to rewrite the role to make sure the audience had empathy for her. As she marched out, the men were confused – they had actually called her in as a possibility for a much smaller role, and weren't considering her for Joanna. 'The Deer Hunter' hadn't been released yet, and nobody knew who she was. "What is her name? Merle?" asked Stanley. But Dustin and Robert had glimpsed that underneath that outer bravado lay a broken heart. She was grieving John's death, and it was that unique mix of strength and emotional vulnerability which ended up making her the perfect choice for the role.

'Kramer vs Kramer' led to Meryl's second Oscar nomination and her first Oscar win. "Holy mackerel!" said Meryl in her speech, before thanking Dustin, Robert, and Stanley for giving her the chance to play the character. After her speech, Meryl was directed to the press room, where she tried to take stock of what had happened. In response to being asked how her win felt, Meryl said, "Incomparable, I'm trying to hear your questions above my heartbeat." She was so nervous that on her way backstage, she'd gone to the ladies' room to have a minute by herself. As she walked out, she heard a voice calling out to her. She realized she had left her first Oscar on the floor of the bathroom._

That same year, Meryl had married. After John Cazale's death, she packed up his apartment, and it was such a big job her brother came to help, along with a friend of his, sculptor Donald Gummer. Meryl and Don began to date and were married six months later, and they are still together now.

Don was by Meryl's side when she got her next Oscar nomination in 1981, for the period piece 'The French Lieutenant's Woman' with Jeremy Irons. And then, a year later, Meryl had her second Oscar win, for the iconic 1982 movie, 'Sophie's Choice'.

Meryl was actually not the original choice to play Sophie. Director Alan J. Pakula had wanted Swedish actress Liv Ullmann, while the author of the book, William Styron, had Ursula Andress in mind. But Meryl knew she could do this role justice, so she campaigned hard. She learned Polish and German so she'd sound authentic, and even begged Alan for the part on her hands and knees at one point.

Eventually, having found nobody else, he gave Meryl the role. And watching her on set, Alan was floored. She completely transformed into Sophie, a Polish Nazi camp survivor who had been through a lot of trauma. For Meryl, all that hard work paid off with strong critic reviews and her second Oscar. "Oh boy!" Meryl exclaimed in her Oscar speech, "No matter how much you try to imagine what this is like, it's just so incredibly thrilling, right down to your toes!"

The following year, Meryl Streep was back at the Academy Awards with another nomination, this time for 'Silkwood'. And then three more nominations followed over the next five years, for 'Out of Africa', 'Ironweed', and 'A Cry In The Dark'. Throughout these movies, Meryl continued to prove herself to be a remarkably versatile character actress, someone who could sink deep to find the emotional core of a character while effortlessly nailing a variety of accents and languages.

In the 1990s, she had three more Oscar nominations, one for Carrie Fisher's 'Postcards from the Edge', where she showcased her singing ability; one for 'The Bridges of Madison County', which showed her romantic side; and one for 'One True Thing', playing a woman stricken with cancer. But Meryl also had a string of movies which weren't as well received, and she noticed her options for roles starting to thin out as she aged. In 1989, the year she turned 40, Meryl was offered three roles as witches. "I was not given any female adventurers, or love interests, or heroes or demons," she said; "I was offered witches because I was 'old' at 40."

Meryl said being cast as witches shows the way Hollywood sees women past this age – wrinkly, monstrous and frightening. Studies by Dr. Stacy L. Smith at USC Annenberg show that Hollywood does have an age problem. Her research looked at speaking roles in the 25 movies which received a Best Picture Oscar nomination between 2014 and 2016. Only 148 of 1,256 characters were age 60 years or older, and in those roles, there were three and a half times more men than women. The majority were white, and none were Latino or LGBTQ. Independent films offered more opportunities, and in recent years we've seen stars like Blythe Danner, Sally Field, Lily Tomlin,

Isabelle Huppert, and Shirley MacLaine in lead roles. But with the exception of 'Elle', starring Isabelle Huppert, these films are often too small to campaign for the Oscars.

In studio films, actresses are cast in mother or grandmother roles much earlier than is realistic. Angelina Jolie was one year older than Colin Farrell, who played her son in 'Troy', and her love interest was Val Kilmer, who is eleven years older than she is. This is fairly typical for love stories in movies; research shows that as leading men age, their love interests remain young. For example, as Denzel Washington advanced from 35 towards age 60, his love interests remained around the age of 30.

A lot of this stems from a lack of opportunities for older female screenwriters who can offer more realistic portrayals of women on screen. So in response, Meryl has used her own money to create a screenwriting lab which focuses on developing scripts written by women screenwriters over the age of 40.

She did manage to find stronger roles in the 2000s with a greater variety of characters, which led to more Oscar nominations. Meryl was a high school music teacher in 'Music of the Heart', an author obsessed with orchids in 'Adaptation', a scary magazine editor in 'The Devil Wears Prada', a vengeful nun in 'Doubt', and chef Julia Child in 'Julie & Julia'. Meryl credits this influx of more diverse roles to the rise of women to powerful executive positions, like Amy Pascal, who was chairman of Sony Pictures, and Sherry Lansing, who was CEO of Paramount. Male executives, Meryl said, don't hire older women because they "don't want to see their first wife in a movie."

One of Meryl's most interesting roles during this time was playing the grey-haired, perfectly dressed, but terrifying magazine editor Miranda Priestly in 'The Devil Wears Prada'. Her character, the devil in the title, could have easily strayed into a caricature of an evil older woman. But instead of portraying that type of one-dimensional "crazy career lady" we've seen many times on screen, Meryl gave Miranda a sense of vulnerability. You saw that just beneath that surface of strict seriousness lay a beating heart with real human feelings.

And Meryl made you understand that Miranda was the result of women being conditioned into believing that they have to be tough in order to lead. It was a performance that was praised by critics, audiences, and the Academy, though she didn't end up winning.

Her third Academy Award win came six years later in 2012, for her incredible performance as Margaret Thatcher in 'The Iron Lady'. Going far beyond any makeup tricks, Meryl completely disappeared into her role as another formidable female leader, and she worked hard to live up to the reputation of the real woman she was playing. "I know that it was very presumptuous to go to England and be the American playing Margaret Thatcher," she said; "but there are elements of all the characters I've played inside me. I don't think I'm that different from elements of her. I tried to swallow her whole."

In 2014, Meryl was again at the Academy Awards with a Best Actress nomination for 'August: Osage County'; she played the meddling mother in the film adaptation of the award-winning stage play. In their monologue, Oscar hosts Tina Fey and Amy Poehler joked, "Meryl Streep is so brilliant in 'August: Osage County', proving that there are still great parts in Hollywood for Meryl Streeps over 60." To which Meryl, in the audience, laughed and nodded.

She did end up playing a witch in 2015, but under special circumstances. She'd dreamt of doing musicals ever since she used to watch them as a young girl; and after the success of 'Mamma Mia' a few years earlier, Meryl jumped at the chance to be in one, even playing a witch, with 'Into The Woods'. And of course, she was brilliant, and her portrayal of The Witch scored her another Best Supporting Actress nomination.

And that year, while promoting her women's rights drama 'The Suffragette', Meryl decided to speak out on another issue which affects women in the business. Telling the press group she was "infuriated," Meryl spoke out about gender imbalance in the world of film criticism and its potential effect on movies with female content. Among the film critics featured on the review aggregator Rotten Tomatoes, Meryl had counted 168 women and 760 men. "I submit to you that men and women are not the same," she told the press conference; "They like different things. Sometimes they like the same things, but their tastes diverge. If the Tomatometer is slided [sic] so completely to one set of tastes, that drives box office in the U.S., absolutely."

Rotten Tomatoes takes all the reviews for a movie from its approved critics, and aggregates them into an overall score, called the "Tomatometer". And Meryl is correct that this score is often used by audiences to judge quickly whether a film is worth their money. Critics don't necessarily go into a movie with a certain bias, but it is plausible that an overwhelmingly male critic audience for a female-fronted film may skew the score without taking into account the tastes of female viewers. And research done by The Center for the Study of Women in Television and Film found statistics similar to what Meryl Streep had cited. Looking at Rotten Tomatoes, they found men made up 73% of the total critics on the site in 2016 and wrote 76% of reviews. Female-fronted films were less reviewed than films starring males, and in each individual newspaper, magazine or website, men outnumbered women in every job title, including freelance writers.

Since Meryl Streep spoke out, Rotten Tomatoes has made a concerted effort to encourage more female critics to join, but this also needs to happen with those review websites, magazines, and newspapers that are its sources. To be accepted as a reviewer by Rotten Tomatoes, a critic needs to be working for an accredited press outlet, so there can't be more female critics represented if they aren't already employed by such a media outlet.

Meryl's 2016 movie, 'Florence Foster Jenkins', was well received by critics, who praised it as a charming "crowd pleaser." And for this role, she received her 20th Oscar nomination. These honors show just what a remarkable actress she is, someone who has built up an unparalleled filmography playing all types of women on screen, from the cold to the compassionate and everything in between. Offscreen, Meryl Streep has been an incredible fighter for women and a strong leader for actresses to look to.

Viola Davis summed up her brilliance perfectly while presenting Meryl Streep with her lifetime achievement award at the 2017 Golden Globes. "She makes the most heroic characters vulnerable," Viola said, "the most known, familiar, the most despised, relatable. Dame Streep. Her artistry reminds us of the impact of what it means to be an artist, which is to make us feel less alone. I can only imagine where you go, Meryl, when you disappear into a character. I imagine that you are in them, patiently waiting, using yourself as a conduit, encouraging them, coaxing them to release all their mess, confess, expose, to live."

PART TWO: THE PRESENT

PART TWO:
THE PRESENT

FILMMAKERS FIGHT BACK

After decades of struggling for careers in the film industry, female directors have had enough. Women are coming forward to speak out more and more: talking to the press, setting up organizations, creating action plans, and taking the issue to the government. And though mini-revolutions have ebbed and flowed throughout the history of Hollywood, this level of conversation, now driven by social media and online press, has never before been seen to this extent.

Dr. Martha Lauzen has been researching gender and racial inequality in Hollywood for almost two decades as executive director of the Center for the Study of Women in Television and Film. Over that time she's looked at the numbers of women working behind and in front of the camera. The average percentage of female directors who work on the top 250 films per year, hovers at around 7 - 9%. There hasn't been much change since Dr. Lauzen started her research. But, she says, this conversation does feel new. "When I first started conducting this research, there was little discussion of women's underrepresentation and underemployment in film and television. Over the years, the issue has experienced a slow build in terms of visibility, aided by shifting demographics. By 2016, the discussion of Hollywood's biggest event, the Oscars, was dominated by a focus on the lack of diversity in film."

Of course, it can't all be talk and no action; this is why it's exciting to see several women taking proactive steps which could make a difference, including filing official complaints of discrimination to the Equal Employment Opportunity Commission (EEOC), which has gone on to conduct a federal investigation in response. "Hollywood in general, and the film studios in particular, will need to be pushed into change," says Dr. Lauzen; "At this point, some kind of external intervention will most likely be necessary in order for significant and sustained change to occur. It is possible that this push will come from the EEOC. Women's underrepresentation is an industry-wide problem in need of an industry-wide solution."

So how did that problem take shape? Well, it would be so much easier if there was someone to definitively blame. The actual reasons for inequality are so much more complex, hidden, and deeply ingrained. The three main areas that female directors seem to have the most trouble navigating are the culture, the pipeline, and the money. (And by the way, everything being said here about women can be applied to both men and women of color, who have even more barriers to climb over.)

The "culture" refers to the boys' club of Hollywood. It's been a slow change for studios to shift from being completely run by men to having women slowly making their way up the ranks into powerful positions. A balance at the top is especially important when you consider these are the people who make the decisions on the type of movies we all get to see. The dominance of one gender at the top (along with ingrained societal ideas about gender roles) creates an unconscious bias that permeates everything. This bias affects the hiring of directors, because as researcher Dr. Stacy L. Smith explains, "When Hollywood thinks director, they think male." There's a feeling, whether it's said explicitly or just implied, that it's much more of a risk to trust female directors with a big movie. It is assumed that they can't be strong leaders. Consequently, women aren't even placed on the lists of potential candidates to begin with, or given a chance to pitch themselves in the rooms where decisions are made.

This is also tied to the "pipeline" - the fact that women don't get an equal chance to progress on their career paths.

The typical path to success as a director generally looks like this:

- Make a short film;
- Self-finance an independent film;
- Acquire financing from other sources (e.g. production companies) to make a bigger film;
- Pitch to a studio to make a larger movie, either your own idea or as a director for hire on their projects.

Each step is vital to prove that a director is ready for a bigger challenge. As the saying goes, "You're only as good as your last movie." Yet research shows women don't progress past the independent film stage. They manage to get their own money together and make a short film and/or indie, and often get their work into festivals. But that's where it usually ends. Female directors find it much harder to get financing in order to make a bigger film, move up the ranks, and gain valuable experience. Because again, it is seen as more of a risk to give money to a woman to make a movie. That experience is necessary in order to get an agent and be placed on the lists for more significant future jobs.

This brings us to the "money" – the business side of making movies. When studios and production companies are considering green-lighting a project, they weigh the possible return on their investment, because films are a financial gamble. There's just no guarantee it will be a hit with audiences. And generally, studios are risk-averse, so if they hold any of the old beliefs, such as, "women can't make commercial hits" or "foreign markets won't watch female-led movies," then that can sway the studio's decision. Most of these market trend ideas about women are outdated and can be disproven. But with only a couple of successful examples to point to (often because of the lack of opportunity to create such exemplars in the first place), these are thought of as exceptions, not rule-changers. This takes us back to the start, back to the culture and bias. These elements all feed into each other.

Anyone who cares about equality and stamping out workplace discrimination, or anyone who simply loves movies, should want this to change. Film is a unique creative medium in the way it combines images, emotions, and storytelling and plays them on a large screen to be seen in a shared experience with other humans. It has the ability to teach audiences about the world and about themselves. Movies can inspire people; films can effect change, open minds, preserve history, and expose the world to a country's culture. But right now, what we are seeing, exporting and learning from, are stories overwhelmingly told from one perspective. And like any art form, films are much more interesting when a variety of people are allowed to tell their stories in different ways and on a wide experiential spectrum.

With all of these unchanging statistics and ingrained beliefs, the problems facing female filmmakers can feel huge and be quite disheartening. What keeps me motivated, excited, and optimistic for the future, is talking to the women who are working hard to change things. The next couple of stories are just a small sample of all the amazing women taking positive actions and steps towards gender balance as well as showing future filmmakers the way forward with their own success. And that is something to celebrate.

Dr. Stacy L. Smith: Information Is Power

Doing any type of research on the current status of women in Hollywood will lead you to Dr. Stacy L. Smith. She is a researcher and educator, working with the Media, Diversity and Social Change (MDSC) Initiative, part of USC's Annenberg School for Communication and Journalism. MDSC describes itself as a "think tank," and since 2005, Dr. Smith has examined the highest-grossing movies to see how equal they are in terms of gender, race, disability, sexual preference, and age. This work has resulted in irrefutable data and a whole lot of headlines, and has given the public a clearer picture of what is happening in Hollywood. It was Dr. Smith's research which first sent me down the path of investigating the lack of women working in film, because once I heard the statistics, I knew I needed to find out more. For Dr. Smith, it all started with Geena Davis.

Geena had been researching the portrayal of gender roles in children's entertainment, and she worked with Dr. Smith to gather data. "I really have to thank Geena for opening the door," Dr. Smith says, "and setting us on a path [so] that hopefully now we're an unstoppable force for eradicating inequality in Hollywood."

According to Dr. Smith, the results of their first study "raised a whole series of questions" and gave her the motivation to keep going; "I decided to write out an agenda of all the studies I wanted to do, and then for the next ten years we basically worked on that list." Dr. Smith's projects include the portrayal of characters on screen, the types of movies audiences choose to watch, plus the barriers and opportunities which affect employment behind the camera. Her reports are a mixture of quantitative data, hard numbers arrived at by statistical analysis, and qualitative research conducted through the findings of anonymous interviews. The studies centered on female filmmakers have been reported on the most widely. This is probably because directing is a less visible job than acting, so many people outside of the film industry may not even think about gender disparity. And it is also because these statistics are quite shocking.

Dr. Smith and the team at MDSC studied the one thousand highest grossing films released between 2007 and 2016 and all the directors who worked on them. For each of those ten years, the average percentage of male directors was 96%. This means only 4% were female directors, a ratio of 24 men to every one woman. That reflects a huge percentage of female directors not being able to work. These figures don't have anything to do with a lack of women who actually want the job, but are due more to a lack of women being considered for these jobs and a perceived lack of experienced female directors.

A newer trend in studio films is to hire directors from the independent film world, plucking them straight from micro-budgets and placing them on big blockbusters. Yet it only seems to be male directors who are selected for this opportunity. As the saying goes, "Men are hired on potential, women on experience."

Here are some examples of that selection on the basis of potential. Jon Watts had just three feature films to his name when he got the job directing 'Spider-Man: Homecoming' for Sony and Marvel Studios. Jordan Vogt-Roberts directed the indie 'The Kings of Summer', which opened in just 65 theaters, before he was selected to direct 'Kong: Skull Island', which was released worldwide. Colin Trevorrow had just one feature film under his belt, the Sundance hit 'Safety Not Guaranteed', when he got the job directing Universal's 'Jurassic World' – and he didn't even need to pitch himself for it.

Producer Frank Marshall says Colin was suggested for the job by Brad Bird, who had passed on directing it himself, but had told Frank, "There is this guy that reminds me of me..."

Being seen as having potential is tied into bias around the very idea of what characterizes a film director. Dr. Smith conducted dozens of interviews with decision-makers from inside the film industry, both male and female, and asked them to describe a director. She found many of the traits attributed to the idea of a successful filmmaker were masculine in nature, with the traits of leadership on a film set being equated to commanding a ship or leading an Army. This association of a particular gender with a job affects who gets hired, because as Dr. Smith explains, "If people are coming up with a list of names, they're going to call up a lot of male names than they would female, if the coupling of director and masculinity is more strongly associated than director and femininity."

Just because this reflects the larger society's view of leadership and gender, Dr. Smith doesn't believe Hollywood should be let off the hook, she says, "What I think is really fascinating is the way in which the industry has anesthetized itself by saying, 'We didn't know, it must be implicit bias,' when the way they make decisions is explicit. I wish we saw more individuals taking ownership for their hiring practices. That personalization is really important as a catalyst for change, and this doesn't happen often enough."

Hiring female directors also may help to increase equality in other areas. The MDSC team researched the correlation between filmmakers and representation on and off screen. As Dr. Smith discovered, "When you have a female director, you have more female leads, you have more female speaking characters, you have more characters that are from underrepresented racial or ethnic groups, more characters 40 years of age or older. You also have more women working in other key production roles."

As we've seen with films such as 'Twilight', 'Fifty Shades of Grey', 'Pitch Perfect 2', and more, women also have the power to influence box office receipts. They buy the majority of tickets to see a film, and that is why Dr. Smith says a large part of the solution to this problem lies with audiences. She encourages viewers to support movies made by women, whether they are playing in the multiplex or the local arthouse theater, and to speak out for change within their own circles, "Take to social media and critique what is seen on film...When portrayals are inauthentic or female directors are missing, consumers need to call it out. These studios, and in particular their shareholders, need to know. These are companies that are not representing the world in which we live."

Dr. Smith points out how audiences being vocal online has already helped in a few cases, such as 'The Great Wall' and 'Ghost in the Shell'. Both of these films were criticized for their erasure of Asian characters and went on to fail at the box office. Dr. Smith contends, "We live in a different world because people have been courageous on social media and they have said 'no more.' I think the millennials and the generation after them, they're growing up with an appetite for inclusion and their concerns are different from previous generations."

This younger age group is what keeps Dr. Smith motivated in the face of statistics which haven't altered since she began her research. She sees hope for the future of Hollywood in her own students, who are determined to take what she's discovered and bring about change for women in film. "I teach a class of about 150 students a term, and they are concerned with issues of diversity and inclusion. They want the world to be a different place. That is so energizing and hopeful. It really pushes us because many of our students go into the entertainment industry, and they want to be informed on all of these issues. As an educator, that makes my day."

Ava DuVernay: History Maker

In examining inequality in Hollywood, Dr. Stacy L. Smith from USC Annenberg wanted to find out the percentage of racial diversity behind the camera. Her team took a sample of the highest grossing films over a decade and looked at the 1,114 directors who worked on them. Only six of all those filmmakers over ten years were women of color. Two of the six were Asian (Loveleen Tandan and Jennifer Yuh Nelson), one was Latina (Patricia Riggen), and three were African-American (Gina Prince-Bythewood, Sanaa Hamri, and Ava DuVernay). Each of these women has had to work even harder than white women do to get a spot behind the lens, with the double bind of dealing with bias against their gender and their race. So it's no wonder that as a child, Ava DuVernay never considered a career as a director in Hollywood or thought that she'd end up making history several times over.

The first time Ava experienced the magic of the movies was when she saw 'West Side Story' as a kid with her aunt Denise. "She really gave me that love of film when I was young," says Ava, "and that was when I became a film person. We're a tribe, film people, we're not just, 'Oh, I like movies,' we really love film. It's in our bloodstream, it's a part of what we need to enjoy life."

Ava grew up in the Los Angeles area, but her suburb of Compton was completely separate from the movie business. According to Ava, "It's a black and brown community that is very far removed. On the map it might look like 15 miles away from Hollywood, but it's another world." With no local movie theater, she had to travel to a mall to see movies on the big screen. At the time, theaters weren't playing any black films, so Ava didn't even imagine the idea of an African-American as a film director until years later.

161

Her interest in film and directing was kindled just before her freshman year at UCLA when she saw 'Mo' Better Blues', directed by Spike Lee. "It was such a strong point of view;" she remembers, "It was black, and I hadn't seen a lot of films with black people in them. I remember seeing it and thinking, 'Oh, a black person made this,' and that created my connection to who a director can be. That's a very old age to be having that revelation."

At UCLA Ava graduated with a double major in English and African-American studies. Initially she wanted to work in broadcast journalism, but being closer to Hollywood changed her mind. "UCLA is very connected to the film industry, and I started to be in the middle of that. Being someone who had always loved films, I was really enamored by the mechanics – the inner workings and the industry behind it." But she still didn't consider a career as a director, deciding instead to work in public relations.

After a few years working as a publicist for 20th Century Fox, Ava left to set up her own PR firm, the DuVernay Agency. This took her onto movie sets around the world, working as a unit publicist for directors like Michael Mann, Steven Spielberg, and Clint Eastwood. It was on these sets that she started to feel a mental shift from just watching movies to wanting to make them. Ava began to observe filmmaking up close, and quietly learned a lot about being a director. She especially learned how not to act if you were one. "I remember more than anything the bad behavior of some directors that I worked with," she says; "There were lessons in people who didn't know your name, who ignored you, or who yelled. Lessons on what you don't want to be, and those lessons were powerful and informative." And she realized that she had never been on a woman director's set in all the twelve years that she had been a publicist.

During her downtime she began writing her own scripts, and in 2003, Ava started to shop around a feature called 'Middle of Nowhere'. Her friends Gina Prince-Bythewood and Reggie Bythewood were filmmakers and producers, and they helped Ava arrange meetings with studios. She already had Sanaa Lathan and Idris Elba attached to star in her film, but found it impossible to get financing for a quiet drama featuring black actors. By 2006, Ava was frustrated by all the doors shutting in her face, so she took matters into her own hands. Her first movie was a short called 'Saturday Night Life' about a single mother; then she directed a feature documentary based on her own community.

To make 'This is the Life', Ava focused her camera on the alternative hip-hop movement which had grown out of Compton. She pulled together a small budget and organized her own distribution, using her skills as a publicist to book the movie into a few theaters and market it herself. It was a success; 'This is the Life' was accepted into several film festivals and won multiple awards. She was then approached by networks like BET to direct music and cultural documentaries.

This type of ongoing work is rare for female filmmakers of color. As Ava remarks, there are "so many beautiful filmmakers who made a first film, women and people of color in particular, and then never went on to make a second one. They put everything they had into the first, and because there was no open door, they set it outside a closed door. Or they got through that door but didn't have enough, whether financially or just emotionally, to keep going and do it again, because it's so hard. I hope we can turn our attention to really trying to create a sustainable environment for marginalized artists, for them to be encouraged to keep going."

For this reason, Ava DuVernay decided to set up the African-American Film Releasing Movement (AFFRM) in 2010. The idea for AFFRM came to Ava while she was attending film festivals with'This is the Life'. She noticed that there was no real plan to get these movies distributed after their festival run was over. And unlike at mainstream festivals, there were no buyers attempting to acquire these black movies and no buzz from the press to push them into theaters. So she got to work establishing relationships with theater owners herself, and tested out her new distribution company with her first narrative feature, 'I Will Follow'. The movie focused on a day in the life of a grieving woman and was released in theaters by AFFRM in 2011. Influential film critic Roger Ebert was a fan, writing in his review that it was "the kind of film black filmmakers are rarely able to get made these days, offering roles for actors who remind us of their gifts."

163

With AFFRM in place and a successful narrative feature under her belt, Ava could finally make 'Middle of Nowhere', nine years after she had tried to sell it to studios. This sensitive drama centered on a young nurse who considers leaving her imprisoned husband for a new man, played by David Oyelowo. It became her breakout film, and premiered at the 2012 Sundance Film Festival. Reaction was extremely positive, and Ava won the Directing Award, becoming the first African-American to win that Sundance prize.

Another few firsts came with her next feature, 2014's 'Selma'. Once again Ava worked with David Oyelowo, who starred as Martin Luther King at the time of his famous march on Selma for voting rights. David actually had a lot to do with Ava getting the job of directing 'Selma'. He had been cast by director Lee Daniels, but when Lee dropped out, David went to the producers to campaign for Ava to direct the picture, knowing she would humanize the iconic man he was going to play.

How David Oyelowo and Ava DuVernay first came to work together is an interesting story in itself. While trying to raise money to make 'Middle of Nowhere' in 2010, her producing partner sent the script to a friend in Canada, who passed it on to his Canadian friends, one of whom ended up sitting next to David on a flight. They started talking, and after David mentioned he was an actor, he was given Ava's script. He loved it, so he got in contact with her and asked to meet her to talk about starring in the film. It was meant to be.

The stars aligned on 'Selma', too; the well-reviewed film grossed over $60 million worldwide and went on to be nominated for many awards. Ava became the first black female director to receive a Golden Globe nomination and have a film nominated for a Best Picture Oscar, although it was notably absent from the Best Director category nominations that year. She received another Academy Award nomination in 2017 for Best Documentary with 'The 13th'. This looked at racism, the number of African-American people in the U.S. prison system, and the role racism plays in African-American incarceration.

Meanwhile, Ava relaunched AFFRM as ARRAY in 2015, widening her mission to include festival films made by people of color and women of all races. That same year, a Barbie doll was designed in her likeness; it featured a mini director's chair as the accessory. The doll sold out within twenty minutes, and in 2016, she made history once again when it was announced her movie 'A Wrinkle In Time' would have a production budget of around $103 million. This meant she was the first woman director of color to break the $100 million budget ceiling. But as Ava was quick to note on Twitter, she was "not the first capable of doing so. Not by a long shot."

This is another reason Ava DuVernay is so inspiring. Despite all of her achievements, she refuses to be singled out, and considers much of her success to have come out of collaborations with talented people. "That's one of my favorite things to do," she says, "working with my fellow artists and comrades on a film. Even if it's someone that I'm meeting for the first time, I consider them to be a friend of mine. And with those close collaborators – visual effects, the director of photography, the production designer – it's important to establish a relationship based on a real rigorous pursuit of what we're doing, and simple human kindness. It's not revolutionary, it's just being a decent human being, and too often we don't see that enough in this industry."

Collaboration was at the forefront when Oprah Winfrey worked with Ava DuVernay to make the episodic television show 'Queen Sugar'. The show is a contemporary drama set in Louisiana, and Ava was determined to hire female directors to helm every single episode. And because women find it difficult to get opportunities beyond independent films, Ava found it easy to fill the slots with talented women. "I mean, everyone was available!" she exclaimed; "It was a real activist effort to say, 'All these women, sitting here, ready, with the knowledge, with the creativity, with the passion, and you won't let them in? You won't give them a chance?'"

But Ava gave them that chance, and this has led to more doors being opened for them. "Literally every single woman that directed on season one of 'Queen Sugar' has gone on to direct a minimum of four other shows in the span of one year," Ava says; "The year before, nobody would even take their call. This industry is so odd and ridiculous. It just took one show saying, 'I vouch for them.' If you work in a sphere where only white men vouch for white men, then how does anyone else get vouched for, if we don't turn back and help each other out?"

165

Being a film lover herself, Ava knows that both the types of stories being told on screen and who gets to tell them matters very much. She points to racism in the 1915 film 'The Birth of a Nation' and the Nazi propaganda in 1935's 'The Triumph of the Will' as examples of just how powerful movies can be. "Our ability to tell stories is the most primitive thing," she says; "It connects us as human beings. To supersize that on a screen, with a sound that surrounds you and the colors that fill every edge of your eye, it goes into your head. This is a serious thing, you're putting ideas and images into their minds, and if you're lucky, into their memory. I take that seriously."

And, she goes on to say, she can relate to that experience: "I've had that in my own life, movies I've seen at a certain time that I needed to see. Movies that soothe, movies that spark curiosity, movies that make you angry, that remind you who you love and that you need to love them more fiercely. All kinds of emotions for me come from that, and I know that everyone feels it when they sit down to watch a movie. Films are very powerful, and it's really an honor to be able to have this job."

Throughout her career, Ava DuVernay has encountered all the road blocks put up in the paths of African-American women who want to direct, from the struggle to get initial financing, to distribution for black films, to trying to sustain a career and being trusted with bigger budgets from studios. But each step of the way, she has pushed through these closed doors, and in the process, she has not only made history, but empowered many others to do the same.

J.J. Abrams and Paul Feig: Men Who Help Women

In their positions as gatekeepers, men can be powerful allies. And behind the closed doors of Hollywood, there are many great male directors, producers, writers, executives, and agents who have been working hard to gain women greater access and allow them to flourish in their chosen fields. Actor David Oyelowo intentionally works with female directors and often pushes for them to be hired. Television show creator Ryan Murphy has a foundation called 'Half' which mentors new directors including women, people of color, and members of the LGBTQ community. Director Joss Whedon says he is asked, "Why do you write strong female characters?" so frequently in his interviews that his answer has become, "Because you're still asking me that question."

There are two men in particular who wield an incredible amount of influence in Hollywood who have had so much success, they could easily sit back and not do anything. But they've made equality their mission. They are J.J. Abrams and Paul Feig.

With billion-dollar movies, multiple gigantic franchises, and countless hit TV shows under his belt, J.J. Abrams is a hot property in Hollywood. He's the man who was trusted with bringing back 'Star Wars', and one of his first decisions was to make sure a woman and a diverse cast were at the center of it. This is nothing new for J.J., who first gained fame as the creator of television series featuring complex women as lead characters with 'Felicity' and 'Alias'.

J.J. knew from the beginning that Hollywood was not an equal playing field. "I don't think it takes much to look around and see how infrequently women get the best roles," J.J. explained; "It is more in their favor now than when I started, but you don't need to be a genius to see it's an uphill battle for anyone who's not a white male."

In 2012 the Walt Disney Company announced a huge acquisition; They had bought LucasFilm, along with the rights to 'Star Wars', for a staggering four billion dollars. The internet was abuzz with speculation. What would Disney do to the sci-fi franchise? Behind the scenes, Disney and LucasFilm got to work planning a reboot. For the acquisition to be successful, the first movie needed to launch an entire series of films and spin-offs, appealing to the existing hardcore fan base and growing a new one.

167

From the very start of writing the script for 'Star Wars: Episode VII', J.J. wanted the lead character to be a woman. For as long as the series had been around, it had been male-dominated, both in terms of onscreen characters and offscreen fans. Princess Leia, played by Carrie Fisher, had been fiercely embraced by female viewers, and J.J. wanted to make sure that a new generation had several characters to look to as heroes. It wasn't just about having a female protagonist, but also a cast which more closely reflected the population of the world. Everybody deserved to have someone they could identify with in the new 'Star Wars' story.

During the casting process, the team thought outside the box. Did Captain Phasma, a villain originally written as male, actually need to be a man? What if the Stormtroopers weren't white underneath their helmets? The resulting cast was the most diverse ever seen in 'Star Wars', and it proved the power of representation. The film was a two billion dollar worldwide smash, with millions in merchandising and girls around the world cosplaying as Rey, the lead character. J.J. says seeing this kind of reaction really touched him. "It's always incredibly satisfying when you see people finding strength in characters they relate to when they see themselves on screen. The idea that there were little girls dressed as Rey walking around for Halloween with their hair in three little buns and their little staffs was so gratifying," he says, adding, 'The idea that anyone, male or female, would find strength in a story about a young female Jedi, a young female spy, a young woman going off to college – these are things that any storyteller hopes for."

His company, Bad Robot, is also a force for change behind the scenes; efforts are made to ensure all of the hiring for their productions is as gender and race-balanced as possible. This is achieved with a diversity quota; J.J. insists that every list of names for potential directors, writers, producers, crew members, or cast that Bad Robot considers represents the population of the U.S. This idea came about after noticing the lack of diversity offered to him on previous lists. "It is important for us at Bad Robot that we are looking at options that are inclusive, and often, the lists you receive are lists of the usual suspects," J.J. says. "Sometimes they're a broader list, but often they are nearly exclusively white men. Men should absolutely be represented, but they shouldn't be solely represented."

This is important, because a chance on a Bad Robot production gives valuable experience to underrepresented people and can at times even make their careers. To make these chances happen,

Bad Robot has been working with Creative Artists Agency on the agent side, and with Warner Bros and Paramount on the studio side. Says J.J., "We have asked our agency, we've asked our studios, that whenever lists are submitted, to simply make sure that they are representative of the population of our country. It's impossible to have lists that are going to make everyone happy, but I will tell you, we have seen so many lists where there aren't women listed as potential directors at all, when there aren't women listed as potential writers, when there are no black directors, no Latino directors, no Asian directors or writers or actors. We are making every effort to ensure that when we are choosing our collaborators, we are choosing them from a wider pool."

J.J. Abrams has become a mentor to many, and he says there are many women to whom he looks for inspiration. This includes LucasFilm president Kathleen Kennedy, who he calls "the hardest working person I know, and one of the most successful, driven, inventive and inspiring producers to work with." He also gives credit to the female film executives, producers, and directors who surround him, "I'm inspired by Nina Jacobson; Ava DuVernay as a director is obviously remarkable. Dawn Gilliam, the script supervisor, one of the saving graces of every project she works on. I love what Megan Ellison is doing as a producer. There are so many people that are doing great work that I would aspire to do, and they definitely inspire me to work harder."

Paul Feig also credits women for inspiring him in his career. As a four-time Emmy nominee and a writer and director of successful TV shows and movies, Paul has been called an "honorary woman" for all of the work he's done to support funny ladies. His love for women in comedy started when he was young, watching classic movies with his mother in Michigan. "I loved Katharine Hepburn, Rosalind Russell, and Judy Holliday," Paul says, "all those women that would show up in movies from the 30s and 40s and were so funny. Then comedians like Elayne Boosler, Elaine May, and the 'Saturday Night Live' gang. There were definitely a lot of funny women. But to me it was never a question of who's funnier, funny people are funny people. That's just how I always grew up."

It wasn't until Paul moved to Los Angeles and started befriending women at his improv classes that he realized there was an issue in Hollywood. "The disconnect for me," he explained, "was seeing them show up in movies. I'd be like, 'Oh good, there's that hilarious woman I love,' and then suddenly she's not being funny. All the guys around her are getting to be funny, and she's a foil, or the mean one they make fun of, or the perfect one who doesn't get to be funny."

This inequality was made even more obvious when Paul began to pitch ideas with female leads. "I was quickly told, 'No, you can't do that, we can't do that,' and I was fresh enough in Hollywood to say 'I'm sorry' and think they knew something I didn't." When he started to ask why, Paul was told "a bunch of business reasons: men won't go see movies starring women, different countries won't go see movies that star women. Then I started to question why we were going take that as an answer, when it means that more than half the population of the planet can't star in a film."

In 1999, Paul created the popular television show 'Freaks and Geeks' with executive producer Judd Apatow. Years after it finished, Judd invited Paul to a table read for a movie called 'Bridesmaids', a comedy with an ensemble female cast written by two very funny ladies, Kristen Wiig and Annie Mumolo. The film languished in development for a couple of years, but in 2010, Paul got a call from Judd telling him the movie had a green light and he could be its director. "I just jumped in and did it," says Paul; "It was just so much fun. First of all, knowing I had all these roles to cast funny women in. And then, once it ended up doing well, it showed me that this excuse of 'people won't see these movies' was pretty much killed."

And 'Bridesmaids' was not only a box office hit that had a big opening weekend and crossed the $100 million mark within 23 days, but it was also something of a cultural phenomenon with its quotable dialogue, its oft-copied poster pose, and its posse of hilarious women. Most importantly, they were women. Here was an R-rated comedy with a female friendship at its center, telling funny, relatable, and sometimes uncomfortable truths about jealousy and growing up. The female characters acted like women, not men.

For a short time, the success of 'Bridesmaids' paved the way for more female ensemble comedies. Films like 'Bachelorette' and 'The Five-Year Engagement' were pitched as the next 'Bridesmaids', with studios chasing that lucrative audience in the same way they had with male comedies like 'The Hangover'. "There's always the immediate response of, 'Oh my god, we gotta get all these female things going!'" says Paul; "But then I feel they quickly change to, 'maybe that was just a fluke.'"

But Paul proved his talent was no accident with his next movies, in which he continued to take genres normally dominated by male characters and turn them on their ear. 'The Heat' recast the traditional male buddy cop comedy with Sandra Bullock and Melissa McCarthy, and it made its budget back five times over. 'Spy' gave Melissa the chance to dive headfirst into an action spy comedy, and it became another smash hit worldwide. And in 2016, Paul made an all-female version of 'Ghostbusters'. Throughout all of these movies, he cast women in comedic roles that were still feminine. "I have no interest in just flipping genders and having women acting like a bunch of dudes," Paul says; "I don't find that funny really."

To make sure the female characters are as real as possible, Paul surrounds himself with women. He works with screenwriter Katie Dippold, most of his producers are women, and he tries to hire a gender-balanced crew, saying it makes for a healthier environment. Plus, it ends up helping his final product. "I always have a lot of women around me, who become my sounding board of, 'does this ring true, does this feel right?' I deputize everybody to call me on anything that doesn't feel like something that a woman would do. That helps, because I'm still a guy, I'm gonna make mistakes."

171

Paul leaned on his team with 'Ghostbusters', which was met with a whole lot of opinion online. Some were simply annoyed that their childhood favorite was being rebooted. But others were horribly misogynistic, and specifically angry that four women were starring in a movie "meant for men." Throughout it all, Paul Feig stuck to his guns, thinking about the wider picture of what this film could do for young girls. "People were like, 'well, it could have been two men and two women.' No. I want to have four women who are either scientists, or who understand science, or who get to learn science and take advantage of it. I'm friendly with Geena Davis and her Institute, and she planted in my head the idea of, 'if they can see it, they can be it.'"

Among the angry tweets were many, many photos of young girls dressing up as Ghostbusters. It made my heart melt to see kids feeling empowered because they saw in his film that women who used their intelligence could save the world. "Every day I get contacted over social media by women and girls," says Paul, "and people send me pictures of their kids dressed up. Women tell me how inspired they were by it. I've had so many women who have written to me, and it makes me sad when they do, but happy at the same time, when they say, 'If I had this movie when I was a kid, I would have been a scientist or I would have been an engineer by now.' I think hopefully history will prove us right in what we did."

Paul Feig has been an important champion for women in comedy, but he knows he's had an easier time getting these films green-lit because of his gender. So he has shifted his focus, determined to use his own success to help more women get into the business. This was a big reason behind the founding of his production company, Feigco Entertainment. "I'm lucky, because since this is what I do, people are more open to it," says Paul. "It's not usually an issue for me to get something made, but it was not my intention to just be the only person to get to do this. That's why with my company, we're trying to get female filmmakers in and produce movies for them to get their stories told."

In addition to this, Paul is working with the organization Women in Film (WiF). Paul has always been a fan of WiF's work, so he contacted them to see if he could join in their efforts. This coincided with a new initiative WiF was putting together called ReFrame. Part of the plan was to enlist established people in the industry to work as ambassadors, people who could approach studios they have relationships with to campaign for equality. Paul explains, "What is so exciting to me is how this is proactively trying to instill a change.

Because nobody thinks they're holding anybody back in Hollywood. This isn't a town where people say, 'Let's keep women out of this,' it's more that in the moment of making a decision, they default to a bias, or to what is the norm, which is, 'We'll go with a guy.'"

Paul Feig knows, perhaps more than most, just how many talented women there are in Hollywood who are waiting for a chance. "It's really just the growing of the pool," he says, "because the fact is, the studios are not meeting all the people who could be right for the job. That's what we're trying to solve with ReFrame."

Keri Putnam: ReFraming The Issue

At the 2017 Sundance Film Festival, I saw twenty movies, as I often do. The difference in this specific year was that half of those films were directed by women. And I didn't have to try hard to make that happen. "That's really as it should be," says Keri Putnam, from the Sundance Institute, "because it reflects the world we live in. And I actually think it's a result of a much larger groundswell of focus, excitement, and building of women storytellers across the board."

As Executive Director of the Sundance Institute, Keri Putnam oversees research studies, programs, initiatives, and workshops, all designed to discover, develop, and champion independent filmmakers. The Institute's efforts include the Women at Sundance program, which focuses on gender inclusion, the Diversity Initiative, and Catalyst, which connects investors with filmmakers.

Making sure the film festival is as gender-balanced and diverse as possible has become of utmost importance to Sundance. Says Keri; "We make sure that we're checking whatever preconceived notions we have about our own curatorial or selection process against the goal of being gender inclusive. I think of it as a subtle directive that comes from prioritizing, rather than mandating, and it's been extremely effective."

But despite making a conscious effort towards balance, Keri says there's still a drop-off for women that is out of their control, an experience gap between directors learning to make films and actually making them. "We've seen in our own data where women fall off the process," she says; "They come to a Sundance lab, which has about a 50:50 ratio with men and women. By the time they get to the festival stage, even with the efforts we've made, we see a decrease in representation. We're below 50% of women directors at the festival. Now, we've improved that over the years, but we're still below 50%, so there is a fall-off happening."

Prior to working at Sundance, Keri Putnam was president of production at Miramax and executive vice president of HBO Films. In these positions, she has seen the pipeline fail women both in the independent world and the studio side, and as she sees it, "To take it to the next step, there are impediments that women face going forward. They have that same mountain, but the access to money is more urgent because they want to make a bigger project, or they want to be up for a bigger job. And whereas we often see men coming through Sundance who've made a terrific first film getting a chance to take a crack at a much bigger film as their second one, we very rarely see that for women directors."

To try and counter this, one of the initiatives the Sundance Institute has put into place is called Film Two, which aims to help filmmakers (in particular women and people of color) to make their second movie. "We select filmmakers who we feel their first work was incredibly promising," says Keri, "and we say to them, 'We're going to give you a year-long fellowship, and we're going to support you in as many ways as we can think of.' There's creative support on script developing, mentorship to figure out what job they could get next, and the chance to work an episodic TV show if that's where they want to go. We help them build their career so that they're prepared to meet that marketplace with the great ideas they have. And having the support from Universal on that program, with the leadership of Donna Langley, it really is great because it sends a message that people do care about these voices."

And over her years in the industry, Keri has noticed a huge shift in awareness and in the conversation around women in film. When the Institute did their first set of research projects with Dr. Stacy L. Smith, she says, "We found the number one problem in women getting employed was the establishment, and people in the field not thinking there was a problem. But I've not heard one person in the last two or three years in any section of Hollywood saying they believe there's not a problem that needs to be solved. There's varying views of how that gets solved and what timeframe that gets solved in, and that's where talk does have to move into action. But I don't discount the value of talk at all."

Keri Putnam and the Sundance Institute have partnered with the organization Women in Film (WiF) for many years, and together they've created a new action plan called ReFrame. This is exciting, because it specifically targets the problem areas for women – the culture, the pipeline, and the money – and to help women in front of and behind the camera to get jobs. "You can't intervene on one side of that triangle and expect to have success," says Keri; "You have to have something that's coordinated between those three, and that's what ReFrame attempts to do."

To tackle these three areas, ReFrame has devised a few different methods. For the culture, they've enlisted a team of 50 ambassadors who are all well-established within the industry and represent different industry positions. They will go into the studios to talk directly to decision-makers about ways they can include more women. ReFrame has also created a special certification stamp which will be given to movies that have a gender-balanced cast and crew in order to better inform audiences. For the pipeline, they're creating a mentor and protégé program to help new voices get into the industry. And for the money side of the equation, ReFrame is undertaking research to prove the financial benefits of making films by women and about women.

The idea for ReFrame sprang from all the studies the two nonprofit partners had done together over the years. "All the research we did was all very much used to apply to the programs that we as a nonprofit built up together with our partner Women in Film," Keri says. "But we realized we were sitting on this trove of knowledge, and we wanted to share it with our peers in the industry on the for-profit side, to try to catalyze a network of people wanting to receive this knowledge and create a peer-to-peer program."

The ambassador program is one of the ways ReFrame is different from other initiatives. Instead of nonprofits coming from the outside, as Keri says, "to wag their fingers and say 'this is what you have to do'," they send in peers, people already working within the film business, to inspire their contacts. This makes the information gathered in research much more personal. It's about "senior people in the field talking to one another about their practices."

Keri Putnam is realistic about the difficulties in changing such an ingrained and long-standing system, but she's energized by the reactions people in Hollywood are now having. "I feel everywhere I go and everyone I talk to, there's so much engagement with this issue," she says; "I don't think it's easy to transition from one system of power to a more democratized system of power. But I think we've got people with a lot of remarkable good will in Hollywood. I don't think there's anyone villainously trying to obstruct change, it's more now a question of trying different tactics and seeing how we get there together. I'm very optimistic."

Maria Giese: Taking Action

For almost an entire year in Hollywood, female directors took turns going into an office building and sharing hours of stories about working in the film business. But this was no press junket, nor was it a pitch for upcoming work; this was a governmental investigation into gender discrimination. And the woman who started it was Maria Giese.

When Maria graduated from UCLA, her film class was approximately half men and half women. Almost all of the movies they had studied were directed by men, and there was only one female directing professor. But she was feeling excited about her new career on the day Francis Ford Coppola presented her with a diploma. Maria had every right to be optimistic, with her first feature 'When Sunday Comes' already financed, featuring a great cast including Sean Bean and Pete Postlethwaite.

Maria's story began like a Hollywood dream. Her first movie had screened in Cannes. Maria signed with a top agent. She was attached to future projects and was observing television shows in preparation to direct. But nothing ever came to fruition. "I would never work again as a paid feature director," says Maria. "I would never be given an episode of prime time TV. I would be dropped by my agency. I watched as my male peers became the cinematic voices of our time. I watched as men who hadn't directed features and had half my training became wealthy and sought-after TV directors."

Maria is one of the "lost generation" of female filmmakers in Hollywood, who have experience, talent, passion, and early success, but without being able to get on lists for future jobs, they slip through the cracks. And in their inability to move forward, we miss out on experiencing their stories. Maria explains, "This is not just a moral and legal problem...it's much bigger than that. The stories and images that emerge from Hollywood help define our national ethos and contribute to the voice of our civilization. If those stories are coming nearly 100% from men, then we are not getting an authentic picture of what our world looks like. We are getting a skewed perspective, skewed to the detriment of women."

So in 2011, Maria decided to do something about it. She launched what The New York Times writer, Manohla Dargis called "a veritable crusade" starting inside her union, the Directors Guild of America. Inspired by the six directors who had compelled the DGA to take two studios to court in the 1980s, she began researching and writing about viable legal strategies to remediate illegal discrimination against women in Hollywood, citing Title VII. In 2013 Maria co-produced the most comprehensive Summit for women directors in US history, and then approached the American Civil Liberties Union (ACLU) with her case.

"I realized I had to. I had to wage a war on Hollywood," she says; "There were many triggers, but the strongest was my realization that the virtual absence of women directors in Hollywood was tantamount to the censoring and silencing of female voices in U.S. media, which is America's most influential global export." Finally, in 2015 after four years of activism, Giese became the person who instigated the biggest industry-wide Federal investigation for women directors in Hollywood history, an action that has rocked the industry and resonated globally.

The ACLU called for more female directors to come forward, publishing a letter in the New York Times which said that any discrimination would be a violation of Title VII of the Civil Rights Act of 1964. This states that no person should lose employment based on race, religion, sex, or national origin. After receiving multiple grievances from female directors, the ACLU of Southern California took up the case. They lobbied the Equal Employment Opportunity Commission (EEOC) to do a full investigation into hiring practices affecting women in Hollywood.

Before the EEOC could do anything, they had to learn as much as they could about the industry, with its complex layers of bias, levels of hierarchy, and multiple unions intended to protect them. They invited a wide range of female directors to help build their case, interviewing them for hours at a time about the specific discrimination they had been subjected to both in hiring and on the job. "Because of Hollywood's longstanding discrimination against women," Maria says, "producers have a rich, deep pool of working male directors to hire from, but a meager and shallow pool of working women. Our industry needs to bring back the lost generation of gifted women directors who have 'disappeared' through gender bias. Thousands of women with exceptional reels and excellent credits remain unemployed, and therefore invisible. These careers must be excavated and returned to the workforce."

As a female director, it's hard to get a job in the first place. And then, even when you do, you face additional barriers. One female director I talked to who didn't want to be named opened my eyes to the type of discrimination some women have to deal with on set. Being branded as the "diversity hire" can actually create resentment within the crew, who may see you as only being there because of your gender and not on merit. This filmmaker told me stories of cinematographers purposely testing her by not changing lenses or setting up the camera in a different position than she had requested. Crew members and actors of both genders often refused to listen to her, sometimes even using bullying tactics like spitting in her coffee. When I asked her what kept her going through these dark times, she smiled sadly and told me she just really loved directing, a thought echoed by Maria Giese. Directing was all she wanted to do with her career, and it seems unfair that she never got a proper chance.

The EEOC is not permitted to comment on their cases, but there have been articles in the press stating they have gathered enough evidence to charge every single major studio with discrimination. Allegedly, the agency is in talks with all of the studios on how to settle the case. This is a big action step towards change, and it represents the first time an outside agency has agreed that gender discrimination does exist in Hollywood, and that it is illegal.

With multiple women breaking down barriers, spreading awareness, and creating initiatives, and with the very real threat of a discrimination lawsuit against the studios, will female filmmakers finally get the opportunities they have always desired? Well, as Maria Giese says, when women work together, we can accomplish great things, "If we do this together – pressing at once on all cylinders – it will not take long. We could do it in just a few years, and then we could all start working on an even playing field where real and fair competition among women, and with our male counterparts, could take hold. Only then will we establish true meritocracy among women filmmakers, and then we will see the best of the best rise, just as we do already see among men. I think that's worth fighting for."

 **ACTING UP**

In Hollywood movies today, there exists an "epidemic of invisibility." This is a phrase coined by Dr. Stacy L. Smith of USC Annenberg to describe a lack of screen representation for several groups, including women. Dr. Smith has done extensive research into the speaking patterns of female characters, counting any role with at least one word to say. What she discovered was that women and girls get less than a third of all speaking parts. This statistic has remained the same for over 50 years, despite women making up over half of the population in the U.S. And for many racial and ethnic groups, members of the LGBTQ community, people with a disability, and anyone over the age of sixty, there are virtually no characters to look to at all.

Representation and why it matters is a common talking point in Hollywood. And it does matter a great deal. It's hard to explain the power of seeing yourself reflected as a hero on the big screen. Films are not just simple entertainment, they can truly be inspirational and life-changing. Watching somebody who looks like you doing amazing things can send a message that you are important, and that you too can do anything. As the Geena Davis saying goes, "If she can see it, she can be it."

Conversely, a lack of representation makes people feel invisible. "Let's say you're an eight-or nine-year-old female," says Dr. Smith, "and you're watching the typical animated movie. Now on average, only three out of 100 of the top films have underrepresented female leads, and rarely in animation. So she might draw the inference that her group doesn't matter, she's not valued. I think the absence of a portrayal speaks volumes, because there's no one to identify with if race or gender is a salient characteristic between viewer and character onscreen."

Without different genders, races, sexualities, disabilities, and ages displayed on screen, audiences miss out on experiencing a variety of perspectives and stories which reflect our diverse world. And a large portion of the world feels unheard and unseen. It doesn't need to be this way. Movies can instantly be balanced by changing a few things in a script. "Hollywood doesn't have to play by the same rules," says Dr. Smith; "There are no boundaries to the imagination; they could make Congress 50:50, and they could make the engineering realm feature a ton of women. Look at 'Hidden Figures', those women were shown in computer science, engineering and math. And it worked! Plus, everyone was OK, the Earth didn't stop spinning..."

Also, the way that these diverse characters are portrayed in movies is just as important as inclusion. The near constant objectification of female characters has been linked in many psychological studies to the lowering of self-esteem in female viewers, along with an increase in body issues and even the increase in sexual violence towards women. Negative stereotypes and practices like cultural appropriation or "whitewashing" are extremely damaging. On the other hand, seeing realistic depictions of a member of an underrepresented group can go a long way to create empathy and understanding.

Similarly, actors in their real lives can be great examples of representation. With the millions of fans who idolize them, these stars are often looked to as role models. They have a big platform to speak out from, and luckily, Hollywood is filled with intelligent, strong women who want to use their fame for a good cause. These ladies are real-life heroes to many. So when they speak up, people listen.

Geena Davis: See It, Be It

At just three years old, Geena Davis announced to her parents in Massachusetts that she wanted to be an actor. "I can't imagine what I saw or how I even knew that that was a job," Geena says, laughing. "It's mystifying to me because my parents only let us see Disney movies when we were kids." Nevertheless, she did watch television, and after school, Geena and her best friend would pretend to be characters from 'The Rifleman'. "It was only about men," she says; "It was about a farmer in the old West and his son. No women at all, like most of the westerns. I was taller, so I would be the father and she would be my son. And there just weren't female characters on TV or movies that we wanted to pretend to be after school."

Geena Davis accomplished her early dream of being an actor, but she also became a powerful leader for changing the very gender imbalance she had noticed. Along the way, she won an Oscar, starred in two feminist film classics, and set up her own Institute on Gender in Media.

Interestingly, Geena's first acting role was in a film all about gender. 'Tootsie' was a 1982 comedy which starred Dustin Hoffman as an actor who assumes a female identity to win a role, but ends up with a greater understanding of women and sexism. On set, Dustin gave advice to Geena about making her own material and how to find books or articles and acquire the movie rights. She tried to do this for the book 'The Accidental Tourist', but someone else had already snapped up those rights. After parts in 'The Fly' and 'Beetlejuice', she was offered a role in the film version of 'The Accidental Tourist' and won the Best Supporting Actress Academy Award for her work.

Then came the movie which, as Geena says, "changed my life profoundly." In the early 1990's, Ridley Scott was on board to produce a script written by Callie Khouri called 'Thelma and Louise'. This was a buddy road movie starring two women, and Callie's script was thrilling, moving, and relatable, with a strong female friendship and complex characters. Geena saw it, and she wanted to be in it. "I read the script and I just loved it," says Geena, "I was so impassioned about it. It was rare that there would be one incredibly well-drawn female character, and yet here there were two. It was very unusual for that reason. I think we all were aware of that."

During pre-production, there were a few different sets of actors attached to play Thelma and Louise, including Michelle Pfeiffer and Jodie Foster, and Meryl Streep and Goldie Hawn. Geena was not about to give up, so she asked her agent to call Ridley once a week for almost a year, to let him know she was interested. It worked, and she was cast as Thelma, with Susan Sarandon as Louise.

When it was released, 'Thelma and Louise' caused a sensation. It received six Oscar nominations, had a Cannes Film Festival screening, made huge box office, caused national debates about feminism, and gained a strong response from female audiences. Even though the script had felt rare, nobody working on the film thought it would become an instant classic. "We were all completely blown away. We were not saying, 'we're making something that's going to have a big impact.' Nothing like that. We thought it was unusual and special in that it had two great female characters, but nothing stood out that told us it would get a reaction," Geena says. "In fact, we just hoped people would go to see it. It had a pretty small budget, and that ending. We were taken by absolute surprise. Susan and I found ourselves on the cover of 'Time Magazine' just two weeks later. It was stunning."

Geena was hopeful that with the success of 'Thelma and Louise', Hollywood would create more opportunities for women to be in interesting roles. And the favorable reaction from female viewers further highlighted why this was so important. "What I realized was how female audiences get so few opportunities to feel empowered and excited by the female characters. And I thought, I am going to think about this from now on when I choose roles. What are women going to think about my character? And when the movie came out, all the media predictions were, 'This changes everything. Now, we are going to see so many more movies starring women.'"

Hollywood didn't change, but Geena kept her promise to herself, and her next movie was similarly empowering for female audiences. She played the lead in the baseball movie 'A League of Their Own', directed by Penny Marshall. Once again, the film made money. Once again, it became a classic, and once again, the talk of the town was the influx of female-led films that would surely follow. "They said, 'This changes everything. Now we're going to see so many women sports movies. It's all going to be different.' I believed that, and I felt that I was getting great parts, that things are going to change and it's all so cool. After five years I thought, 'Have things changed? I'm not sure, I hope so.' Then ten years, and then fifteen years, and then I finally started saying, 'You know what, I'm going to Google it. It doesn't seem like it.' And when was the last female sports movie? It was 'A League of Their Own."

What Geena realized was that Hollywood believed that it had changed, when nothing actually had. "I got disgusted that people weren't speaking from facts, but just trying to say, 'Doesn't it seem like it's changed?'"

With no tangible way to prove the lack of female roles, Geena got back to work finding her own. She had great characters in a couple of projects, like the action thriller, 'The Long Kiss Goodnight', the family movie 'Stuart Little', and the television show, 'Commander in Chief', where she played the President of the United States. But these interesting offers were few and far between. And when Geena became a mother, the gender imbalance of entertainment was impossible to ignore.

Watching G-rated content with her young daughter, Geena plainly saw a lack of girls represented in television shows and movies. "I was absolutely floored," she says, "and I think I noticed because of the 'Spidey' sense I developed over all those years. I noticed there were profoundly fewer female characters than male characters in things aimed at the littlest of kids. There certainly were some exceptions, the 'Teletubbies', for example, is gender balanced, but I was absolutely horrified that in the 21st century we would be showing kids these worlds nearly devoid of female presence." Seeing a lack of female characters from a young age can warp a child's perspective on the world. There is a strong tie between self-esteem and the type of media consumed, and if girls see less positive representations of themselves, it tells them they can't be important. It tells them they can't be heroes. At best, they're sidekicks; at worst, they don't exist at all. As Geena says, "We are in effect acculturating kids from the very beginning to see women and girls as not taking up half of the space."

Geena's friends hadn't noticed the problem until she pointed it out, and when she did, they were also shocked. So she thought she'd do the same thing from inside the business. "I decided, I'm going to bring it up at meetings all the time. I'm going to see if anybody in the industry notices. Not one person had noticed, and in fact they argued with me that it was still a problem. I would say, 'Have you ever noticed how few female characters there are in movies for kids?' and they would say, 'Oh no, that's not true anymore, that's been fixed.'"

Of course, Geena was not about to simply accept this as an answer. If the creators of children's entertainment didn't believe her, then she would get undeniable proof to show the existence of the gender imbalance. "I said, 'This is crazy, I really am sure I'm right, so why don't I get the data?' Really I just wanted to know how right I was, and then go back to the creators and share it with them. Maybe that will make a difference. So, that's exactly what I did. I raised a bunch of money and sponsored the largest study that had ever been done on gender depictions in children's movies and TV aimed at kids 11 and under."

Her research project proved exactly what she had predicted. On average, male characters outnumber female characters 3 to 1 in family films. Female characters were four times as likely to be shown in sexy attire and nearly twice as likely to be unrealistically thin. The statistic which really surprised me, because it's so needless, is that in any crowd scene, there is an average of just 17% female extras. "It was just as appalling as I thought it was going to be," Geena says, "so I called the studios, and they put together groups spanning from 20 to 200 to hear what I had to say. I had no idea how they were going to react in the beginning, I thought maybe they'd be insulted... but the reaction has been the same every place, which is, their jaws are round."

185

Geena knew she was onto something. In 2004, she set up the Geena Davis Institute on Gender in Media to conduct further research and to educate the industry about her findings. The initial focus on children's entertainment was purposeful, knowing this was an area which desperately needed change; also, it was a way to talk about gender representation on a larger scale. "If I was going in asking 'Do you realize you make more movies starring male characters than female characters?' The answer would have been, 'Yes, we know, and it's very deliberate because we believe men and boys don't want to watch stories about women and girls. But women will like everything, so that's what we do.' I figured there was no upside to talking about that. I'm not going to change their mind about it." But with children, "They are horrified, because most of the people who make kids' entertainment do it because they care about kids. It is kind of an easy sell to say, 'Kids are getting harmed by the stuff that you're making.' I've had people with their heads in their hands saying, 'We're supposed to be good for kids. How did we never think about this?'" Since its inception, the Institute has focused on research, education, thought leadership, and advocacy. Geena and her team have spoken to movie studios, visited production companies, met with television networks, talked to universities, and appeared on press outlets all over the world. Their work has gone a long way to raise awareness and create change, all under their motto, "If she can see it, she can be it."

There's something known as the "CSI Effect," where forensic science experienced an influx of women wanting to do the job after seeing it portrayed on TV. I think there should also be the "Geena Davis Effect," with more interesting female characters appearing in film and television after Geena has visited those companies. "A number of things have come up that we know we've impacted," she says; "If we keep on this problem with the intensity that we have used so far, I feel like we can make dramatic change in the next ten years. It will be dramatically different in the world of kids, movies, and TV."

The achievements Geena and her institute have made includes the first-ever global gender in media study, showing the full scope of inequality around the world. Also, the creation of the Geena Davis Inclusion Quotient (GD-IQ). This is a remarkable piece of audio-visual recognition software which is able to analyze films and TV shows to accurately calculate the amount of speaking and screen time given to each character. The films are analyzed at a rate of about 15 minutes per 90-minute movie, which means the sample of movies researched for these studies can increase dramatically. Geena also launched the Bentonville Film Festival, which screens movies made by women and diverse voices and awards a prize of theater distribution to the winning film.

All of this has made Geena very excited and passionate about the future. "I'm very optimistic based on the reaction that we've gotten every time and from everywhere. I've realized that this is pretty much the one sector of society with profound gender inequality that you can change overnight. That's what I tell them when I meet with them, I say, 'It's so easy and fun to gender balance.' The easiest thing to do is just go through and cross out a bunch of first names and change them to female. 'Now it's gender balanced!' And to fix the problem of being so few female extras, background characters, and women in group scenes, all you have to write in the script, is, 'A crowd gathers, which is half female.' And you did it!"

For many people around the world, including myself, Geena Davis is a role model. She is someone who had a dream, made it happen, and then when that dream wasn't quite as equal as it could have been, she got to work. Her passion for change comes from pure joy, and it is infectious to hear her talk about it. It's not about pointing a finger at anyone, it's about empowering people to want to fix it. "There's lots of little victories, but I was very proud when I heard that there's one company that makes preschool shows," says Geena, "After we had visited we heard that with everything they develop now, they pause and say, 'What would Geena say?' I actually couldn't have a better goal! If I could get everybody to adopt gender balance, that would be great, but 'What would Geena say?' As a motto? That's a good start!"

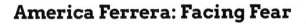

187

America Ferrera: Facing Fear

As an actress, producer, director, speaker, activist, humanitarian, and triathlete, America Ferrera is the type of person who doesn't let a new challenge get in her way. She faces the fear and moves through it, as a dreamer, a doer, and a defier of categorization.

Her determination might come from the strength of her mother, an immigrant from Honduras and a single parent to six kids. Perhaps her dreams were created by watching television, looking for examples of what she could be. "We spent a lot of time at home, as 'latch-key kids,'" says America. "I know that so much of what I thought was possible for me and what I thought was possible in the world came from television and film. The messages I took in about the world and my place in it, it compelled me to think really big for myself. But I also know it had its limitations."

America's ambition saw her land a lead as her very first acting role, in 'Real Women Have Curves,' a 2002 drama/comedy selected to play at the Sundance Film Festival. It must have been a daunting experience for the new actor, who was still in high school when she made the film, but America ended up winning the Special Jury Prize for acting.

A few years and a few more independent films later, America was cast in the big, studio ensemble film, 'The Sisterhood of the Traveling Pants.' The film was a massive success; it was about four young women and their bond with each other. Audiences embraced America's character, who challenged stereotypes assigned to Latina characters. This was a stark contrast to one of her early auditions, where the casting director instructed her to "sound more Latino". America was confused, asking if that meant she should speak Spanish. But the casting director insisted again on "Latino", as in, speak with a broken accent. America was 16 at the time, and remembers realizing that in Hollywood, "there's a certain box or a certain way that you're seen, which I didn't feel growing up."

That box was well and truly smashed with her lead role in the primetime television show 'Ugly Betty'. Very quickly, the show was a hit, and 22-year-old America was thrust into the spotlight. The media hailed the series for being progressive and groundbreaking, and America's Betty became a beloved and unlikely small screen hero. She must have felt the pressure, with the world looking to her to be a voice for underrepresented actors, but she handled herself with absolute grace and won an Emmy and a Golden Globe. By age 23, America was listed in Time Magazine as one of the 100 most influential people in the world.

The show filled America's life for five years, and when it wrapped, she set up a production company, determined to push herself and defy expectations in new ways.

She'd always had a dream of performing in London's West End in a musical, despite a fear of singing in public. In 2011, she accomplished her goal by starring as Roxie Hart in a production of 'Chicago'. America felt the fear, but she did it anyway. "I definitely am someone who persists in spite of the fear," she says; "I've never had an experience of fearlessness, maybe there are people who don't experience fear. But my experience is that any time I'm doing anything new, or challenging, or even exciting, there is an element of fear that is there, just of the unknown. I definitely have come to notice the fear, acknowledge the fear, and try to move forward anyway. I do think that whenever I take on something that is challenging, that element of fear is almost a positive indicator that I'm moving in the right direction."

That direction saw America tackling everything from playing a cop in 'End of Watch' to portraying the wife of a civil rights activist in 'Cesar Chavez', lending her voice to the animated movie 'How to Train Your Dragon', and starring in two films directed by her husband, Ryan Piers Williams. America didn't let any fear stop her from producing her own projects and creating documentaries and series which focus on important issues, such as women's rights and the plight of undocumented immigrants. Nor has she let fear stop her from using her voice on the world stage as a political activist, protesting and speaking out on issues she's passionate about, while also encouraging others to do the same. America spoke at the Democratic National Convention in 2016, and she was co-chair of the Women's March on Washington and co-chair of the Artist Coalition of Voto Latino, which empowers young Latinos to be agents of change. America also founded the organization Harness with Ryan and actor Wilmer Valderrama, which aims to connect communities through conversation in order to inspire action and empower change. And when America appeared on 'Who Do You Think You Are?' she discovered where some of this revolutionary spirit comes from. The television show looks into the ancestry of a different guest star each

189

week, and America was curious about her father's side of the family. "My parents are immigrants, so I didn't know a lot about their family history," she explains, "and my father wasn't very present in my life, so I knew even less about his family and history. There was always a lot about my own interests and passions and characteristics that didn't make sense in the context of my family."

She had heard stories as a child about her great-grandfather, and the show was able to verify them. Gregorio Ferrera had been a general in the Honduran army and was a well-known revolutionary in the early 1900's. He spoke out about important issues and fought back against the Presidency. Just as America has been doing, a hundred years later. She says that when she learned about her great-grandfather, "it explained a lot for me. Who he was and what he did in his life did validate a lot of things to me about who I am. And it made me believe there's something to this idea of inherited things in your blood."

America has taken on another leadership role as a director on her TV show, 'Superstore'. Ticking off this long-held goal "was definitely a challenge, and a bit scary," she admits, "but I worked really hard to prepare myself. I definitely felt nervous about doing something that I had never done before, plus wanting to do it justice and to succeed in the role of director. Luckily I have a lot of female friends who have taken on the role of directing on shows that they acted in, and I was able to ask them what their hesitations were, and how they got past any mental blocks or fears."

America's determination to face fear is also apparent in her offscreen life; for example, she competes in triathlons. America wrote a piece for the New York Times sharing how her first triathlon helped her to overcome the inner critic which had told her she wasn't good enough. She is also passionate about spreading body positivity on social media and talking about the need for gender and racial equality in entertainment.

America Ferrera is like a real-life superhero who reminds all of us that fear doesn't have to be completely crippling or hold us back from our goals. Instead it can be used as a superpower, and as fuel for the fire of ambition.

And America is excited for the future female superheroes of the world, who may be inspired by women seen on the screen, superheroes like Wonder Woman and female protagonists in 'Star Wars'. "I sat through 'Star Wars: The Force Awakens' with my two young god-daughters. And I just sat there weeping. They were looking at me like I was crazy, they didn't understand what the big deal was. And this made me cry even more, because they will never have to even think about why this is such a big deal. They'll get to grow up seeing women in roles that are actionable, and powerful, and strong, and it matters that they grow up seeing that it is possible for women to be heroes."

Mya Taylor: Transforming Hollywood

Growing up in Texas, Mya Taylor knew she wanted to be an entertainer, but she never expected she would end up making Hollywood history. The idea of Hollywood felt very far away when Mya's mother was arrested when Mya was 13 and she was sent to live with her grandparents. Mya was born male, but identified as female from a young age. This did not sit well with her grandmother, who kicked her out of the house at eighteen years old.

Mya moved to Los Angeles, but Hollywood was still very much out of reach. In fact, she found it impossible to get any kind of a job. Mya applied for every single position she saw, no matter what it paid. In one month she applied for almost 200 jobs, and she was denied every single one. "I was transitioning," says Mya, "and I was discriminated heavily against. I couldn't get a job." Mya had begun to look like a woman, but her ID hadn't been changed to reflect her new name and correct gender. Changing gender on identification records is expensive, and Mya just couldn't afford it. So, with each job application, she'd have to disclose she was transgender, and then the doors would be shut in her face. Eventually, desperate for money, Mya turned to sex work.

And then, Hollywood came to her. One day, Mya was at the LGBT Community Center, when director Sean Baker approached her and offered her the chance to star in a movie. "It didn't feel like it was meant to be. It just felt like something to do," says Mya. "I didn't really have any idea it would be huge at the box office. I didn't think anything like that. I thought it was just going to be some regular project." The film was 'Tangerine', a movie about friendship which follows a day in the life of two characters as they go on a mission through Los Angeles. It is full of vibrant life, and shows a side of L.A. transgender culture that had never been explored on film. The two stars, Mya and Kitana Kiki Rodriguez, play their parts with absolute realism, probably because they crafted the movie alongside Sean. And it was entirely shot on an iPhone 5. "Sean is extremely professional," Mya says, "he's not outspoken; he's really quiet. But he's a good listener, and he doesn't make you do anything that you don't want to do. When he was writing about Santa Monica and Highland for 'Tangerine', he didn't know anything about that area. But he did a lot of research by asking me, my co-star Kiki, and a bunch of other people, and that's how he came up with his story. He didn't just go in assuming that the area was about one thing, and that's what made it so perfect. What he put on screen is actually what it was like. It was raw."

'Tangerine' was entered into Sundance, where it gained buzz, picked up distribution, had positive reviews and eventually was part of an Oscar campaign. For Mya, going from the L.A. streets to fancy award season lunches was a crazy ride. "It didn't hit me that I had become an international star, that the film was released in Korea, England, and Taiwan, all these different places. That didn't hit me for a long time. I guess I somewhat loved the attention, too, but I didn't get into it for the attention," says Mya. "then I felt like I started to lose my mind. And the reason was because of the people around me. I felt that if I hadn't become this actress in this film, people wouldn't treat me the way that they did. All of a sudden, I was being told what to wear, and what to eat, and [that] I needed to lose weight, and it just really got to me. That's not who I am."

All of this pressure was made even tougher by the fact that Mya was still transitioning. "I had insecurities while making 'Tangerine'.

I was really emotionally abused by a family member, and the street harassment that I would have at that time, that kept me so insecure. Underneath all of those nice clothes they put me in, I just felt like I was screaming. I hated the way I looked. I felt disgusting. I felt ugly. I felt so inadequate;" Mya says, "I didn't feel like I wanted to commit suicide or anything, but I didn't want people to look at me. I think that I'm beautiful now. I'm really happy with what hormones have done for me."

In early 2016, Mya Taylor made Hollywood history as the first transgender actor to win an Independent Spirit Award for Best Supporting Actress. "Before I got into the business, I did not know what an Independent Spirit Award was. I thought, it's all just about the Oscar and that's it. But I learned the Independent Spirit Awards are just underneath the Oscars. And then it hits me that I have made history; I've made some serious history. And I felt accomplished getting on stage."

Unfortunately, Mya missed out on an Oscar nomination that year, but someone who was nominated was English actor Eddie Redmayne; he was nominated for his role as a transgender woman in 'The Danish Girl'. "It is a problem," Mya says, "because they come in, dress up, and call themselves transgender, and then they go on screen and win awards. But it's not the same when we, as transgender women, do really well on a film. 'The Danish Girl' was a very good movie, I love the cast and the director and producer. But 'Tangerine' should have gotten a nomination at least. I might not have won, but I would have been known as an 'Oscar-nominated actress' and I needed that. But they put him inside a wig and women's clothes, and then that movie gets nominated."

If it's hard for a white cisgender women to get interesting roles in Hollywood, imagine what it must be like to be a transgender woman of color. Visibility has increased slightly for transgender roles on screen with actresses like Laverne Cox in 'Orange is the New Black', but there is still a lack of representation in movies. And if transgender characters do appear, then cisgender actors usually get to play them. We saw this in 'Boys Don't Cry', 'Albert Nobbs',

'Transamerica', and 'The Dallas Buyer's Club', with each of these roles leading to Oscar nominations. But at least these characters were portrayed with care. And just seeing them on screen is a first step towards inclusion for a community so often left out of the narrative.

The organization GLAAD has researched the presence of LGBTQ or anti-LGBTQ characters in the highest grossing movies. In 2015, only 11 roles in mainstream films were identified as female LGBT characters, and one featured a transgender woman character. But a majority of these had screen time of less than ten minutes.

Representation is particularly important for these communities, because visibility helps to make the unfamiliar more familiar, and exposure to different groups through mainstream media can begin the journey towards acceptance. And this may go some way to help end violent hate crimes against these communities.

"But it's really been hard," says Mya; "You would think that I would have people just breaking my door down because I've done all of this and broken all these barriers, but it has not been like that. I've been asked to audition for so many prostitution roles, and I've turned them down. I cannot represent the transgender community like that. Every transgender person does not go into prostitution and sell their body. And you know, it's sad. I don't get offered roles to be a lawyer or a doctor, or a role where I have family. I don't get roles like that. I always get prostitution roles. I think out of all the auditions that I've done, which has been a lot, I've only had two offers where they were not prostitutes. That's sad."

What Mya really wants is to be selected to play female roles. She has transitioned to be a woman, and doesn't want to always be placed in the box of portraying a transgender role. "I have had maybe two offers to play a woman. Sometimes this business, it's disgusting to me, quite honestly. And you know what? There are some moments where I've said, 'I'm tired of this business. I'm just going to go back to school.' But I still have a lot of energy and life in me, and I'm not the type of person to give up. It's just been frustrating because it's so hard."

The type of transgender characters that Mya would love to see on screen are pretty simple. "Just a trans woman who's living life as a woman, and she has a family and everything, and she goes through normal problems and things. We need to see more roles where trans people are going to be more normalized instead of people always making fun of us and saying mean stuff."

Since the success of 'Tangerine', Mya has used her platform to be an advocate for the rights of transgender people. And if she sees them being bullied online, she makes sure she sticks up for them. "I was watching this video on YouTube about a trans woman who spent a hundred thousand dollars to have her dream body. She is extremely gorgeous. And then in the comments, it says, 'Shaking my head. What an abomination,' and 'Transgenders are disgusting,' and so on and so forth. So I came in and wrote my comment, 'These comments are so nasty and hateful. How can anyone say these awful things about any human? You should be ashamed of yourself. All of us need to remember that if you don't have anything nice to say, then don't say it at all. And if transgenders are so disgusting, then what are you doing watching this whole video?' That was my comment. Because I saw some of the negative comments about me after I won the Spirit Award, like 'Mya's not a woman,' and 'This award was supposed to be for a woman.' And they did hurt my feelings. So I can't imagine with this girl, if she goes on here and she reads all these comments, and all of them are negative. And it's stuff like this which keeps transgender people in hiding. It's bullying. There are kids in school that are committing suicide because of the negative stuff that people say."

Mya Taylor is the type of role model we need to help transform Hollywood. She speaks with refreshing honesty and a determination that is powerful to hear, and with just one role she has made a difference to people both inside and outside the transgender community. Imagine what she could do with more opportunities.

Octavia Spencer: Scene Stealer

No matter the size of the role or the amount of screen time, Octavia Spencer never fails to make an impression. She's been a stealer of scenes ever since her very first role in 'A Time to Kill' back in 1996. Octavia had been working behind the scenes in production, and she asked director Joel Schumacher if she could read for a small part. He said that her sweet face would be suited to play the nurse, and she ended up with that character. But Octavia had really wanted the role as the woman who starts a riot. This sums up Octavia Spencer to me. She is a strong woman who creates her own opportunities, makes the most of every single one, goes for the unexpected and her infectious energy makes it impossible not to be drawn to her. She is a riot.

Octavia met Tate Taylor on the set of 'A Time to Kill'. He was also working in production, and the two became fast friends. In 1997, Octavia moved to Los Angeles on his advice, and started to get bit parts in television shows and movies. She played more nurses, plus a bank worker in 'Drag Me to Hell', a check-in girl in 'Spider-Man', and a woman in an elevator in 'Being John Malkovich'. Each part was tiny, with only a few lines, but Octavia worked hard.

Hollywood has had a long history of giving actresses of color meager parts to play. Diversity in film roles has increased over the years, but not by much. A study by Dr. Stacy L. Smith at USC Annenberg looked into the number of speaking roles for non-Caucasian actors. They took the top 100 films from the year 2015, and found that almost half did not feature any female African-American speaking roles. And by the way, to be counted as a speaking role, the character only needs to say one word. Also, 70 of those 100 films did not have one female Asian or Asian-American character who spoke.

Eventually, Octavia Spencer got her chance to show exactly what she could do, thanks to a little help from her friends. Tate Taylor had acquired the movie rights to a book called 'The Help', written by his childhood friend, Kathryn Stockett. Tate was adapting the book into a screenplay, and planned for the movie to be his directorial debut. Tate and Octavia were roommates at this time, and she reminded him that there was one role in it made for her – quite literally, because Kathryn also knew Octavia, and wrote the character of Minny with her in mind, infusing the role with Octavia's sass and wit. Tate didn't need reminding, because he too had written Minny for Octavia. And in 2010, DreamWorks came on board to produce, and Octavia had her role. She was joined by Emma Stone, Jessica Chastain, Viola Davis, and Bryce Dallas Howard. It was meant to be.

Octavia earned rave reviews as Minny, the maid who takes revenge on her racist former boss by giving her two slices of humble pie – chocolate pie with a special, unsavory ingredient. The moment is funny, but Octavia adds a real sense of pain underneath, a glimpse of Minny's life as someone who has been so downtrodden.

Octavia says she gets so invested in a moment like that, she never knows if she has nailed a scene. "If you're truly emotionally immersed, there is no way to tell," she says; "Whatever state of mind your character is in, hopefully you are there as well when the scene ends. That's why I work with directors that I trust, because I need someone else watching the performance so that I'm free to exist in the moment."

'The Help' was a big success, and soon Octavia found herself on multiple red carpets around the world, culminating in the biggest one of all, the Oscars. She swept award season, winning the Golden Globe, the Screen Actor's Guild Award, the BAFTA, and Best Supporting Actress at the 2012 Academy Awards. And Octavia was so in that moment, she cannot tell you exactly what happened.

The character of Minny was a black maid role, but there was nothing stereotypical about Octavia's portrayal of her. But after her Oscar win, maid roles in historical movies were all that she was offered. Period pieces are so often given to African-American actresses. These can be important stories, of course, but are fairly limiting in an acting career, given that the parts are small and in subservient ocupations.

Octavia turned down those maid roles, instead choosing a variety of films, like the indie 'Smashed' about alcoholism and 'Fruitvale Station', a biopic of a young black man shot by a white officer. This also gave Octavia her first feature film producing credit, because when the production needed more money, she jumped on board to help raise it. Then came the Korean thriller about the class system, 'Snowpiercer', the dystopian young adult science fiction film 'Divergent', an animated flick about racism called 'Zootopia', and the comedy 'Bad Santa 2'. Octavia says she chooses projects based on whether they "resonate with me on a personal level... I look for things that first and foremost allow for entertainment and escapism; but if they educate or enlighten in some way, that's even better."

We can add to Octavia's eclectic filmography the title of author, because Octavia has also written a series of children's books called 'Randi Rhodes: Ninja Detective'. These center on a young girl who loves karate, idolizes detectives, and solves mysteries in her small town. Octavia has also optioned the rights to a novel about Madam C.J. Walker, the first female self-made millionaire. And she produced another movie, 'Small Town Crime', starring her friend John Hawkes.

Outside of work, Octavia is focused on giving back and works to support victims of domestic violence through the Jenesse Center. This nonprofit gives free housing to women and families who have suffered, and Octavia set up a Learning Center within the apartment complex to provide education to everyone living there.

Friendship is also important to Octavia; she takes her friends to events and works with them on movies. "I believe that my true friends are family," she says; "I subscribe to the idea that one's biological family is one chosen for them by the divine, and one's friend family is their choice by design. All of those relationships are necessary and have been touchstones for my personal life and my career."

It's only fitting that the movie that took Octavia back to the Oscars was about three friends who worked together. 'Hidden Figures' was based on an inspiring true story with Octavia, Janelle Monae and

Taraji P. Henson playing three women who worked in the space program at NASA in the 1960's. This is a great example of positive representation. Here were three non-stereotypical lead roles which were all empowering and showed African-American women working in STEM fields. The cast knew it was special, I remember seeing footage at the Toronto International Film Festival, which included a Q&A with the cast. The three actors could not stop crying with happiness, because it felt like a momentous moment.

'Hidden Figures' was nominated for multiple awards, including three Oscars for Best Picture, Best Adapted Screenplay, and Best Supporting Actress for Octavia Spencer. And it was a box office smash worldwide, disproving the idea that foreign audiences won't watch movies with black female leads. Octavia, Taraji and Pharrell Williams also bought out some theatrical screenings and gave tickets away for free so that lower-income families could see the movie. It's inspired girls to seek out careers in STEM fields, and many young women attended special panel discussions on science and math organized in conjunction with the release of 'Hidden Figures'.

Speaking to young girls who want a career in the movie business, Octavia says, "Do it. Be prepared to fail a hundred times, but you only need to succeed once! The question is, are you up to the task?"

Octavia Spencer certainly was, and in the past two decades she has carved out a wide-ranging and award-winning career. And she's only just getting started. Along the way, Octavia has refused to let other people place her into any specific group, because as she says, "The minute you allow someone else to define you, you've lost all of your power."

Jennifer Siebel Newsom: Using Her Voice

On Oscar morning in 2015, Reese Witherspoon posted an Instagram. She was getting ready to walk the Academy Awards red carpet, where the world's media would be lined up to interview her as a nominee. Reese was up for her second Academy Award for her role in 'Wild', playing a woman who overcomes her inner demons by taking on an extremely challenging hike. Her character goes through a huge journey, in more ways than one. That day, Reese used her voice to post a request to interviewers: Ask Her More. She was referencing a campaign by The Representation Project, calling on the media to ask female Oscar nominees about more than just their dress. Reese's post had some suggested questions, such as, "What's the biggest risk you've taken that you feel has paid off?" and, "What accomplishment are you most proud of?"

The woman behind the idea for Ask Her More is Jennifer Siebel Newsom, a former actress and a businesswoman with an MBA from Stanford. When Jennifer was considering having a baby, she started to become hyperaware of the world she was about to bring a new life into. She looked at films, watched television shows, saw ads and billboards, and read magazines; and everywhere she looked, she saw toxic messages that challenged a woman's worth. Such as overtly sexualized characters in movies, violence against women in video games, models reduced to body parts in advertisements, actresses scrutinized for their weight in magazines, women pitted against each other in reality television shows, and the nightly news commenting on the appearance of female politicians instead of what she had to say. "Since media is the greatest cultural communicator of our time," explains Jennifer, "media normalizes culture for us. What's damaging is how this media communicates to young girls this is what it is to be a woman. A woman's value lies in her youth, her beauty, and her sexuality, and not in her leadership capacity, her intelligence, her voice, or her other talents."

Jennifer decided she wanted to do something about this, and came up with the idea for the documentary 'Miss Representation'. She would produce the movie, and enlist experts and celebrities to talk about the dangers associated with misrepresenting women in media. Jennifer started searching for a female director and approached numerous women in Hollywood, but "everyone loved the idea, though they were afraid of being blacklisted for making the film. So I ultimately decided to direct it myself."

She had been a producer and actress, but directing was a completely new experience for Jennifer. The film screened at the 2011 Sundance Film Festival, and it was here that Jennifer realized how making this film had actually changed her life: "At our Sundance premiere, Gloria Steinem, Geena Davis, and a bunch of incredibly powerful women were in the audience, and a woman who is on the Board at the Women's Media Center asked me a question, 'So, Jen what did you discover making this film?' I didn't even blink, out of my mouth came, 'I found my voice.' And it was in that moment I realized how powerful it is to have a voice. Since then, there's been uncomfortable moments, because I think a lot of people aren't used to women having such strong opinions. But it's gotten me to where I am today, and I'm so grateful to have had the opportunity to actually discover my voice, even at the later age of my mid to late thirties."

After the release of 'Miss Representation', Jennifer started to receive multiple requests from people all over the world, asking her to continue to speak out beyond the movie. This led to the creation of 'The Representation Project', with Jennifer pledging to explore issues of gender representation and create campaigns for social action. I remember seeing 'Miss Representation' in 2011, and it absolutely opened my eyes. I liken this experience to the sunglasses in John Carpenter's 'They Live'. Once you put them on, you see all of the toxic messages in movies, hidden in plain sight. "It's hard to ignore," agrees Jennifer, "to the point where sometimes it's hard to watch certain films, or it's hard to watch the news. I definitely don't subscribe to, or ever purchase, tabloid magazines. I rarely pick them up. Even though they are everywhere in nail salons and hair salons. It's challenging."

In Hollywood movies, female characters are often reduced to an object to be gazed at or acted upon. A research study by USC Annenberg showed how women are three times less likely to speak on screen, but three times more likely to be presented in sexy clothing or partially nude. To say it bluntly: women on screen don't talk, they strip. Another study by the Geena Davis Institute looked at popular films from 11 countries around the world, and the character group which was the most sexualized on screen were female teenagers. They also found that female characters were five times as likely to have their appearance commented on in movies than male characters.

So much of the focus of a female character is her appearance. This happens even with powerful female action heroes, who are usually placed in impossibly tight clothing and high heels. It's not about making them look strong, it's about looking at their body. Men too are also objectified in these movies, with shirtless scenes being added just so we can see their chiseled abs.

Yet the objectification of male and female characters doesn't quite happen in the same way. For example, when a male character is shown shirtless, it's usually in a full shot that shows their face as well as their abs. In all likelihood it happens during an action or sex scene, where the character is actively doing something. When a female character is objectified, her body is usually shown in a series of close-ups of her various parts, sometimes without including her head. Usually, this happens while she is doing something passive, is not speaking, and is not aware that she's being watched. This reinforces the idea that a woman's body is separate from her person and also subconsciously encourages voyeuristic attitudes toward women.

Far from this being just a bit of fun, a research study published in the 2016 Archives of Sexual Behavior psychology magazine found that, "The more that men are exposed to objectifying depictions, the more they will think of women as entities that exist for men's sexual gratification, and that this dehumanized perspective on women may then be used to inform attitudes regarding sexual violence against women."

Movies and other forms of mass media also play a big part in shaping the ideal view of what a woman looks like. In movies, female sexual attractiveness is often linked to having a thin body. By using this as a point for comparison, women feel an enormous amount of pressure to conform to this type of beauty. When this is internalized, it leads to body monitoring, shame, anxiety, eating disorders, and more. They say on average, women think about their bodies every 30 seconds. That's a lot of brain power that could be spent on productive thought. "Women deserve to be treated equally to men," says Jennifer, "and that means not holding them to these ridiculously sexist messages that they are objects and things to be acted upon, rather than agents for their own destiny."

Body distortion is especially outrageous in animated movies aimed at young kids. Male characters are depicted as large and muscular with giant hands. Female characters are drawn with tiny hands, big eyes, and impossibly small waists. The comedy site Above Average studied eleven Disney Princesses and found their eyes were quite literally bigger than their stomachs.

Girls as young as 6 years old are unhappy with their weight, and this is a trend in all countries around the world wherever media culture is prominent. Jennifer says the voice of the media is particularly dangerous for young kids, because, "Our brains are not really fully formed until our late 20's. And what that means is – young people are malleable. The media tells boys that their value lies in dominance, aggression, and control, and not in their empathy, caring, [or] nurturing capacity or capabilities. And it tells girls that their value lies in sexuality. So you see issues such as eating disorders amongst very young girls, plus anxiety and depression, and violence against women from young boys. Not only does it put our kids into these boxes, but it puts pressure on them to conform."

These messages are also conveyed and reinforced with movie promotions. If you ever want to see the difference in the type of questions male and female actors get asked by the press, Google interviews with Scarlett Johansson from any of 'The Avengers' press tours. While her co-stars were asked (somewhat) deep questions about their characters, Scarlett is constantly questioned about whether her tight costume means she can't wear any underwear. "This is important to note," says Jennifer, "because again, it normalizes women to sexual objects. Scarlett Johansson is a brilliant young woman with a strong voice and an activist mindset. She's a powerful being and deserves to be treated as such. They really need to see her as more than a thing or an object for the male gaze, and really listen to her and hear her. Unfortunately, historically, we haven't given women with a voice the time of day."

This is the most noticeable on the red carpet for award shows. While male actors are asked about their nomination and work, women are asked, "Who are you wearing?" and required to twirl for the camera and explain how long it took them to get ready; they have every tiny detail of their bodies studied with sweeping camera movements and "mani" cams to see their nail polish. Sometimes, female nominees don't even get the chance to talk about their role. Obviously, fashion is big business during these events, and actors may have to give a shout-out to a designer in return for borrowing clothes, but when the source of their outfit is the only question being asked, it sends the message that woman are just there to look pretty. As journalist Hadley Freeman from The Guardian puts it, "The red carpet is a strange zone in the western world, one utterly untouched by feminism...it is a place where there is a tacit agreement that both celebrities and the public are idiots and will be treated as such by entertainment journalists."

In the last few years, there has been more awareness, more conversation, and a bit of a change in the way red carpets are covered. A lot of this is due to Jennifer Siebel Newsom's Ask Her More campaign. "I really am so proud of this,' she says; "Every year, we reach around 25 million people, and during the Oscars it trends nationally on Facebook and Twitter. Aside from that, I feel like the campaign has really inspired everyone to speak out, from Shonda Rhimes to Meryl Streep, Patricia Arquette, Octavia Spencer, Kerry Washington, and Reese Witherspoon, who has been an incredible supporter of our work. It's created the conversation that women should be seen for more than 'who we're wearing,' but really acknowledge these fully realized human beings with power and capacities, in an industry where they have not been celebrated and reviewed that way."

In the few years since the making of 'Miss Representation', the conversation around women in film has gained momentum. Actresses are speaking up about the way they are depicted onscreen and how they are treated offscreen. Rose McGowan tweeted out a sexist casting notice, Jennifer Lawrence has written about pay inequality, Jessica Chastain has addressed the treatment of female characters at the Cannes Film Festival, and Jennifer Aniston has penned an essay about the focus of tabloid magazines on whether or not she is pregnant, writing, "We use celebrity 'news' to perpetuate this dehumanizing view of females, focused solely on one's physical appearance, which tabloids turn into a sporting event of speculation. The sheer amount of resources being spent right now by press trying to simply uncover whether or not I am pregnant (for the bajillionth time... but who's counting) points to the perpetuation of this notion that women are somehow incomplete, unsuccessful, or unhappy if they're not married with children."

These are just a few examples of the actors who have chosen to use their voices, and they make Jennifer Siebel Newsom hopeful for the future. "What is so exciting is that there are so many women in the entertainment industry who are discovering their voices outside of being actresses, directors, producers, and female icons. These powerful, intelligent human beings are speaking up in powerful ways, perhaps in some cases for the first times in their lives. That's super inspiring to me!"

Debbie Reynolds & Carrie Fisher: Mother-Daughter Icons

205

When Debbie Reynolds died just one day after her daughter Carrie Fisher, it was tragic, but also quite beautiful. Their closely timed deaths seemed to speak to their unique bond. They'd had many parallel moments with each other through most of their lives, from their careers to their fame, their bad luck with men, and now their deaths. It was as if their relationship was so deep, their fates seem to have been entwined together from the beginning.

They both became icons after appearing in hit movies at the age of 19. Debbie was launched into fame after starring in the classic musical 'Singin' In The Rain' in 1952; 25 years later, Carrie became a phenomenon from her role in the sci-fi smash, 'Star Wars'.

Debbie (or Frannie, as she was called as a child, for Mary Frances,) originally wanted to be a gym teacher. But in 1939 her family moved to Los Angeles, and at age 16, she entered a beauty contest that would end up changing her life. "My mother didn't believe in luck," says Todd Fisher, son of Debbie and brother to Carrie. "Debbie believed in making your own luck. She believed in having a dream and making it happen, but she didn't dream to be a movie star. She didn't plan to win the Miss Burbank contest. But she did an impression of singer Helen Kane, and that's part of why she won. It wasn't because of her body, because she was wearing this second-hand, hand-me-down bathing suit that had a hole in the butt. And she wasn't the most beautiful girl there, but there was a quality about her."

Winning the Miss Burbank title led to a contract with Warner Bros, in which they changed her first name and promised film roles. But nothing came along for her, and by 1950, they let her go. She was then offered a long-term contract with MGM, which led to her role in 'Singin' In The Rain', despite Debbie not knowing how to dance at the time. The film was a smash, and she became a star. She went on to have other great roles in 'How the West Was Won' and 'The Unsinkable Molly Brown', for which she was nominated for an Oscar, but 'Singin' In The Rain' remained her most famous role.

Debbie gave birth to her daughter Carrie Fisher in 1956, and Carrie joked about this moment in her autobiography, saying the doctors and nurses were so enamored with movie star Debbie Reynolds and her handsome crooner husband Eddie Fisher that "When I arrived I was virtually unattended. And I have been trying to make up for that fact ever since."

Carrie grew up knowing her mother was famous and that she "belonged to the world," and she dreamed of looking just like her. "I think it was when I was ten that I realized with profound certainty that I would not be [like Debbie]," wrote Carrie, "I was a clumsy-looking and intensely awkward, insecure girl...I decided then that I'd better develop something else – if I wasn't going to be pretty, maybe I could be funny or smart." She buried herself in reading books and writing, and at 14 years old realized she suffered from bipolar disorder, just like her father. "I accommodated it by developing a very big personality," Carrie said.

She had been performing in her mother's show since she was a teenager, but was never quite comfortable singing next to the iconic Debbie Reynolds. In 1973, Carrie enrolled in the Royal Central School of Speech and Drama in London, and then in 1975, made her feature film debut in the romantic comedy 'Shampoo'. "When she did it, it was just for fun," says her brother Todd; "Warren Beatty had to talk Debbie into it because [Carrie] had to use the F-bomb, and my mother really didn't dig that. Carrie was very young at the time, and needed her permission in those days. And then we didn't really know what was going to happen next with Carrie. She was given this little opportunity to do this little reading on this little, weird, science-fiction thing, where you got this crazy guy, George Lucas. Who is that? He's looking for a princess to be in this movie. It's like a cartoon science-fiction film, and she wasn't even a science-fiction fan. She barely knew a science-fiction movie. She knew '2001: A Space Odyssey.' She maybe knew 'War of the Worlds' from literature. And that was it."

Her screen test for the role of Princess Leia in 'Star Wars' is widely available online, and in the video you can see just how confident she seemed at 19 years of age. Carrie did the audition opposite Harrison Ford, and they had an immediate chemistry. "George Lucas saw something in Carrie that, I guess, those people at the beauty contest saw in Debbie," says Todd. "There was just a spark, and Carrie was this princess, because her whole life was being the daughter of this glamorous movie star. My sister said we were constantly on a photo shoot. There's truth to that. We spent a lot of time dressed and getting photographed. My mother was proud of us. Some of it was for her, some of it was for these magazines, but she wanted to share us with her fans, in an innocent, cute way. She just felt this connection to these people always. She shared everything with them."

After their first roles propelled them to extraordinary fame, Debbie and Carrie each amassed a huge fan base. This shocked both of them at first, but they each made sure to give back as much as they could. Debbie performed live shows around the country, singing and entertaining on stage and taking pictures with fans on the street. "I remember one time when Carrie and I were very young," Todd says, "and we were wanting to go to the toy store. We were right out the front getting ready to walk in the door and some fans came up to my mother and stopped the whole process. It was very frustrating as a child, Carrie and I were pulling and pulling. She says, 'Oh, no. This is the priority. You have to take the time for these people. These are the people that make us who we are.'"

This was something that Carrie didn't forget, and when it was her time in the spotlight, she traveled the world visiting 'Star Wars' fan conventions, posing for official photos, and signing autographs.

Nonetheless, they each had very different approaches to fame, which in a way, represented the eras in which they had become icons. Debbie Reynolds was a star of classic Hollywood, from an era when actresses were shaped by their personas. She was a product of the 1950s, representing the squeaky-clean, virginal housewife that was idolized at the time, as a contrast to the other popular persona, the sex goddess like Marilyn Monroe. This contrast also played out in her real life when her husband Eddie Fisher left Debbie for her best friend, the sexy Elizabeth Taylor. It was a scandal that rocked Hollywood — Debbie was left to look after her two children as a single mother, while tabloid magazines looked on. Throughout this ordeal, she smiled, posing with Carrie and Todd, sharing their lives with her fans. And whenever Debbie appeared in public, she was the picture of a perfect movie star — always well-dressed, with her hair and make-up done, a warm smile, and plenty of well-rehearsed jokes at the ready. And audiences loved her for it.

In contrast, Carrie was a star of the 1970s and 1980s, when Hollywood became a bit more real and gritty. Gone was the veneer of perfection, if an actor was struggling, people knew about it. Carrie was as real as it got. She was an open book, sharing her vulnerabilities, her addictions, her troubles with men, and her battles with bipolar disorder. She performed her own one-woman comedy shows and wrote several honest books about her life. Carrie became the public face of issues many people were dealing with in their own lives, and because of this, fans formed a strong bond with her. "Carrie played the princess, but she became an icon," says Todd. "She earned that position through life and through survival. You don't get that stuff. That's not a handout. Carrie used to be nervous early on in her career, and she wasn't totally comfortable with who she was until later. That didn't happen easily, she struggled with it, she struggled through."

Both Carrie and Debbie dealt with a lot and were tough in different ways. Female fans were especially drawn to the mother-daughter duo. They were approached more by women than by men, Todd says, because women were "inspired by their strength. They were inspired by their 'pick yourself up.' Both Carrie and my mother lived complex lives. And both of them didn't do well with men. They were both special, amazing women, and the idea that they couldn't find a man, they couldn't understand that, but it's complicated. Being Mr Reynolds. Being Mr Fisher. It's complicated."

Throughout it all, they had each other, even when they were fighting. Carrie's book and film 'Postcards from the Edge' satirized their relationship, but the two bounced back to be closer than ever, and moved next door to each other in their last few years. They had, Todd says, "a complicated relationship. But it evolved. It was very tumultuous, but in some ways, it looked like every other house and mother/daughter across the world. But I saw this evolution of respect and adoration. There never seemed to be an end to my mother. No one ever thought it would ever end. I think Carrie started to have the epiphany that Debbie wasn't forever. It changed the way that she approached and listened and interacted with her, and that was not a forever deal. Fortunately, the last 10 years of our lives together, certainly the last five years were in complete appreciation of who she was, and they had this much, much deeper understanding of each other."

On December 27, 2016, Carrie Fisher died after suffering a heart attack while on a flight from London to Los Angeles. And on December 28, 2016, Debbie Reynolds suffered from a stroke, and passed away as well. The world mourned this mother/daughter iconic duo, who represented so much of Hollywood history for multiple generations. Both Debbie Reynolds and Carrie Fisher meant a lot to the people who loved them, and their generous spirits made each of us feel as if we knew them personally.

As to how Carrie's brother and Debbie's son Todd Fisher would describe them, he said, "Carrie put it best. She said, 'Debbie is Christmas.' Debbie was just a big, giving thing. There was just no end to that gift. When Carrie said that, it was an absolute truth in a moment. And Carrie was like that. She had a lot of blinding truths. She would say something in a sentence, a group of words that nobody could spin the way she could. And that unique perspective she had, that was her gift to us all."

 # BELOW THE LINE

When we talk about women in Hollywood, the focus is often on actors and directors. But a film production unit consists of many talented, passionate, and hardworking people, who all make their mark on American film.

Dede Gardner is a great example. As president of the production company Plan B Entertainment, she has a proven track record of producing diverse films and taking them to the Oscars. She made history at the 2017 Academy Awards as the first female producer ever to win two Best Picture Academy Awards, for 'Moonlight' and '12 Years a Slave'. Her productions have been nominated for Best Picture every year since 2012.

Another successful woman is Donna Langley, chairman of Universal Pictures, who has final authority on green-lighting movies, and whose forward-thinking leadership has seen films such as 'Straight

Outta Compton' become hits. The movie was dropped by other studios due to its R rating and because it's an honest look at the world of gangster rap. Plus the other studios had doubts that it would translate to overseas dollars. 'Straight Outta Compton' went on to become the highest-grossing musical biopic of all time.

Cinematographer Autumn Eakin is another woman of note; her project, Cinematographers XX, is a beautifully designed website which works as a resource to find talent to hire. She set up the site to advocate for her fellow female cinematographers, so that, as she says, the industry can see "there have been women shooting, telling stories, for decades, at least. We are here!"

Then there's ten-time Oscar-nominated sound engineer Anna Behlmer. And Colleen Atwood, who has won four Oscars for costume design. Also Ruth Carter, the first African-American nominated for a costume design. And documentarian Barbara Kopple, who has two Oscars. I could go on.

While there are many women who are successful in film production, a gender imbalance definitely exists within film crews. This is sometimes dubbed the "celluloid ceiling," because crew positions on Hollywood movies aren't equally distributed by gender, despite an even split in numbers of male and female film school graduates. The Celluloid Ceiling is also the title of a yearly report examining employment behind the scenes, put together by Dr. Martha Lauzen at the Center for the Study of Women in Television and Film. The Center's research has found that in the top 250 highest grossing films each year, women represent less than 20% of all directors, writers, producers, executive producers, editors, and cinematographers. The job most filled by women is producer with 24%, and the least is composer, with 97% male composers compared with 3% female composers.

There is a gendering of certain departments, with roles such as make-up seen as more feminine, and positions like camera operator thought to be more masculine. This bias excludes accomplished women from getting those positions, and it also disregards men who are highly skilled at make-up and costume design. Interestingly, films which feature a female director employ dramatically more women crew members.

The Academy Awards reflect how far there is to go for gender equality in craft positions, with an average of 80% of all nominees being men. This is mostly due to a lack of opportunities in the first place, but some categories have also been gendered. For example, there has never been a woman nominated in the Best Cinematography category in Oscar history, despite many female cinematographers having worked on movies which were nominated for Best Picture.

Taking the research one step further, data analyst Stephen Follows looked into the gender of crew roles on 2,000 of the highest grossing films between 1994 and 2013. Overall, he found that women held less than a third of the behind-the-scenes jobs during those 20 years. The only departments to feature a majority of women were make-up, casting, and costume, and those with the most men were camera and electrical. The film with the highest overall percentage of female crew in those 20 years was 'Mean Girls' in 2004. The movie had a crew makeup that was 42% female and 58% male.

Labor unions and guilds representing artisans across all departments – from drivers to wardrobe to accountants – are important to helping to change this trend, as they stand between the industry's employers and crew members needing employment. The various unions and guilds often don't tabulate exact numbers of who makes up their membership, as this data is collected voluntarily, and they've found that many artisans don't want to be categorized by gender or race. But these unions know they have a way to go before it's truly equal, and many have started diversity programs to help.

One example is the International Cinematographer's Guild, of which Rebecca Rhine is the first woman to be the executive director. She's trying to help bring balance to these positions by focusing on training and being a resource for studios by providing lists of available cinematographers. The Motion Pictures Editors Guild has a Diversity Committee which runs open discussions; created in response to a survey where 60% claimed that lack of diversity was an issue and 36% said they had been discriminated against in post-production, including pay differences for women and minorities.

There are also mentorship organizations such as Women in Film, The Alliance of Women Directors, Film Fatales, Film Independent, and companies that offer grants to female filmmakers, like Chicken & Egg Pictures and the Women Cinematographers Grant.

Gender and racial equality is an important issue for below-the-line craftspeople. Achieving a balanced crew can be done, it just takes a bit of concerted effort. For example, Paul Feig always aims to have his crews as equal as possible, and makes sure he's picking from a wider range of people. He says this "just makes it a healthier environment. There's no competition because the crews are so mixed, so everyone is relying on everyone else, and that's how it should be."

Amy Powell: The Risk Taker

When Amy Powell was placed in charge of the brand new television and digital division at Paramount Pictures, she'd never created a TV show, let alone a company. "I really just dove into it headfirst!" she says, laughing. But like everything in Amy's career, this leap worked. She brought a fresh perspective to the studio with her out-of-the-box ideas and kept a big focus on supporting women. Under her direction, Paramount won five Emmys for 'Grease Live', and had a successful collaboration with Selena Gomez for the series '13 Reasons Why'; and their micro-budget production company Insurge had a worldwide hit with 'Justin Bieber: Never Say Never', plus several viral marketing campaigns. And throughout it all, their TV department maintained a 50:50 gender balance.

213

Amy's role at Paramount reflects the shifting paradigms within the movie industry. Not too long ago, the division between what a TV show is and what a movie is was quite clearly defined. Movies had a certain level of budget, a certain depth of story, a certain production look, and a certain type of star. But now, it's all quite blurry. Television shows have become more like feature films, with big name actors and slick production. We watch movies on streaming services, and popular digital platforms like YouTube have led to a complete rethinking of what "content" can be. The rulebook of format has pretty much been thrown out.

Thinking outside the box is something Amy Powell has done her whole life. She went from journalism at CNN in Atlanta to launching a digital department at Sony Pictures in Los Angeles. At Sony, she worked closely with people who would end up ruling the internet. "As a young executive, I had the opportunity to be in meetings with the people who had founded these companies," said Amy, "whether it was YouTube, or Yahoo, I was sitting in the room with these people, and nobody had any idea what those companies were about to become. I reflect back on it now and I just realize how fortunate I was."

This knowledge came in handy when Amy moved to Paramount Pictures to work in interactive marketing. Her campaigns made use of the popularity of the internet and were completely unique, which helped to turn small budget films into big box office successes. 'Paranormal Activity' is a great example of this. It was a tiny horror film with a little bit of buzz from film festivals and midnight screenings, but it exploded into a viral hit when the website offered audiences the ability to demand screenings at their local theater, which they did in droves as curiosity spread about this terrifying movie. And the marketing for 'Cloverfield' also relied on curiosity and using the internet, in a way that was completely opposite to the usual movie campaign. Whereas most films are launched with a lot of detail about the plot, 'Cloverfield' had mysterious trailers with no film title, but links to connected websites.

In her own career Amy loves the idea of curiosity. She describes herself as being a "very curious person" who is always interested in learning more. "Curiosity is really one of the best systems of motivation that you can have, because it keeps you asking questions, keeps you researching, keeps you reading, keeps you meeting people, traveling, exploring, or having adventures in general."

At Paramount, Amy worked under CEO Sherry Lansing, the highly regarded executive who in 1980 became the first woman ever to run a movie studio. Sherry had a huge influence on her, both as a woman in the film business and as a manager who took a special interest in every member of her team. "One of the unique things about Sherry is the human side of her," says Amy; "She always knew when it was your birthday, she knew when it was your wedding anniversary. She sent you flowers, she sent you hand-written notes. She was the first to ask you about your weekend before discussing the box office. And her ability to connect with people on a very human level and her sincere interest in you as a person, versus as an employee, was really eye-opening for me. I think up until that point, I had felt like I was a cog in the system. But she really made you feel like you were somebody incredibly special, not only to the company, but to her. And as a result, you worked hard, because you wanted to be somebody who deserved the respect and admiration of Sherry."

Sherry led the way for Amy and for many other women making their way up the ranks in Hollywood. According to research, women hold around a quarter of the very top executive slots at the movie studios, along with slightly more than a quarter of executive vice president positions and more than a third of senior vice president positions or their equivalent. These numbers are far from parity, but still encouraging, because it shows just how many qualified women are currently in positions at the top or just one or two steps down from it. Every woman in a powerful role encourages more to move up. "My first boss at Sony Pictures was an incredibly strong woman," says Amy, "and then I went to Paramount to work for Sherry. So my formative years, if you will, were spent working for these two super-dominant, really impressive, strong women."

When Amy was hired as president of Paramount Television and Digital, her biggest focus was building a team that was gender balanced. With every single hire, she has been cognizant of inclusion, saying it makes for a more positive, encouraging, and equal environment, "Since we started this company from zero, I have literally hired every single person who works on my team from the start. Women are important leaders, an important part of the work force. I do have a fifty percent rule, which is that fifty percent of my team [must] be comprised of women in each of the various roles. And also on set the goal is to have fifty percent directors, fifty percent writers, et cetera. I think it's incredibly important. And I probably have, on my own staff, a higher than fifty percent rate."

Her care in hiring has led to a supportive department which fosters interesting ideas. This is why Amy Powell stands out in Hollywood. Movie studios are usually male-dominated, but her team has more than half women. The business is traditionally risk-adverse, but Amy is someone who is willing to try new things. She takes chances to see what works, and isn't afraid to fail. Along the way, she has nurtured and empowered women below her to follow her lead, just as leaders like Sherry Lansing did for her. And Amy's advice for young women is to be bold and learn as much as possible. "I think that you should try to educate yourself, whether that means getting a degree, or asking somebody out to coffee, or talking to someone you're intimidated by, I guarantee you, you will learn something from that person. They'll be valuable to you later in life. And no one's ever offended by being asked for a meeting or for time to imbue some wisdom upon you. And I think you just have to be okay with putting yourself out there."

Denise di Novi: From Producer To Director

A quick look at the posters hanging in the office of producer Denise di Novi shows the number and variety of movies she has been involved with. On one wall, there's 'Edward Scissorhands' and 'Heathers', on another, 'Crazy Stupid Love' and 'The Sisterhood of the Traveling Pants'. Many of these posters reflect her collaborations with director Tim Burton. All of them show how long Denise di Novi has been a power player in Hollywood. But despite always loving movies "more than real life," making them was not what she originally intended to do.

As a child, Denise remembers watching old movies every afternoon with her mother. They especially loved the women's pictures of the 1940s featuring strong protagonists like Katharine Hepburn. But she knew she didn't want to be an actress, and she didn't consider any other career in the movies, so after school, she studied journalism. "At first I wanted to be a straight news journalist," Denise says, "and then I became a features story journalist, and then I moved to Canada to be a TV reporter. There were a lot of movies being made in Toronto because of the tax shelter, so I started asking to cover stories about them and interview filmmakers."

On one of her interviews, it was suggested she could use her film knowledge to work as a unit publicist. "I was like, 'What's that?'" says Denise, "'it's on a movie set? Oh my God! I'll take it!' I had this promising career as an on-air reporter, but I left to be a unit publicist to get involved in production." When Denise moved back to the U.S., she lived in Los Angeles and started to write, but found that "I did not love the isolation of it. I'm a people person and a coordinator person, so I just got into producing. I produced 'Heathers' and then my career as a producer took off."

Though she makes it sound easy, Denise started her career in the 1980s, when a female producer was still a rarity. "They'd say to me, 'How can a woman be a producer?' Because it's such an authoritative job. And I'd say, 'I don't understand how a man can be a producer.' Because to me, it's a completely maternal job. When I started, there were less than a handful of women producers, I didn't even know if there were any. And I did come [up] against a lot of pushback, but I didn't take no for an answer. It didn't make sense to me, I didn't see any reason why I shouldn't do what I wanted to do and make films. I couldn't see any logic, so I thought eventually 'I'm just going to push through this', and luckily it happened."

These days, out of all the powerful positions in Hollywood, the one most filled by women is that of producer. Research by the Center for the Study of Women in Television and Film shows that currently around 24% of all producers are women. This figure has remained unchanged since 1998. It's still obviously far from equal, but the level of bias against female producers has definitely changed for the better over the years.

Denise di Novi has over 35 film producing credits to her name, with a combined box office of over $1 billion. One of her biggest successes was producing 'Batman Returns' with director Tim Burton, who Denise describes as a genius, saying, "Tim is an artist who transcends filmmaking." As a producer who works with filmmakers like Tim, Denise says you still "have a lot of influence, but at a certain point it's the director's movie. If you have too much influence while the director's shooting, it's not going to be a good movie. A director has to be in charge, has to be zealous and very relentless about holding that vision and making it happen in that way."

This is why after over three decades in the industry, Denise decided to start directing. Her directorial debut was on a drama called 'Unforgettable', about a mother who becomes unhinged when her ex-husband gets serious with another woman. Denise was only going to produce the film, but when the original director dropped out, Warner Bros suggested she should take over. And she was excited by the idea of being a female director who gets to show an unlikeable woman on screen. "There's a feeling that if you're going to get a shot to make a female movie, it should only be something that celebrates the strength or integrity of women. I love those movies, I'm a big champion of them, but I think the really great thing will be when women can play psychotic people, or women who are complex and who do crazy things, do complicated things, and be flawed," says Denise, "and I think as a director, that fascinates me more. There is a dark side that comes out for women based on, or because of, our social conditioning, and how our culture is. And to expose that is important."

With years of experience on a movie set, Denise says directing "came very naturally, because I'm probably more at home on a film set than anywhere else to be honest. I knew how movies were made, I had watched so many directors, but it is different when you do it yourself," she explains. "The analogy I use is you can have 15 nieces and nephews and say, 'I know what it's like to have kids.' But until you have kids, you don't realize. So that first day, when I was the one calling 'Action!' and everyone was looking at me, I thought, this is a bigger responsibility than I realized until I was standing in those shoes. But I loved it, it was thrilling to be that intimately involved with the movie. As a director, I'm the closest person to the storytelling. Me and the actors. And I really loved it."

Denise di Novi is hoping to continue her career as a director, but will also produce films. Producers are important power players in Hollywood, because they have a vital role in pushing for an increase in diversity and the variety of roles we see on screen. Denise is optimistic about more inclusion of women in the future, and says having people talk about gender equality helps a lot, "The thing that is most exciting to me is that there is a lot of conversation. The more that we talk about it, the more women speak up about it and the more conversations we have about it, the more that people's inherent sense of justice and decency will prevail. They just need to be educated and think about it."

Nicole Perlman: Writing Her Own Script

Despite having nine worldwide smash hits to their name, Marvel Studios still viewed 'Guardians of the Galaxy' as a bit of a risk. For one, the comic book series was quite obscure, much less known than the popular Iron Man or Captain America. For another, it was set entirely in space and it also had to introduce a completely new set of characters into the established cinematic universe, including a talking raccoon and a tree.

Of course, 'Guardians of the Galaxy' ended up being another huge win for Marvel, even outdoing the success of the original cinematic universe film, 'Iron Man'. And most surprising of all, the script began in a writer's program. The woman responsible went from being relatively unknown to making history as the second ever female screenwriter on a Marvel Comics movie, the first having been Jane Goldman on 'X-Men: First Class'. The fact remains that without Nicole Perlman, the film might have never happened.

For Nicole, the script was the perfect blend of everything she had loved since she was young. She wrote plays in high school, enjoyed movies with great dialogue like 'The Hustler' and 'Sweet Smell of Success', and wrote her thesis on the cinematography of 'Citizen Kane'. Additionally, she was a huge fan of science-fiction, and had entered writing contests where she won a trip to space camp. Unfortunately, jaw surgery prevented her from going.

Nicole made it to NYU, and moved from Colorado to New York to study film. She was inspired by the city and the movies she watched. Nicole remembers going to the cinema one weekend to see a movie by a female screenwriter; "Erin Cressida Wilson's 'Secretary' was in theaters," she says, "and it blew me away with its boldness and originality. The fact that Erin wasn't playing it safe with her debut film reminded me how important it was to write something to please yourself, first and foremost."

This was advice she followed for her first script, based on the Challenger Space Shuttle explosion. Her screenplay, 'Challenger', ended up on the 2005 Black List, an annual survey of the best unproduced screenplays making their way around Hollywood. Being featured on the list gave Nicole a good amount of positive buzz, and she moved to Los Angeles to start working on an adaptation of a Neil Armstrong biography.

A few years later, Nicole enrolled in the Marvel Writing Program, which was a short-lived enterprise by the studio. This was a two-year paid internship of sorts, where screenwriters were charged with going through the Marvel Comics back catalogue and looking for new stories for their feature films. Out of all the comic titles to choose from, the one that appealed to Nicole was 'Guardians of the Galaxy'. It wasn't known to many outside the inner circle of comic book readers, but it appealed to Nicole straightaway because it was set in space.

Nicole's first task was to learn about the property, and she spent months reading through the comic books and finding out as much about the characters as she could. All of the writers in the program were given a lot of creative freedom, and because this was 2009, at the start of the Marvel cinematic universe, there wasn't much of a thought that these projects would ever see the light of day. But Nicole was smart. She had an inkling the series would move to space one day, and zeroed in on a couple of key characters who she thought would be the most interesting on film. Nicole thought the Infinity Stones would make for a fun plot device, and that Thanos should be the big bad villain the Guardians were fighting.

At the end of the program, Nicole submitted her script for 'Guardians of the Galaxy'. Six months later, she was called back to work on rewrites. That's when she realized the film might actually happen. Another year later, writer/director James Gunn was attached, and the movie was on the official slate.

As a female writer in Hollywood, it can be extremely tough to get jobs on studio movies. Out of the 250 highest grossing films of each year, approximately 13% are written by women, while 87% are by men. Female screenwriters have the extra battle of bias about what type of movies they should write, and are often tasked with romantic comedies, dramas, and other female-skewing content. But writers like Nicole Perlman, Jane Goldman, and Katie Dippold are proving that women can be successful in all genres, and this is important for the future generation to see. "So many young women have approached me at Comic-Con and Austin Film Festival to say they never thought girls could write science fiction," says Nicole. "I think the perception will change, now more and more women writers are becoming more visible as writers of genre films, but it has been a slow progression." She advises girls to "write the stories they want to see on the screen. No matter the genre or subject matter."

221

Nicole also encourages young women to find "a group of other writers they trust and get used to giving and receiving feedback on your work - the earlier the better." She had support inside the Marvel writers program, but says, "It wasn't really until 2015 that I found myself a part of a large group of screenwriters who were all working within the same circles. Most of this was as a result of working in feature writer rooms, where you get to meet some truly mind-blowing talent."

Out of all the talented people she's worked with, Nicole says writer Meg LeFauve is especially inspiring. Meg was behind Pixar's 'Inside Out', and she has been working closely with Nicole on 'Captain Marvel'. With this film, Nicole will make history once again; it is the first Marvel movie to feature two women writers. Star Brie Larson, who will play the title character, has been vocal about wanting to explore what a female superhero may look like, not simply a woman with male characteristics.

"I think any writer, regardless of gender, has a responsibility to depict their characters in a well-rounded way, to treat their characters as if they are human," says Nicole. "If I were male, I would have just as much responsibility to portray women thoughtfully and take pains to avoid dehumanizing them. Which means not reducing them to a function or a caricature. This is a challenge for a lot of people, not just on the page, but in life as well."

Taking on a career as a writer can be extremely isolating. And when you do reach out for feedback, you have to be careful who you trust. "The most important relationship you will have as a writer isn't with your agent or your lawyer," explains Nicole, "it is the relationship you have with yourself. Plenty of people will be there throughout your career to doubt you or cut you down, you have to be a friend to yourself and be able to develop a thick skin. The film industry is not for the faint of heart, so try to enjoy the writing process as much as the hoped-for result, because there are a lot of twists and turns on the road to getting a film made."

With her success in the male-dominated arena of comic book movies, Nicole Perlman has broken down barriers, challenged stereotypes, and become a role model for young female writers. She's also "written a comic book series for Marvel, helped a season of television in a writers room, been a consulting producer on a large scale action movie franchise, participated in a director's fellowship in New York, and run a feature writers room for 'Sherlock Holmes 3'." Nicole Perlman says she's proud of "the breadth of work experiences I've sought out. With the acknowledgement that I have a tremendous amount still to learn."

Joi McMillon: Editing History

The most talked about moment from the 2017 Academy Awards involved 'Moonlight'. The small, powerful drama won Best Picture... after a mix-up of envelopes saw 'La La Land' being announced at first. It was an unfortunate (and unusual) event in Oscar history, but on the positive side, it ensured 'Moonlight' would stay in everyone's memories, with that moment to replayed over and over.

It was a history-making night for another reason too, one that also involved 'Moonlight'. In the Best Editing category, Joi McMillon was nominated alongside Nat Sanders, making Joi became the first African-American female editor to ever be nominated. It's an honor she doesn't take lightly. "I believe this distinction not only holds a special resonance but also a special responsibility," says Joi; "When your nomination marks a historical first, then people look to you to continue to be a catalyst for change."

The rest of the nominees were all male. That's nothing shocking as far as the film industry goes. Research studies by Dr. Martha Lauzen at San Diego State University show the average percentage of female editors who work on top-grossing films is around 17%, and overall, editing rooms are predominately white. Being the only person of color is something Joi McMillon is used to; she grew up in a mostly white neighborhood in Florida, and was the only African-American working on her school yearbook. Joi was planning to study journalism after school, and the film industry was not on her radar at all until a class trip that changed everything.

223

For career day, Joi's school went on a tour of Universal Studios. There she observed an editor working on 'Animal Planet', and as she watched him work, she was transfixed. In that moment, Joi knew she wanted to become an editor. "What struck me was the ability the editor had to rewrite the story by rearranging the images," Joi explains; "Witnessing that continues to stay with me to this day. Being a part of the evolution of a film is the act of editing that still enthralls me. To watch a film take shape and finally become what it's supposed be never gets old." As soon as she got home, Joi started to look into film schools, and ended up at Florida State University. It was there that she met a young man by the name of Barry Jenkins, as well as a fellow editor, Nat Sanders.

It wasn't until Joi moved to Los Angeles that she realized the lack of diversity that existed in editing rooms. The job of an editor is somewhat invisible, and you shouldn't notice the editing on a film, unless a stylistic choice asks you to notice it. But editors are key to shaping a story; their DNA is almost as woven into the film as a screenwriter. Given that, it's surprising that many films that tell stories about women and people of color still have editing rooms full of white men.

For inspiration, Joi looked to a few women in her profession, such as Sally Menke, Quentin Tarantino's long-time editor, who sadly passed away in 2010; and Thelma Schoonmaker, who continues to work with Martin Scorsese. "I've been inspired by many female editors [including] Sally and Thelma," she says; "In addition to that, I've had the great fortune to work with inspirational female editors like Mayise Hoy, Terilyn Shropshire and Nancy Richardson."

Collaboration is a vital part of being an editor, and establishing a strong relationship with the director is essential. Once these partnerships are created, many filmmakers stay with one editor across multiple movies. Despite the low number of female editors with jobs in Hollywood, some of the most iconic movies have been edited by women, including 'The Wizard of Oz', 'Singin' in the Rain', 'Lawrence of Arabia', 'Star Wars', 'Apocalypse Now', 'E.T: The Extra-Terrestrial', 'Raging Bull' and many more.

Many of the biggest male directors have been long-time collaborators with female editors. Lisa Lassek worked with Joss Whedon on 'The Avengers' and 'The Avengers: Age of Ultron'. Margaret Sixel won an Oscar for editing 'Mad Max: Fury Road', her third time collaborating with her husband, filmmaker George Miller. Dede Allen collaborated with Sidney Lumet for 'Serpico' and 'Dog Day Afternoon', while Peter Bogdanovich hired Verna Fields for

'Targets', 'What's up Doc?', and 'Paper Moon'. Steven Spielberg worked with Verna on 'Jaws' and 'The Sugarland Express'. And on 'Star Wars: The Force Awakens', J.J. Abrams enlisted his go-to editing team, Mary Jo Markey and Maryann Brandon. These two have also worked with J.J. on the first two 'Star Trek' "reboot" movies, plus 'Mission Impossible III' and 'Super 8'.

And one of the most successful collaborations between director and editor in the history of cinema is of course Thelma Schoonmaker and Martin Scorsese. The two met during a summer course at NYU in 1963, where Thelma salvaged a cut of Scorsese's short film. Their first feature together was 'Raging Bull' in 1980, and this partnership proved so valuable, Scorsese hired her for every single movie he has made since. Together they've created a cinematic style which has been studied by and remains influential for many other filmmakers and editors. Thelma's use of freeze-frames, jump cuts, and speed changes shows her technical mastery, but Scorsese says he relies on Thelma to uncover the emotional heart of his films. The secret to their partnership, according to Thelma, is maintaining a trusting relationship. Joi McMillion agrees, "The key ingredient for a successful collaboration between an editor and director is trust."

Joi established that level of trust with Barry Jenkins during their university years, and he hired her to work on 'Moonlight', along with their other FSU friend, Nat Sanders. This was Joi's first feature film as editor; she had previously been working in the editorial department, editing short films. 'Moonlight' changed all of that, and the film itself was special – it tells the story of a black man in Miami who is struggling with his day-to-day life while questioning his sexuality. It's elegantly told and beautifully put together in three sections played by different actors, one showing him a young child, one as a teenager, and the third as an adult.

'Moonlight' is a stand-out film because it's the type of story and character that are so rarely seen or explored in cinema. Movies which show audiences a person's experience – one they might never come across in their own lives – can help to create empathy and understanding towards a whole community. "Many of the films

I watched as a child," says Joi, "allowed me to discover worlds that I'd never been exposed to. Telling diverse and cultural stories allows for us to better understand each other and open the lines of communication that have yet to be used."

After finishing on 'Moonlight', Joi moved to another editor position working for director Janicza Bravo on 'Lemon', an off-beat film about a struggling actor in LA. The movie has screened at multiple festivals, including Sundance and SXSW, where it was well-received. Joi says she is grateful for the freedom these directors have given her, "What I love about working with Barry and Janicza is that they both don't like to follow the rules when it comes to filmmaking. This gives me license as an editor to color outside the lines. For me, I love to use cuts that disorient the audience and often take them where they least expect to go."

As you can tell, Joi's passion for editing has never waned, and I love the way she talks about the moment everything comes together. "The feeling you experience when a scene or cut finally starts to work," she says, "is one of both relief and utter joy. It's quite hard to explain, but it's definitely one of the best feelings you can experience as an editor."

The statistics for female editors working in Hollywood might be horribly low, but it's women like Joi who are showing future editors what is possible with a lot of hard work and passion. As to the advice she would give young girls wanting to get into editing, Joi McMillion says, "The road may be long and hard, but if you can endure it, then you will arrive to where you want to be."

Rachel Morrison: Striking Images

On the big budget blockbuster 'Black Panther', director Ryan Coogler made history by doing something that has never happened on a Marvel movie before. He hired a female cinematographer, his frequent collaborator Rachel Morrison.

Over the past decade, Rachel has made a name for herself in the art of cinematography, thanks to her striking work, where she uses a variety of film stock, colors, lighting, and shadows. Rachel's love for images was fostered at a young age, growing up in Massachusetts with an interest in photography and cinema. "I can't say that any one film made me realize there was this incredible art form called cinematography," Rachel says, "but I remember the day I fell in love with foreign cinema, and I realize in retrospect that so much of what I was responding to was the image. I must have been around 13, and everything at the multiplex was sold out, so I stumbled into this French Canadian film called 'Leolo', and I walked out mouth agape, mind blown."

After school, Rachel moved to New York to study photography and film at NYU, and then to Los Angeles to get a Masters of Fine Art in cinematography at the AFI Conservatory program. Rachel was drawn to the gritty dramas of the independent world, and one of her first jobs as primary cinematographer was on 2007's 'Palo Alto' with director Gia Coppola.

Over the next few years Rachel worked in television and on commercials, with seven Sundance premieres, and now the grand-scale 'Black Panther'. Her body of work is very wide-ranging, and each film is unique in its look. For example, her list of feature films includes the harrowing drama 'Cake'. Jennifer Aniston stars as a woman suffering from grief and chronic pain who becomes obsessed with a stranger's suicide. This is one of Jennifer's best performances to date, and Rachel's camera was key to showing a different side to the popular star. She had never been shot in such a naturalistic way,
with her flaws and vulnerability on full display. This allowed a level of believability not usually associated with very famous celebrities.

In contrast, Rachel filmed the indie favorite 'Dope' using a hand-held camera and colors inspired by the 1980's to bring a vibrant sense of life to this movie about coming of age in L.A. And her imagery on 'Dope' is completely different from her work on the period piece 'Mudbound'. This historical drama about racism in the South was directed by Dee Rees, who worked with a largely female crew. Dee and Rachel pulled inspiration from painters, documentaries, and photographs, using vintage lenses to create a beautifully bleak portrait of a mud-covered landscape. When I saw the film at Sundance, I wanted to pause each frame to take in the details, then print each of them out to put on my wall. "I get inspiration from everything," Rachel explains, "photography of course, and fine art, but also a conversation I might have with my two-year-old, or a sunrise surf session. Music will often be a big influence on the look and feel of a film, and that is why some are so different than others. We tend to make 'look books' because they are easy for everyone to understand, but I could just as easily break the three acts of a film into three songs that represent the tone and rhythm for each section."

Some of Rachel's best collaborations have been with director Ryan Coogler, who she has worked with twice. The first was the powerful 'Fruitvale Station', based on a true story about a racially charged police shooting. Here, Rachel used grainy film stock to reflect the grittiness of the story. The next will be 'Black Panther', her biggest budget film to date, an industry step-up that has been a long time coming. "Marvel was very supportive actually, especially Victoria Alonso, the executive vice president," Rachel says; "But I don't doubt for one second that Ryan made it part of his deal and thus enabled me to shatter the glass ceiling of big-budget superhero films. Hopefully nothing will be off limits to me now, but again, we will never know why the phone doesn't ring."

Ryan Coogler has worked with female cinematographers on each of his feature films – with Rachel on 'Fruitvale Station' and 'Black Panther' and Maryse Alberti on the boxing film 'Creed'. As Ryan explained in an interview, "You're absolutely missing something in a room that's all men...Everybody's a prisoner of their own perspective. I can only see the world through my own eyes. The last few times I made a movie, I had a cinematographer who was a woman. And my editors, one of them is a woman, and the way those two view things and give notes are radically different, and when you have that balance, it's really an asset."

Rachel says her collaboration with Ryan "means more than I can possibly put into words." She continues, "Besides the fact that he truly is one of the kindest, most humble, and most brilliant people to walk this earth, he also has become the sibling I never had but always wanted. He has shown more faith in me than I had in myself and fought for me like no one before. And I would do the same for him in a heartbeat. We challenge each other to step outside our comfort zones – to experiment and explore, but also to stay true to our own instincts and to the truth inside the narrative. Ryan is a magical being and genuine to the core. He never ceases to amaze and inspire me, and I am a better cinematographer and better person for knowing him."

According to research, cinematography is one of the roles which is still most often filled by men. The Center for the Study of Women in Film and Television's study shows the percentage of female cinematographers working on studio movies to be between 2% and 6% since 1998. Because of this low percentage, whenever we talk about directors of photography who are women, the qualifier of "female" is usually needed in front of the job title. This used to frustrate Rachel, who says, "For once, just once, I'd like to be referred to as a DP and not a female DP. We don't use qualifiers when we refer to doctors or lawyers or teachers. Can you imagine if I asked for a recommendation for the best female realtor or female knee surgeon on the East Side? It all seems incredibly antiquated."

But Rachel knows why this happens. "Unlike these other professions," she says, "we are nowhere near the 50/50 mark. Quite the opposite. So I have come to realize that part of the solution is being willing to acknowledge that there is indeed a problem, and that has made me far more vocal and willing to be recognized as the anomaly we are. That said, I still believe the only way people will start to think of the terms 'cinematographer' or 'director' as being genderless is if we start seeing three, four, five, even six women on every list of 10 cinematographers to watch... it needs to be normalized so that we can start being part of the rule and not the exception to it."

Rachel says she's been fortunate to have never experienced any overt sexism on set, even though on every job people are shocked to discover she is the DP, she simply finds it amusing at this point. Instead, "The only bias I can speak to," she explains, "is a much less tangible form – the kind that goes on behind closed doors with studio heads and agency producers... I've watched countless times as my male counterparts lensed one successful indie movie and got a phone call from a studio saying something to the effect of, 'We loved what you did with no money, we'd like to see what you can do with a budget.' Those are words no woman I know has ever heard. We have to earn that trust ten times over. Literally. I think I must have shot five movies under a million dollar budget before I got a five million dollar feature. Then two five millions before I got a 10."

This is a complex problem to solve, made tougher by the fact that crew members like Rachel never get to meet the people in charge. "Studio executives are like the Wizard of Oz behind the magic curtain. If you can't see them or speak to them, then how can you possibly change their perception of you? How can you show them you have a solid head on your shoulders and a kind demeanor and the confidence and capabilities to get the job done? I've been saying for years that cinematography is the art of translating emotion into imagery, and who [is] more qualified than a woman who is historically more in touch with their emotional side? And yet there are still so few of us."

Something that is hopeful is the growing community of female DPs. Though cinematography is a solo job, women working in these roles are starting to come together and help each other out. "Several groups have emerged in the last few years attempting to disprove the common statement – 'We would have considered a female cinematographer, but there were none to choose from.' The idea is that a director or producer can go to the site and explore different reels and resumes and see just how many talented professional DPs are female." Rachel says; "I admire so many other women in this business. From the trailblazers like Nancy Schreiber and Sandi Sissel and Amy Vincent, to Ellen Kuras and Mandy Walker, who have been idols for years, to amazing contemporaries like Lisa Wiegand, Natasha Braier, Monika Lenczewska, and Polly Morgan."
One of her friendships in particular is an uplifting example of women

helping each other. "Perhaps no cinematographer (recently turned director) has been more of an inspiration and source of moral support than my 'sister from another mother', Reed Morano," said Rachel. "We were among the only women in cinematography classes at NYU, and we have been close friends ever since. For years we have checked in on each other, shared advice, and even recommended each other for jobs when one of us was not available. Reed was the first person I called when I wanted to have kids in an industry that can be very tough on families, because she had been down that road. I asked questions like, 'Should I tell people I'm pregnant, risking nine months of involuntary bed rest, or wait until the baby pops so I can keep working?' (I opted for the latter.) As women we really need to support each other and create an aggregate of shared experience and advice. I try to mentor up-and-comers as well as hire women in my departments whenever possible."

Rachel Morrison is fast becoming both a star and a role model in the world of cinematography. Through her work, young women wanting to be cinematographers have a powerful and talented example to look to for inspiration. Her advice to them is to be "patient, persistent and polite." Rachel explains further, "Patience, because success doesn't come overnight, especially if you are female. Persistence, as you have to be willing to commit to the long haul. Try to remember to enjoy the journey because it's usually far better than the destination. And politeness – the biggest double standard in this industry is attitude. Dudes can be assholes and they are considered geniuses. If they are meek, they are considered artistic introverts. Women can be neither of the above. You have to toe the line between strong and engaged but also kind and compassionate. The artistic talent alone is not enough in this industry, because we don't operate in a bubble. It is a collaborative medium and at times a political environment, so practice your social cues along with your grip, lighting, and camera work and eventually you will rise to the top."

PART THREE: THE FUTURE

The Future is Female

I strongly suspected when I started writing this book that my final chapter would be all caps and yelling. Between the disappearance of those early female directors and the dismal statistics of today, I started to feel a little despondent.

But after interviewing so many brilliant women and men who are working hard to make Hollywood more equal, I feel incredibly optimistic. I have real hope for the future when I see people like Geena Davis, with her work at her Institute on Gender in Media. I find hope in male directors like J.J. Abrams and Paul Feig, who are leading the way with inclusion. I am hopeful that the EEOC investigation, the Representation Project, the Sundance Institute, and Women in Film continue to create conversation and change. And I believe in the power of audiences to take these conversations and turn them into action.

And this action is important. Right now, Hollywood is skewed towards one gender. There are many talented women who are out of work, both in front of and behind the camera, because of outdated, inbuilt biases towards the gender of roles. This seems all the more ludicrous when you read those stories of women in Hollywood's past. If it wasn't this way in the 1900s, why is it now? As audience members, we deserve to see stories told from all perspectives, featuring characters who represent us. This is the culture we export to the world, and movies have a unique power on us. If we can see it, we can be it.

In digging through the stories of women in early Hollywood, I have been inspired by their courage, strength, and determination to make change. And in looking at the new generation of young actors and directors, who are bold, brave, and refuse to be placed inside one box, it's hard not to have hope. Like Emma Watson who has used her 'Harry Potter' fame to spearhead the UN's He For She campaign. And Rowan Blanchard, a young film star in the making who writes Tumblr posts about inclusive feminism. Also Amandla Stenberg, who played Rue in 'The Hunger Games' and created an incredible YouTube video explaining cultural appropriation. And Yara Shahidi, another activist actress who gives inspirational speeches about diversity and the effect media images can have on young audiences. To see these women is to know Hollywood is in good hands; they are setting great examples for viewers by being heroes both on and off the screen.

And mostly, I believe in people like you. Yes, you. You film geeks, passionate viewers, and supporters of equality. Let's make sure women get their point of view on screen, because Hollywood will listen to their audience. So vote with your money, support filmmakers who deserve it, and call out inequality by using your voice on social media to stimulate conversation and debate. As these collected stories show, women or men working individually can have an impact, but together we are unstoppable.

SELECT BIBLIOGRAPHY

Alice Guy Blaché: Lost Visionary of the Cinema, by Alison McMahon

Women Filmmakers in Early Hollywood, by Karen Ward Mahar

Lois Weber in Early Hollywood, by Shelley Stamp

Mary Pickford: Canada's Silent Siren, by Peggy Dymond Leavey

Pickford: The Woman Who Made Hollywood, by Eileen Whitfield

Women Film Editors: Unseen Artists of American Cinema, by David Meuel

Without Lying Down: Frances Marion and the Powerful Women of Early Hollywood, by Cari Beauchamp

A Short History of Film, by Wheeler Winston Dixon and Gwendolyn Audrey Foster

Movie-Made America, by Robert Sklar

The Genius of the System, by Thomas Schatz

Directed by Dorothy Arzner, by Judith Mayne

Feminism and Film Theory, edited by Constance Penley

Scandals from Classic Hollywood, by Anne Helen Petersen

Mae West: It Ain't No Sin, by Simon Louvish

Hattie McDaniel: Black Ambition, White Hollywood, by Jill Watts

Hattie: The Life of Hattie McDaniel, by Carlton Jackson

The Tool of the Sea: The Life and Times of Anna May Wong, by Jennifer Warner

A Woman's View: How Hollywood Spoke to Women 1930 - 1960, by Jeanine Basigner

Stars for Freedom, by Emilie Raymond

City of Nets: A Portrait of Hollywood in the 1940's, by Otto Friedrich

Hedy's Folly, by Richard Rhodes

If This Was Happiness: A Biography of Rita Hayworth, by Barbara Leaming

You Must Remember This podcast, by Karina Longworth

Conversations with Wilder, by Cameron Crowe

Barbara Stanwyck: The Miracle Woman, by Dan Callahan

Bright Boulevards, Bold Dreams: The Story of Black Hollywood, by Donald Bogle

Ida Lupino: A Biography, by William Donati

Marilyn: Norma Jean, by Gloria Steinem

From Reverence to Rape, by Molly Haskell

My Life So Far, by Jane Fonda

Jane Fonda: The Private Life of a Public Woman, by Patricia Bosworth

Foxy: My Life in Three Acts, by Pam Grier

Women of Blaxploitation, by Yvonne D. Sims

Leading Lady: Sherry Lansing and the Making of a Hollywood Groundbreaker, by Stephen Galloway

Her Again: Becoming Meryl Streep, by Michael Schulman

Wishful Drinking, by Carrie Fisher

Unsinkable: Debbie Reynolds, by Dorian Hannaway

Reel Inequality, by Nancy Wang Yuen

USC Annenberg Research Studies: http://annenberg.usc.edu/pages/DrStacyLSmithMDSCI

Center for the Study of Women in Television and Film: http://womenintvfilm.sdsu.edu

ACKNOWLEDGEMENTS

First off, I want to give a huge thank you to all of the women and men who gave their time and insight to me for this book. Each of the people I interviewed I've admired for a long time, and it means so much that they agreed to be part of my project. They are: Geena Davis, Ava DuVernay, Maria Giese, J.J. Abrams, Paul Feig, Octavia Spencer, America Ferrera, Keri Putnam, Dr. Stacy L. Smith, Todd Fisher, Jennifer Siebel Newsom, Melissa Silverstein, Joi McMillon, Nicole Perlman, Rachel Morrison, Denise di Novi, Amy Powell, Jeanine Basinger, Shelley Stamp, Karen Ward Mahar, Nancy Wang Yuen, Cari Beauchamp and Diane Baker.

I also owe a gigantic amount of gratitude to Scott Mantz, Ngoc Nguyen, Charlie McDowell, Sean Cameron, Scott McGee and Kendel White, who gave me contacts, wrote emails, made calls, campaigned and vouched for me to get these interviews in the first place. Thank you! You get all the hugs!

Thanks to my writing mentors Lyndal Garrett and Brett Paesel, for checking my work, giving me guidance and making me feel like I could actually do this. Thank you to my editors at Mango for helping me through my first book, especially Hugo Villabona.

Also a shout out to my amazingly supportive friends, who gave me pep talks, sent me "you can do it!" texts, read chapters, picked me up when I was down, and were really understanding as I completely disappeared from existence for five months to write: Amirose Eisenbach, Maude Garrett, Hema Patel, Lucy Armstrong, Ashlea and Robin Burke, Matt Perez-Mora, Nadia Neophytou, Roth Cornet, Jacqueline Coley, Sean Carey, Chad Byrnes, Miri Jedeikin. My family for giving me the love of movies in the first place, and especially to Sue and Brian for their support. And thanks to all my social media friends who cheered me on virtually! It helped!

Thank you too, to my places of work, who were really flexible when I needed time off to write, Gina Sirico, Shane Abad, Harry Medved at Fandango, Sean Cameron, Scott McGee, Brandy Austin, Susana Zepeda, Pola Changnon, Jennifer Dorian at FilmStruck, Andy Signore, Roth and Justin Lamb at Screen Junkies.

I obviously couldn't have done this book without the inspiration of all the ladies in my stories, both living and dead. Thank you for showing me the way and inspiring me to make my own way through Hollywood.

And finally, thank you to coffee, Red Bull, Tim Tams and wine for getting me through some long nights!

Author Bio

Alicia Malone is a film reporter, host, writer and self-confessed movie geek. She first gained notice hosting movie-centric shows and reviewing films in her native Australia, before making the leap to Los Angeles in 2011.

Since then, Alicia has appeared on CNN, the Today show, MSNBC, NPR and many more as a film expert. Currently, she is a host on FilmStruck, a cinephile subscription streaming service run by the Criterion Collection and Turner Classic Movies, and she is the creator and host of the weekly show, Indie Movie Guide on Fandango.

Alicia is passionate about classic films, independent movies and supporting women in film. In 2015, Alicia gave a TEDx talk about the lack of women working in film and why this is important to change. In 2017, she was invited to give a second TEDx talk, where she spoke about the hidden stories of the earliest women working in Hollywood. Alicia has also spoken at conferences around America, and because of this, was named of one the 100 Worthy Women of 2016.

Alicia has traveled the world to cover the BAFTAs, the Oscars, the Cannes Film Festival, Toronto Film Festival, Sundance Film Festival, Telluride Film Festival and SXSW. She is a member of the Broadcast Film Critics Association, and over the years has interviewed hundreds of movie stars and filmmakers.

She also wrote this bio, but knew it would sound way less egotistical if written in third person.

Publisher's Note

Thank you for reading.

In writing *Backwards and in Heels*, Alicia Malone did her very best to produce the most accurate, well-written and mistake-free book. Yet, as with all things human (and certainly with books), mistakes are inevitable. Despite the publisher's best efforts at proofreading and editing, some number of errors will emerge as the book is read by more and more people.

We ask for your help in producing a more perfect book by sending us any errors you discover at errata@mango.bz. We will strive to correct these errors in future editions of this book. Thank you in advance for your help.